DEAR

My Life with ADHD

DON K POTOCHNY

ISBN 978-1-60145-622-9

Library of Congress Control Number: 2008908715

Printed in the United States of America.

Booklocker.com, Inc.
2008

Cover design by Todd Engel
Cover photo by Stephen Potochny
Title page photo by Stephen Potochny

For My Parent’s 50th Wedding Anniversary

“Discovery consists of looking at the same thing as everyone else and thinking something different”

-Roger Von Oech

CONTENTS

PREFACE

I met Mary Packard on a chilly October evening at the Drake University Phi Delta Theta fraternity house. A group of Delta Gammas came over for an extemporized night of socializing with the brothers. I was apprehensive about attending the impromptu event, since it involved women who lived down the street from me. Unlike fraternity-sorority exchanges, the informal mingling of the sexes consisted of an alcohol-free environment. I was without my social crutch.

The Police's "Message in a Bottle" pulsated from within the fraternity house as I tentatively walked up the steps towards the front door. Upon entering, I made my way to the second floor bedroom that I shared the previous year. Young men and women packed the bedroom while raucously conversing over the blaring stereo. I immediately headed towards familiar faces, a pattern of behavior I displayed whenever anxiety exploded into my social environments.

I made my way past a woman who was standing by herself next to a stereo. She danced in place while singing the lyrics from "Walking on the Moon." Before I could move past her unnoticed, she stuck out her hand and warmly said, "Hi ya! I'm Mary Packard." Her smile was so radiant that it would have melted Dick Cheney's heart. I immediately felt at ease with Mary because of her smile. We spent the rest of the evening chatting about a number of topics, always coming back to the central theme of politics.

I did not see Mary much for the rest of the fall semester. After winter break, I garnered enough nerve to call her. I asked if she wanted to go out in the near future. The near future was the next day. We started dating and a wonderful friendship blossomed.

Mary always provided unconditional love, unbridled support, and ardent compassion. She never asked, "What's wrong with you?" or talked down to me with any vexation reflected in her voice. She never tried to change me or offer wisdom on how I should improve my life. She accepted my quirks as well as my inconsistent behavior. She did not know about my ADHD, and it would not have mattered if she did.

Mary was always the encouraging beacon in my life, even when I slipped into a drug-induced morass during the four years that I lived in Chicago. I reached out to her during my moments of desperation and she comforted me when we spoke on the phone. I am not sure if she ever realized this, but her words of reassurance pulled me back from the brink on more than one occasion.

Mary demonstrated her acceptance of my behavior on the night I tried to cook dinner for her at my apartment on 34th Street in Des Moines, Iowa. I planned to make Turkey Tetrazini, along with a couple of side dishes that I cannot recall. Mary helped with the sides dishes while I finished preparing the main course.

I placed the piping hot casserole dish on the table and Mary immediately scooped out a portion onto her plate. She made a crunching sound with her first bite, which I thought was odd considering I did not add Grape Nuts to the recipe. I asked her how it was and she said it was delicious. I took some out of the casserole dish and noticed the noodles were uncooked; I did not boil the linguini before I layered the noodles into the casserole dish. I was embarrassed, but Mary reassured me in the most soothing way that the dish was "tasty." I will never forget her kind words.

Mary was quite the letter writer; I never met someone who wrote such inspirational letters. This is my letter for her. Lengthy, but I hope inspirational as well. This is for her supporting me while I struggled with emotional issues in college. This is for her cheerful work with Gary Hart's presidential campaign. This is for her tireless efforts to make the world a better place. This is for her always greeting me with an infectious smile and caring warmth, whether it was on a daily basis or for the first time in twenty years.

Writing this book was an intense emotional experience, sometimes draining me to the point of mental exhaustion. When I thought about quitting, I thought about Mary Packard.

She inspired me to finish what I started.

INTRODUCTION

"Why do you want to write this book?" I would not make progress with the project of my life until I answered the why question.

Publishers strongly urge writers to delineate their reasons for writing a book. One company recommends prospective writers to envisage themselves wrapped in an Oprah moment, when she asks for an explanation of the book in less than two minutes.

I need more time than that.

One of the purposes of this book is to educate and provide perspective for those in the general population who do not have ADHD. By telling my story, I hope to dispel the myth that ADHD is not a real condition. Nothing changes perceptions more than an intimate personal account shared from the heart. I bare all of my heart in this book.

I describe my journey with undiagnosed ADHD for those who had an association with me in some form or another over the course of my life. This book is an explanation of undiagnosed ADHD, not an excuse for abhorrent displays of recalcitrant behavior. I want my family, friends, former employers, and teachers at every level of my education to realize how undiagnosed ADHD influenced my life. I undeniably accept full responsibility for my past actions and hold myself accountable for future behavior. I am not making excuses or blaming others. I am just telling my story.

Up until ten years ago, ADHD research focused on how it affected children. There was the notion among leading researchers and medical professionals that ADHD diminished in intensity, or even disappeared, as the people who had it entered adulthood. The perception changed as more and more adults started realizing that some, if not all, of the behavior displayed by their ADHD offspring reminded them of how they acted in their daily routines.

If left undetected, adults with ADHD may develop a variety of secondary problems as they move through life. I hope the greatest benefit derived from this book will be that my story motivates other undiagnosed adults to seek more information about ADHD and then circumspectly consider a consultation with a qualified professional. I stress the word circumspectly because after participating in the initial stage of the current ADHD diagnostic process, I am not convinced the current criterion used for a diagnosis is credible. The diagnostic interview opened my eyes to the subjective ADHD diagnosis.

The ADHD diagnostic process requires a second interview. I was so dismayed with the initial interview that I shunned a second encounter with a certified psychologist. ADHD professionals want to gather evidence in the second interview to make a conclusive diagnosis. This is my second diagnostic interview, sans the exorbitant consultation fee and mandatory attendance of a significant other to validate my ADHD symptoms. My story needs an audience of more than one certified ADHD clinician or a small group of support group participants. I can help those who struggle with ADHD because I am pouring my heart out, while risking unadulterated scorn discussing the impact of undiagnosed ADHD. Helping others is worth the risk of ridicule.

I want the intimate story I tell in this book to be the impetus for a second book that pushes for physical evidence to validate an ADHD diagnosis. I also want to explore why the ADHD medical establishment promotes controlled substances when there are a combination of alternative treatments and interdictions that may work for an individual.

ADHD is a big gray area, and I am not talking about the gray matter in our brains. While I never received the official stamp of an ADHD diagnosis, I did go through enough of the process to realize I have, or had, some type of brain aberration. Call it what you want. Use any acronym you want. There should be a number of psychologists and psychiatrists clawing at my front door after reading my story and the detailed explanation of symptoms and events.

I experienced the gamut of emotions while writing this book. Some were so painful that I had to walk away from the keyboard and take a few deep breaths. I had a tough time coming to grips with the wild vacillations in my life, from the poignant moments of euphoria to the destabilizing quiet episodes of despair. I realized about halfway through writing the book that I was in the midst of an introspective psychotherapy session. Living with undiagnosed ADHD caused confusion, frustration, and low self-esteem. This book cleanses my soul of those self-imposed demons. Once I finished the initial written draft, I understood that one of the motives for writing the book was to purge the negativity that infested my life for forty-six years.

I did encounter periods of immense doubt, that what I was putting into words was a hunk of horse manure. It still may be in some people's eyes, but I am proud I stuck this one out. This book project proves to me that people who have ADHD can make significant contributions with their lives as long as they are cognizant of the condition and develop an intervention strategy.

There is a surfeit of books written by professionals on a variety of ADHD topics. Most of the pertinent information about ADHD has not made it into a book. Instead, the information is stored in the minds of the people who have ADHD. I have the memory to convey how ADHD affected my life for the past forty-eight years, forty-four of which I spent in the dark not knowing I had it. The time has come to share what has been stored inside of my brain.

I rarely collect photographs from the prominent events of my life. They are merely snapshots of a particular moment in time that may have captured an amusing pose or displayed our entire family at a holiday celebration. I do not need a digital camera so I can download photos to be stored in a computer's memory. My eyes are the camera; my brain is the computer memory. I recall flash images of past events and splice them together like a skilled movie producer.

Memory was the agent for my literary transformation and the main reference for this book. It remains the primary building block of my visual communication and is the foundation of my cohesive consciousness. I unambiguously remember, down to the finest detail, what transpired during the events that I describe on the following pages.

Whether I tell the story of how I grappled with the moral question of cheating in Dr Francois Wilhoit's modern political theory class, or detail the events leading up to the day I had to answer for my truancy in sixth grade, I tell the story the same way today as I did ten, twenty, or thirty years ago. There was never a need for embellishment, because I have the gift of pristine recall. I do not use the James Frye salacious method of recounting events.

Most of all, I strived to complete the first lengthy project of my life and, with the culmination of the book, overcome one of ADHD's most common behavioral traits. I cannot enumerate the times I wanted to quit, frustrated with my lack of written clarity and purpose. It was also difficult to shed the image of being someone who tells people he is going to do one thing, and then repeatedly stop midway through a project or commitment to start on something else.

This book does not describe how to overcome ADHD. There have been dozens of ADHD coping strategies that worked for me. That is important to remember: they worked for me. ADHD is like most other medical conditions. People have varying degrees of ADHD and they have dissimilar methods of coping with the symptoms.

This is not a technically written research book about ADHD. While I scrutinized hundreds of ADHD documents to educate myself about the condition, I disseminate little information about what I have read. What I describe are the experiences I had living with undiagnosed ADHD for the first forty-six years of my life. Still, I provide some valuable information about ADHD that is integrated within my story.

Three people have pseudonyms. Dr. Kia is the professional who conducted the initial ADHD interview. My visit with Dr. Kia started the mental wheel for writing the book. T.H. is the acronym for Trojan horse. There are people who claim to be compassionate, supportive, and empathic. Just like the Trojan horse, appearances are deceiving. I write about one Trojan horse who played a minor role in my ADHD discovery journey. Barney Chiselhead is one of T.H.'s business sidekicks. Dr. Kia, T.H., and Barney Chiselhead have pseudonyms because like the television show *Dragnet*, the identities of those involved shall remain anonymous. Every other person mentioned by name is the real deal.

Within most chapters and sub-chapters, there are interspersed sidebars called **Frustration** and/or **Irritation**. The **Frustration** sidebars are activities, events, or people that frustrated me because of ADHD. The **Irritation** sidebars are commentaries, comprised of unique viewpoints that evolved from my challenge the status quo mentality. A handful of sidebars combine both emotions.

At the beginning or within most chapters, I match one or more ADHD symptoms with the topic at hand to buttress my case under the current ADHD diagnostic process. The symptoms I list in each ADHD Epoch chapter denote the strength ratings for that particular period of my life. The symptoms I list in the other chapters indicate strength ratings when my ADHD was at its apex. Most of the symptoms no longer make a significant impact on my life.

The symptoms are from ADHD surveys created by Dr. Daniel G. Amen, and the team of Larry Jasper and Ivan Goldberg. I give full credit, with the requisite contact information requested by the copyright holders, at the end of the book.

The Amen survey uses the following frequency scale for the symptom list:

0=never
1=rarely
2=occasionally
3=frequently
4=very frequently

The Jasper/Goldberg Screening Quiz asks about behavioral situations and gives six options indicating the extent for which a particular behavior is true:

Not at all
Just a little
Somewhat
Moderately
Quite a lot
Very much

There are quotes placed at the beginning of most sections and chapters. The quotes are generally from prominent historical figures. Most of the quotes relate to the theme of the corresponding section or chapter. Some are quotes that I just like and have no connection to the corresponding topic. My favorite quote of all begins this book. I want the quote on my tombstone.

Five sections divide the book. **Discovery** is a synopsis of my journey to ADHD awareness. **Impact** describes how ADHD affected virtually every aspect of my life. **Runaway Brain** highlights four scenarios that heightened my ADHD to the point of it being out of control. The section also includes a brief chapter about other conditions associated with ADHD. **ADHD Epochs** chronicles certain periods when my ADHD symptoms were omnipotent. **What All of This Means** is the last section, a four-chapter compendium of redemption and renewal.

Finally, I refer to both ADD and ADHD in the book. The current acronym of ADHD has gone through multiple names over the past fifty years. ADD was the official designation up until about six years ago, and it appeared on some of my earlier recorded tapes and in the research that I uncovered when my discovery journey was in its infancy. Experts sometimes refer to ADD as ADHD without the hyperactivity component. I am sure the name will change as we move forward with a better understanding of what goes on inside of our brains.

I offer one caveat: some of the following passages contain profanity. When I wrote the first draft, the profane words did not come out of my fingertips by premeditation, but in a naturally flowing and descriptive way. Profanity has always been a part of my vernacular and it is included as an accurate depiction of my life story. There is less profanity in this voluminous work than there is in a standard rap compact disc. Nevertheless, I do not recommend this book for anyone under the age of 16.

This book is for adults.

DISCOVERY

"Success is measured not so much by the position one has in life as by the obstacles one has to overcome while trying to succeed."

-Booker T Washington

I see the tiny feet scurrying up a driveway. The footsteps make an entrenched sound on the gravelly asphalt. A light gasping sound intersperses with giggling, as a small arm reaches up to push the doorbell. A woman answers the door and looks down at a grinning four-year-old boy.

The young boy screams, "You're a shit!" He slams the screen door into the woman and runs frantically down the driveway towards his home, wildly cackling over the use of his newly discovered profanity.

Waiting for the boy at home is his displeased mother, who has just received a phone call from her neighbor three houses down on Rucker Street. The little boy's mother is astonished that her first-born son has learned such foul language. She is even more at a loss to explain why he used the profanity in such a flippant manner.

The punishment for cursing in the boy's household is to have his mouth washed out with soap. Not a bad punishment, the little boy thinks to himself, as it beats a spanking, or worse, being the recipient of the dreaded belt strap. Having his mouth washed out with soap was a punishment repeatedly implemented during his early childhood years.

The woman on Ruckert Street was accustomed to me asking for permission so I could retrieve balls from her backyard. She must have expected a similar query when she opened the door and looked down at me. Instead of a ball query, I called her a shit and if I had known the word fuck, I would have certainly said, "Fuck You!" For the cursing incident, I received the first rebuke of "What's wrong with you," a statement that should have been tattooed on my forehead.

I was more hyperactive than the average child. The hyperactivity exploded during kindergarten nap time. A secluded Harvard scholar who thought children should fall asleep after a physically active lunch recess must have devised the concept of nap time.

I feigned nap time until the teacher left the room, when I then sprung to my feet to disturb the other kids. I noticed my classmates actually rested during nap time, which I found troubling and realized for the first time that I was participating in an activity by myself. School officials attributed my hyperactivity to normal childhood exuberance. They believed my behavioral problems were a part of the growing up process.

I am sure my parents referred to numerous child psychology and rearing books. Child rearing books could not explain why I jabbed an umbrella into a classmate's left eye. The school sent me home, where a belt strap stung my buttocks. I do not remember if mom washed my left arm with soap, since it was the perpetrator of the scandalous umbrella incident.

The report cards and the comments on them by my first two grade school teachers suggested I was a good boy with a bright future. The encouraging comments belied the restless motion of a distracted child. There were several signs of ADHD during my childhood. The signs became warning sirens when our family moved to a new neighborhood before I finished the first grade.

The journey towards ADHD awareness was just beginning.

****

FRUSTRATION

One of the reasons I detest November is because every day is a ceaseless stream of gloomy weather. The main reason I detest November is the annual ritual of raking leaves.

Leaf raking is a mind-numbing task for someone who has ADHD. Rake a pile here and rake a pile there. Bag the leaves. Take the bags to the curb. Leaf raking was especially frustrating when a gust of wind unexpectedly blew away a newly created pile. I hated starting over, especially when I had a hard time finishing a project.

I last raked leaves when I was a college student in Des Moines. I responded to a job board to do some yard work on a Saturday morning. The yard work was to rake leaves for an elderly woman near campus. She paid me twenty dollars up front because she was going to be out of town for the remainder of the weekend. The yard was huge, much larger than the ones I was accustomed to raking back home. I figured I would start at 9AM and be done by noon, just in time for the opening kickoff of the Drake University football game.

By noon, I was barely halfway finished and I could hear the crowd roar in the distance. The woman paid me up front, so I dropped the rake and furiously ran into the woods towards the stadium.

I spent the twenty dollars on beer by halftime.

****

"What's wrong with you?"

Adults frequently asked me the question. As I entered early adulthood, the question turned into the more definitive statement of "You're not right," which was a declaration uttered by my co-workers, family members, and friends.

The confusion of not knowing about ADHD had a deleterious effect on the quality of my life. The unremitting criticism from adults and peers, and the perception I lacked discipline and maturity, led to low self-esteem, bouts of depression, and frantic mood swings. ADHD has so many symptoms and associative problems that it is hard to determine which ones have made the most impact on my life. I emphatically declare that not knowing "What's wrong with you?" is at the top of the list.

I spent a considerable amount of time with career counselors, therapists, and psychologists trying to ascertain the root causes of my behavior. The professionals never remotely mentioned ADHD as a possible explanation. My behavior was associated with a general lack of self-discipline. The more I attempted to find answers to the meaning of my mixed up life, the more I became confused and withdrawn.

Two particularly painful events highlight my tumultuous history. The first event occurred while I attended North Glendale grade school. The brain trusts of the school decided the reason for my sloppy handwriting was that I used my left hand. They tried to force me to write with my right hand. I was so distraught that I went on an ADHD rant. The emotional eruption caused the school to call in my father, who convinced the principal to let me write and draw with my left hand. It was the first misdiagnosis of my ADHD.

The second painful event was my first and only visit to a sexual therapist. Nothing breaks down a man's self-esteem more than a sex shrink appointment. I went through my sexual intimacy history with him for over an hour, and all I got was an occasional affirmation. He never inquired about what transpired in my brain during moments of intimacy. I left the visit two hundred dollars poorer and no closer to an ADHD diagnosis.

The frustration of those who interacted with me reached a point when they stopped trying to figure out "What's wrong with you?" "I've had enough of you" was usually the last declaration before people ostracized me. A childhood understanding of ADHD would have precluded a lifetime's worth of emotional misery.

****

FRUSTRATION/IRRITATION

ITEM: "No Blood for Oil" bumper sticker

FRUSTRATION: I have a hard enough time focusing on the road. I do not look at tattoos on people. Why would I want to look at tattoos on a car?

IRRITATION: The "No Blood for Oil" bumper sticker was on a SUV

****

I am sure I have met people who had ADHD throughout the course of my life. The problem was nobody discussed his or her ADHD. It was not until 1998 that I had my "Ah ha!" moment. The revelation about ADHD came from a young man who I worked with at Longhorn Steakhouse.

He reminded me of what I was like when I was twenty years old, dominating conversations and butting into ones where he was not invited. He spoke without thinking about the implications of his words. He constantly displayed an uncontained hyperactivity that got him trouble at work and in relationships. He made impulsive decisions without clearly thinking about the consequences. His attention span was non-existent.

One of his close friends told me the co-worker had ADD. His close friend went on to describe-during several discussions-that my newly discovered ADD friend received a diagnosis in childhood. He had always been a behavioral problem. He started taking prescribed Ritalin in high school, which seemed to diminish the more prevalent symptoms. He had numerous scrapes with the law that included spending time in a Missouri penal institution.

My co-worker was reluctant to discuss his ADD in detail when I asked him questions. I left him alone and marveled at the similarities between his behavior and mine. "Ah ha!" was the common refrain every time I heard a story or observed a personality quirk of his that resembled my personal history. The once flickering light bulbs in my brain brightly illuminated the possibility that I had ADD.

I only worked with him for about six months, but those six months set the stage for me to begin the road to awareness. My "Ah ha!" moment was a gift, albeit an unanticipated gift discovered thirty years too late for me to rectify how undiagnosed ADD negatively affected my life. I spent the next five years learning more about ADD. Over the course of five years, ADD changed into ADHD in order to include the hyperactivity component.

CBS's *60 Minutes* ran an enlightening segment on ADHD in 2004, interviewing medical professionals and people who had ADHD. *US News and World Report* featured an exhaustive article, also in 2004, that tackled the many elements of ADHD and the controversial techniques used to treat it. One of the article's recurring themes was that many people were not aware of their ADHD until they were well into their adult lives. They discovered ADHD by taking online surveys and completing behavioral checklists that prompted them to seek professional help.

My "Ah ha!" moment morphed into an astounding revelation.

****

FRUSTRATION

Teachers must have been demented to force their pupils to endure a forty-minute lecture before administering a quiz. They must have been just plain stupid to begin a lecture after administering a forty-minute test.

I sat at my desk, squirming as if someone shoved a piece of glass into my ass. I only focused on the quiz, blocking out every word the teacher said during the lecture portion of the class. I was relieved after the test, my mind a complete vacuum unable to soak in any more information. It must have been difficult for most kids to endure these teaching tactics. It was pure torture for someone with ADHD.

****

Thank you, Google.

After making a number of fruitless trips to the library, the time came to type the acronym ADHD into Google's search engine and tear down all of the psychological barriers that inhibited me for over forty years. At least that is what I optimistically thought.

I found my first online ADHD checklist, a brief six-question survey that touched on the major components of ADHD. I searched for a more comprehensive test and found Dr Daniel G Amen's ADHD checklist. The checklist was a thorough progression of questions organized by symptom.

After conservatively answering Dr. Amen's checklist, I realized my erratic behavior corresponded to ADHD. To be sure, I feverishly took other surveys and completed numerous checklists. A consistent pattern developed, one that firmly established I had ADHD. I scored high on all three of the major ADHD components: distraction, impulsiveness, and hyperactivity

I began to understand why my legs shook when I sat for lengthy periods. I understood why my mind wandered when given explicit instructions in the classroom, on the job, or in a sporting competition. I finally realized why I suddenly shifted gears and engaged in a completely different activity, or started a project after abandoning work on another task. The online questionnaires were helpful in moving me towards closure.

My **first online ADHD screening survey**

ADHD Screener Result Page — Page 1 of 2

Center for Adult ADHD Answers

Adult Self-Report Scale (ASRS) Screener

Back to the Center for Adult ADHD Answers

This questionnaire, though not a substitute for a clinical evaluation, is designed to help you recognize if you may have symptoms of ADHD and would benefit from further assessment by a physician.

The responses you have provided indicate that your symptoms may be consistent with Adult ADHD. It may be beneficial for you to talk with your healthcare professional about an evaluation.

Only your doctor can make a definite diagnosis. If you have concerns about ADHD, discuss your results and any concerns with your physician and/or other healthcare professional.

Use the print button below to print out your responses to the questionnaire and take it to your doctor.

PRINT

Your responses to the questionnaire:

	Questions	Your Response
1.	How often do you have difficulty getting things in order when you have to do a task that requires organization?	Rarely
2.	When you have a task that requires a lot of thought, how often do you avoid or delay getting started?	Often
3.	How often are you distracted by activity or noise around you?	Often
4.	How often do you leave your seat in meetings or other situations in which you are expected to remain seated?	Very Often
5.	How often do you feel restless or fidgety?	Often
6.	How often do you have difficulty waiting your turn in situations when turn taking is required?	Often

The 6-question Adult Self-Report Scale (ASRS) Screener is a subset of the WHO's 18-question Adult ADHD Self-Report Scale (Adult ASRS) Symptom Checklist. Adult Self-Report Scale (ASRS) Screener

Only your doctor can make a definite diagnosis. If you have concerns about ADHD, discuss your results and any concerns with your physician and/or other healthcare professional.

Use the print button below to print out your responses to the questionnaire and take it to your doctor.

PRINT

https://signup.webmd.com/adultadhd/adhdres1.html — 6/23/2003

****

IRRITATION

Rich Hall calls someone who checks out more than ten items in a ten item or less grocery express lane "expressholes." Add to that moniker someone who writes a check in the express lane.

****

After forty-two years of dwelling in an ADHD cave, and another two years getting up the nerve to do something about it, I finally made an appointment with a local psychologist. I went directly to the Yellow Pages and searched under a variety of classifications. The Yellow Pages were my only source for prospective certified clinicians, since I did not ask for referrals from friends or my physician. I let my fingers do the walking and that was another impulsive ADHD decision.

A few days before my appointment, I mulled over the reasons why I desired a professional's official diagnosis. I was not going to meet with a professional after forty-four years because I wanted some type of direct intervention to alleviate the stronger symptoms. The time for direct intervention was twenty-five years ago. I wanted validation that I had a very strong version of the ADHD condition. I also wanted to explore the possibility of being part of a brain imaging study.

I showed up five minutes late for my session, ensuring that the first box the psychologist checked was "lacks time management skills." I signed some medical related forms and the receptionist handed me a psychology exercise. The psychology exercise was a forty-sentence form that required me to complete simple phrases. I used a blue ink pen until it ran out. I muttered an expletive and got *the look* from the receptionist. *The look* she gave me was the look I have gotten thousands of times. It was the look of unreserved disapproval. She gave me a black pen and I started in on a test that was going to give Dr. Kia some indication of my personality.

I breezed through the form, writing down the first thing that came to me. Most of the sentences required some type of opinion to complete the blank section. Since I am full of opinions, those questions involved little contemplation. The sentences that did make me think a little before responding were the ones that delved into my personal feelings, like the sentence completion to the phrase "I failed." It took me awhile to fill in the sentence since I had a host of failures to draw from.

I finished the exercise and waited for the doctor to summon me for our interview session. A short time passed before a disheveled looking man greeted me and invited me into his office. The brevity of the wait impressed me, since I was used to spending over an hour waiting for a physician or dentist. Maybe the good doctor realized, I thought to myself as he shut his office door, that people with ADHD do not like to wait for anyone or anything.

Dr. Kia reviewed my personality profile answers and we discussed those for ten minutes. He circled my answer, which was "are heights," to the sentence that began with "My greatest fear." He made his first association between ADHD and other psychological and physical phenomenon by declaring that many people with ADHD have a fear of heights. He asked about a couple of my other answers, dwelling on one in particular. He wanted to know about my answer to "What annoys me," which was, "are people who use drinking fountains to fill their water bottles."

He wanted to know if I was a smart ass and I said yes. I purposely put down some sarcastic responses on the form as I do for any written question and answer format. I told Dr. Kia that I did not on the "What annoys me" sentence and he seemed perplexed by that. He made a few more insights about my form, mentioning people with ADHD can be smart asses, and that we are highly intuitive. We discussed a few more of my sentence completions before Dr. Kia began his rant. He lambasted people he called normal, meaning the people who do not have ADHD.

"The *normals* don't get our wit and sense of humor," he said as he showed signs of perspiration.

He mentioned he had ADHD and could relate to how the *normals* treat people who have it. This began a pattern of him railing about the *normals* for the balance of our session. It seemed Dr. Kia had it out for the *normals*, the people who are able to sit still, not blurt out answers before a question, and stay focused during a fifty-minute lecture. Dr. Kia was pissed and wearing his forty-plus years of dealing with the *normals* on his sleeve. He became so agitated that saliva poured from his mouth during the harangue. I smelled rising tension on his fetid breath.

The rant became complete outrage when he started talking about medication for ADHD and how "the goddamn Republicans keep shutting down funding for ADHD drugs." His outburst would have been hysterical except I was paying $110 for an initial diagnosis, not a forum for one Dr. Kia's political rants. He threw in some derisive comments about religion in his diatribe, which made sense since he prominently displayed *The DaVinci Code* on his desk. He settled down after awhile, but he looked like I felt after a harangue. I should have treated him and charged the $110.

Finally, I went into a room for a computer test, where I was supposed to touch any key on the keyboard when the letter X appeared on the screen. I guess that was the ADHD litmus test. I did well when the X's flashed at a rapid pace, but I floundered when the pace slowed down and my mind began to wander. I reflected on the past hour and wondered if I made the right decision in choosing Dr. Kia for a diagnosis. I became so bored that I hammered the keyboard without rhyme or reason. After about fifteen minutes of keyboard madness, Dr. Kia charged into the room with his prognosis.

"I'm eighty percent sure you have ADHD, so we need to set another appointment. And make sure you bring a significant other."

I researched the diagnostic process prior to the Dr. Kia consultation and understood that a second appointment meant bringing a significant other to provide further evidence of my ADHD behavior. Dr. Kia asked me to bring report cards, disciplinary reports, medical records, and any other documents that might shed some light into my past. He also gave me the contact information for a group of specialists who could prescribe Ritalin for me, and yet he was only eighty percent sure I had ADHD.

Why did he give me the medication contact information if the diagnostic process was incomplete?

Before the receptionist cleared me for departure, she asked for a payment of $330. I expected to pay $110 and now the medical mafia hit me for $330. They could claim that someone with ADHD forgot the price quote. On the other hand, maybe I *did not pay attention* to the receptionist's price quote during our phone conversation. My initial diagnosis from Dr. Kia was that he was eighty percent certain I had ADHD, which meant he wanted twenty percent more of my money.

ADHD affects people in different ways, at varying degrees, and under different circumstances. All I wanted was to get an idea how strong my ADHD was when I was a child and possibly receive some networking on participating in a neurobiological brain imaging study.

All I got from Dr. Kia was a pounding headache and a Ritalin prescription.

****

IRRITATION

Local governments should pass an ordinance requiring health clubs and the YMCA to install filling fountains along side drinking fountains. It is frustrating enough to wait behind someone who takes a long time to gulp down water from a drinking fountain, all the while muttering under my breath, "What are you, a fucking camel?" It is downright irritating to wait behind someone who fills his or her water bottle at a drinking fountain. People should realize that a drinking fountain is not the last stop in the desert for them to fill up their water bottles.

****

I thought about my meeting with Dr. Kia for days, as I usually do when ruminating over a complex topic. My visit with him qualified as complex.

I was on the verge of impulsively making the decision to take the next step in the interview process, the step that required me to bring a significant other to meet Dr. Kia. Reason won over ADHD. I decided to forgo the standard ADHD diagnostic process and move forward with more research and self-analysis.

Dr. Kia's rant did not piss me off. Neither did his one-size-fits-all Ritalin panacea that he forced down my throat. I scoffed at the $330 Ritalin prescription. The sheer lunacy of his statements provided the motivation that I needed to challenge the ADHD diagnostic status quo and forge a different approach to the condition.

He instructed me during our session "to beware of snake oil salesmen," the clinicians who advocate treatment outside of a strict Ritalin regimen. I found his whole shtick to be one of a snake oil salesman, from his restless and agitated diatribes, to his assertions that many of the things that I described about myself were typical of people who have ADHD.

There was no way I was going to drag my parents to a second interview. My parents have been a shining beacon in my life, steadying me when I wavered and providing unrestricted love and support when I faltered. Without a strong two parent household providing guidance, I might have ended up in the prison system before I was old enough to drive. I imagined dad cringing at the first words that exploded out of Dr. Kia's mouth. Things might have gotten ugly.

If you believe that you have ADHD, ask your general physician for a referral. After all, we have made enough bad decisions in our lives to regret one that requires choosing a psychologist. Also, make sure the psychologist understands what you want out of the visit. Make it clear that you are not interested in meeting with a Ritalin sales representative, but wish to speak with a medical professional who will keep his personal feelings to himself.

A year after consulting with Dr. Kia, I came across an announcement in our local alternative newspaper. The announcement listed a monthly support group meeting for adults with ADHD. A few months passed before I called to confirm my attendance. On the day of the meeting, my mind raced with the same two thoughts.

I was finally going to discuss my ADHD and I hoped Dr. Kia was not running the show.

****

FRUSTRATION

My brother occasionally suggests a movie to me, one he thinks I would enjoy for its political wit, gaudy humor, or dark story. *The Dark Knight* was the latest thumbs up from him.

I make excuses to him and other people about why I do not go to movie theaters. I mention my antipathy for Hollywood's political perspective. I mention the outrageous prices of the oversized popcorn and soda. I mention the lack of quality storylines in today's flicks.

Those are nothing but excuses. I have not been to a movie theater in over ten years because I cannot sit still for two hours without fidgeting or squirming in my seat. I leave my seat to buy soda and candy which, for a person with ADHD, is akin to throwing a match into an oil drum. I bounce around between the other big screens in the building, catching five minutes of a flick here, ten minutes of a flick there.

I miss important parts of the plot because of distraction. Someone's conversation in front of me or a movement that catches my peripheral vision distracts me. I miss integral parts of a movie that everyone talks about afterwards. Movie theaters frustrate me because I cannot stop a scene, rewind it to the appropriate point, and then review the scene again.

The Usual Suspects and *The Sting* took me at least three sittings and hundreds of pauses and rewinds before I understood what went on. The only three movies I have ever sat straight through are *The Godfather*, *The Deer Hunter*, and *Animal House*.

****

I attended the ADHD support group meeting at a suburban St. Louis community center. CHADD-the national ADHD support and resource organization-sponsors affiliated support groups throughout the country, though none located close to the St Louis region. A local organization ran the support group meeting that I attended.

A member of the local organization and a psychologist were the moderators of the ninety-minute session. Ninety minutes for an ADHD meeting seemed strange, considering people with ADHD cannot pay attention for longer than ten minutes. The main task of the moderators was to keep our group on topic, which was a Herculean task for any mortal human being. There were eight of us participating in this particular session, which was a comparatively large group. The number of participants changes month-to-month, an expected outcome that comes from a group of people who are impulsive and easily distracted.

I thoroughly enjoyed the session. The moderators instantly made me feel comfortable. I was the first person introduced to speak about my high priority ADHD concerns. The primary focus of the session was a discussion about the three areas of our lives where ADHD has the biggest impact.

The diverse contributions made by each member of the panel surprised me. Some members of the panel sought advice on their current malaise and others provided helpful hints to combat ADHD symptoms. Others were not paying attention at all. The two moderators did a splendid job of not parting with advice or therapy, but letting us hash out our own way of dealing with ADHD.

The problems, as told by our panel of eight, ran the full gamut of ADHD symptoms. One man in his early fifties told us that he spent the past week camping out in a local state park in order to clear his head and address his job situation. A woman who worked for a local municipality had the combined problems of a very cluttered home and a job where she talked too long on the phone. She was unorganized and had no sense of time. Another man, probably in his twenties, had an ostensible tic movement and interrupted people throughout the ninety-minute session.

The psychologist obviously had a professional relationship with some of the panel. He remained reticent during our discussions, unless brevity was clearly required to move the conversation along. He stressed during our ninety-minute session that the best way for us to cope with our ADHD symptoms is to lean on other people. He also made a compelling point about ADHD that may summarize the entire phenomenon.

He said, "People with ADHD are consistently inconsistent in all aspects of their lives."

The epitaph on my tombstone will read, "Here lays a man who throughout his life was consistently inconsistent!" My relationships, job attendance and performance, and sports participation all had remarkable points of achievement along with desolate periods of failure. I finally understood why people invariably asked, "I wonder what Don we are going to get today?" I always thought I lacked the self-discipline and maturity needed to produce a stable performance record. After the support group meeting, I understood that undiagnosed ADHD played a prominent role in causing my consistently inconsistent behavior.

I was thoroughly impressed with the doctor. His calm demeanor and measured advice was in stark contrast to Dr. Kia's diatribes. I left the support group meeting with a renewed faith in the ADHD medical establishment. The five dollars I spent for the support group meeting was a much better investment in my mental health than the $330 I forked over to Dr. Kia for a Ritalin prescription.

Since there are a plethora of tests and surveys on the Internet to determine the presence of ADHD, maybe it makes more sense to take those tests and share the information with others in a support group setting. Every self-assessment survey I took on the Internet had a disclaimer that stated the surveys were not a definitive diagnosis of ADHD. If deemed definitive, the surveys would put frenzied psychologists like Dr. Kia out of work.

IMPACT

"A life spent making mistakes is not only more honorable, but more useful than a life spent doing nothing."

- George Bernard Shaw

A childhood ADHD diagnosis can lead to a number of treatment options. Adults living with undiagnosed ADHD are not so fortunate. The inability to meet other people's expectations consumes their lives. The longer ADHD goes undiagnosed, the longer pain lingers from unceasing rejection.

Undiagnosed ADHD adversely affects the quality of relationships. It hinders the attainment of sexual intimacy. It stifles educational achievement. It expunges any chance for developing a stable career. It causes such poor money management skills that a game of Monopoly is a fiscal challenge. It precludes athletic success, particularly in the realm of team sports. It causes a nefarious cycle of self-medication to control the rapidly firing thoughts that percolate in the brain. It disrupts a restful night of sleep and who knows what it does to the dream sequence. It increases the incidence of accidents that have physical repercussions. It is the impetus for risk taking and thrill seeking behavior.

Undiagnosed ADHD affected all of the aforementioned areas of my life. The dagger in my heart was not knowing why I behaved the way I did. I cannot enumerate the times I heard stinging statements like "Sit still," "Settle down," "You're not listening," "You're not reaching your potential," "Wait your turn," "I've had enough of Don to last me for awhile," and "What's wrong with you?"

****

Do you know what it is like when a woman tells you that your love making skills are inferior?

Do you know what it is like when your high school basketball coach cuts you, not because you lack physical skills, but because you cannot follow directions to run simple plays?

Do you know what it is like to fail a job interview because you cannot pay attention and ramble on with your answers?

Do you know what it is like to wake up one morning and impulsively quit a job?

Do you know what it is like when your family and friends do not want to be around you?

Do you know what it is like to rush through the car buying process and purchase a lemon, or purchase a reliable car with a loan you cannot afford?

Do you know what it is like to continually sit through group education or work training sessions and draw mental blanks?

Do you know what it is like to live with unfounded peer labels throughout your adolescence?

Do you know what it is like to rush through a school test and put your answers with the wrong questions?

Do you know what it is like to have a teacher tell the class she gives extra credit points to students for putting their names on a paper or exam because you frequently forgot to do so?

Do you know what it is like when other children ignore you during pick up games because they are wary of your temper?

Do you know what it is like to be home alone on Christmas Day and muse about all of your failed relationships?

Do you know what it is like to be eight years old and drop motherfucker on your grandmother after she beats you in crazy eights?

Do you know what it is like to contemplate ending your life because you cannot make your brain slow down the rapid-fire thoughts?

Do you know what it is like to enthusiastically start a project, then lose interest and impulsively decide to start another one?

Do you know what it is like when people perceive you as an overly animated person who exaggerates?

Do you know what it is like when your immediate family or few close friends have reached the point that they no longer have confidence you will accomplish anything in life?

Do you know what it is like to have a credit score so low the credit bureaus do not give you a number, but instead mail you a picture of Death Valley?

Do you know what it is like to self-medicate with cocaine in order to concentrate on banal tasks?

Do you know what it is like to wake up in the morning with acute anxiety and spend the rest of your day rushing through activities?

Do you know what it is like to be engaged in conversation when suddenly, without any warning, your mind starts to aimlessly search for a missing ball in the handball court that is your brain?

Do you know what it is like when people repeatedly tell you that they are disappointed in you?

Do you know what it is like to have ADHD for forty-four years and not know it?

"It's not what you do, but how much effort you put into it that matters."

-Dad

FAMILY

I am the oldest of three boys, born on a sultry August afternoon during a St. Louis rush hour.

The oldest sibling faces a Catch-22. Expectations for a vibrant and successful journey through life are high, much higher than for the siblings that follow and take root on the family tree. The other side is the affectionate attention lavished on the only sibling. I soaked in all of the unmitigated love as if I was a new vacuum model scouring the length of a shag carpet.

Then one day, my parents walked through the front door with a baby. Much to my chagrin, the baby never left our home. I thought we were borrowing the baby for a while or keeping it until someone wanted him back. The baby was my brother Gary. It was the first time I had an entrenched animus towards someone for stealing some of the attention previously bestowed on me.

My erratic behavior never had any visible impact on my parents until the day I unleashed the profane barrage on our Ruckert neighbor. I am not sure if there ever was a pivotal point when my parents decided that something was different about me. It was not until my family moved to our new home on Edwin Avenue that undiagnosed ADHD started to affect my parents, particularly trying my father's patience.

****

Dad came from an impoverished background. He worked hard to break through socio-economic barriers, culminating his hard work with a MBA from Washington University in St. Louis. He met mom at the Washington University library, where she worked as a librarian. They were married in 1956 and decided to start a family four years later.

Dad and I share some common traits. We both have disdain for chest-thumpers, the people who always try to be the center of attention. We are both skeptical of establishment dogma. We are fiercely independent and equally fierce in maintaining independence. Our political views are similar, though I tend to challenge the status quo more than he does. We are not particularly social people-for different reasons-and we both enjoy bourbon.

In the ways that Dad and I are alike, our differences are far more numerous and significant. Dad has always been fiscally responsible. He is a meticulous person who loves to work on projects, mostly long-term projects that entail fixing up things or building some type of contraption for the house. He has always been a man of his word, a man who fulfilled the many commitments he agreed to make. He spent what little free time he had coaching little league baseball and was involved in my extra curricular activities.

I am sure Dad had a completely different vision for our family than the one he left behind in Pennsylvania. His own father, who passed on before I was born, was strict according to dad's account of his childhood and adolescence. Alcoholism was a common feature on his side of the family. There are no signs from him or any member of his family that ADHD was a genetic trait passed down to other generations.

As I grew older and eventually moved out on my own, dad addressed the episodic downward spirals in my life with reasoned discourse. He immediately drove to Chicago when he found out I was in jail. Not many fathers put their professional responsibilities on hold while their son sits in a cell 300 miles away. His discussion with me later that day was one of the most measured pieces of advice I have ever received. I did not listen to him, but at least he tried.

Mom raised three boys in the era of stay-at-home mothers. She definitely should have received a bonus for raising me because she was first to hear about my misbehavior whenever a teacher, neighbor, scout leader, or best friend's mother called to complain. With a teaching background, she understood my troubles in school and helped me with homework and school projects. I performed much better under her guiding hand than I did in a classroom setting, which leads me to believe I would have prospered in a home school environment.

My brothers and I were blessed to have the singular attention mom gave us. She set the guidelines and standards in virtually every aspect of our lives, making sure not to smother our personal growth or hinder our natural curiosity. She was the first person to address me as "Donald" when I was in some sort of trouble; I still cringe when someone addresses me by my birth name. I am grateful that she was meticulous in watching what we ate by limiting our sugar intake and introducing us to healthy foods like fruits and vegetables. I think she had an intuitive reason for limiting my sugar intake, realizing the motor I had running did not require additional fuel.

Mom was a teacher and librarian, which should tell you whether she has or ever had ADHD. She does not. She displays anti-ADHD behavior, which throws a wrench into any genetic predisposition theory. She is mild mannered, soft spoken, very organized, and about the only thing she has ever been impulsive about were the times she decided to let her right hand meet my ass. She constantly worried about me and rightly so.

It is fair to say that without my supportive parents, I would have landed in the penal system at an early age. They were my balance, the only two authority figures I respected enough to walk the tenuous line that bordered the dark side. God knows I tried to cross that line.

Great Expectations

****

FRUSTRATION

Family vacations were a great time to bond. However, I squirmed, writhed, and moved about in our fully loaded family sedan to the point of driving my parents crazy. I do not like being in a moving automobile for long distances, unless I am the one driving.

****

The closest relationship I have ever had is with my brother Gary. There have been times when we drifted apart. For the most part, we have enjoyed a strong brotherly bond and tight camaraderie.

I wonder if Gary has or ever had ADHD. We shared similar ADHD personality traits: wound up disposition, social skills deficit, and unpredictable behavior. His temper was evident when he threw a toy gun at me that left a deep gash just above my eye. He exuded impulsiveness, especially when he was in high school.

During the spring semester of my junior year at Drake University, I received a call from my parents that Gary had been away from the house for a few days. The few days turned into two weeks as he traversed the middle section of the country, sleeping in his car and finding nourishment at fast food restaurants. He also climbed down from our bedroom window in the middle of the night so he could join his friends for a night of mischief.

Gary has not impulsively hopped from job to job. He fulfills most of his commitments. He has been part of the same group of friends for over twenty-five years. Except for a semester during his first year at Bradley, he was a good student and got better grades than mine. His grades were also consistent, not all over the place like mine.

He completed the Appalachian Trail in 2005, an immense feat that challenges the emotional, physical, and mental aspects of our existence. He told me he would not have accomplished the feat when he was younger, during a time when he was more impulsive and hyperactive. There is no way someone with even a diminished version of ADHD could start the Appalachian Trail and finish it within six months, or even finish it at all. I probably would have ditched the trail and stopped in the first town that had a bar. After spending some time in the bar, I would have thrown on an apron and bartended for the rest of my life in the backwoods of America.

I know my ADHD had an affect on him. He was supportive of me when I was looking for a place to live in 1991. Little did we know that my stay would last over eight years; the eight years took its toll on him and our relationship. I was a good roommate, but my ADHD behavior eventually drove him to the point of issuing a move out edict. Then again, we had many similar ADHD characteristics, which is a volatile combination for two people living under the same roof.

Since 1999, when I moved out of his condominium, we have not had the same kinship that we did when we were younger. One reason for the distance was my over extended stay. The primary reason was he got tired of me butting into conversations, haughtily sharing my self-acclaimed superior intellect in his presence. He got tired of the irresponsible Don, the one who lost his driving privileges with a second DUI and had to walk to a Laundromat with a backpack full of clothes in order to do his laundry. ADHD can wear down anyone, even your closest friend. Maybe I am trying too hard to be Dr. Phil, but one incident in our childhood set the stage for our relationship.

I was sitting on the living room sofa, feigning to be engrossed in a children's book. Out of the corner of my eye, I watched Gary gently put together a rather elaborate Lincoln Log structure. I never had the patience to build anything, much less a house out of a bunch of hollow wood pieces.

Gary was humming along with his creation, laboriously placing each piece in a perfect spot that provided a resting place for the next piece. I was ready to burst out of the sofa and destroy his creation, but I showed unusual patience and waited for him to finish.

When he was done, he left the room to tell mom about his accomplishment. I jumped off the couch and quickly assembled a Hot Wheels track that started at the top of the sofa and went as far as the log cabin's front door. I took one of the cars and pushed it as hard as I could down the track. As soon as I released the car, Gary ran back into the room without mom. The Hot Wheels car crashed into the cabin, instantly destroying the hour plus work Gary put into his little project.

I will never forget the stunned look on his face. He cried out for mom and told her what I did, the little ratfink that he was. I did not get my mouth washed out with soap, but I do remember a stinging sensation on my butt cheeks.

****

My brother Tom does not have a hint of ADHD. Tom is an electrical engineer for the Navy and he has breezed through some tough undergraduate and graduate programs. He is, however, a sneaky son of a bitch. He waited until Gary and I were both off to college before he pilfered our burgeoning collection of baseball cards. Sometimes, the normal ones exhibit the bad behavior.

My Grandfather supposedly displayed a raw temper, though I never saw it. He was unlike any of my other relatives, always goofing with somebody and making wisecracks. I was his favorite grandchild, the first to be born on the maternal side of the family. He spent his entire lunch break every Wednesday sharing his time with me. The first thing he did every week was hide my stuffed bear. He always hid it on the top of my bedroom door. If anyone in my immediate family showed signs of ADHD, it was my grandfather.

I always had a close relationship with both of my grandparents. Neither of them seemed affronted by my behavior. I may have modified or even restrained my behavior knowing that I had a good thing going with them. I have vivid memories of walking through the park on the way to the ice cream store. It was like being king for a day, or a weekend, if they chose to take me in for that length of time. Of all the people I have known in my life, my grandparents were the ones I was the most excited to see.

"If a man does not keep pace with his companions, perhaps it is because he hears a different drummer. Let him step to the music which he hears, however measured or faraway"

-Henry David Thoreau

RELATIONSHIPS

Developing, growing, and nurturing a relationship is the primary wiring mechanism in human beings. We immediately attach ourselves to our mothers to be comforted and nourished. We trek through life meeting new people, forging new bonds, and sustaining close friendships. The reason we are here is to love one another, except on Super Bowl Sunday when there is money on the line.

Research verifies the inability for someone with ADHD to develop and maintain relationships. We do not develop the social skill set necessary to thrive in a relationship. We do not keep commitments to other people. We display impulsive fits of anger that alienates anyone who is close to us. We are distracted in conversation, sending a message to the other person that we do not care about what they have to say. We have mood swings that confound other people. We build a wall of defensive responses to criticism.

The biggest failure of my life has been the inability to build lasting relationships. I do not attend reunions because there will not be one person attending who I have been able to maintain contact with for a long-term relationship. I am also wary of the pedestrian question, "So, what have you been up to the past quarter century?" I do not have to worry about that question.

I have detonated so many relationships that nobody would give a shit.

****

ANGER

Amen-Quick responses to slights that are real or imagined (4)

Jasper/Goldberg-I have a quick temper…a short fuse (Quite a lot)

ADHD is widely recognized by experts to contain three major components: distraction, impulsiveness, and hyperactivity. Of the three, impulsiveness has impelled the most chaos on my relationships. At times, I was able to hyper-focus and pay attention to someone in a one-on-one conversation. I could also force myself to slow down and take five, so to speak, when I was blazing my trail through life.

Impulsive anger is the fundamental reason I have been unable to sustain long-term relationships. My short fuse has alienated friends, family, and coworkers. The short fuse response often included an intense rage that triggered a biting harangue. There were times when I resorted to physical retribution. My short fuse erupted so fast that I had little time to think about the consequences of my actions.

The girl I poked in the eye with an umbrella was the first act of rage I remember committing in response to a perceived slight. Soon thereafter, I swung a five iron that severed a small section of Dick Fiala's ear. I do not know what Dick did to warrant such an anger driven action, but I remember turning around and swinging the five iron towards his head.

A group of girls felt my wrath after another eventful day at North Glendale grade school. They followed me home from school, mocking me about a number of subjects that included the lunch box I carried under my right arm. I ran up to one of them and shoved her head into a mailbox, running away as she lay motionless on the ground.

If I did not get my way on the playground, I blew up and took care of business on the spot without any contemplation. In an intense argument with a classmate during a soccer game, I picked up a large handful of stones and hurled them directly at his face. I smelled blood when he ran away from me.

I got the reputation in grade school for having an explosive temper. I was so unpredictable with my anger driven emotions that even though I was physically talented in a variety of sports, I was usually the last one picked because nobody wanted to deal with my incendiary behavior. I hated to lose, whether it was a simple game of crazy eights with my grandmother or competing in pickup basketball games on the school playground.

My anger did not only lead to spontaneous retributions. I was at my most dangerous when I took a perceived slight and let it simmer inside of me like a hearty stew. My devious intentions to get even surpassed my instantaneous rage in severity because of the time I had to devise a plan of attack.

My reactions to not getting my way as a child and my responses to perceived slights in competitive environments should have been another sign that I was different from my peers. Instead of trying to figure out why I had rage, most of the people close to me decided that the best form of treatment was outright avoidance. My issues were not about taking anger management classes to rectify the spiteful behavior. My impulsive, angry reactions to events that hurt or offended me were a direct result of a functional imbalance in my brain.

****

FRUSTRATION

I have pre-paid for gasoline and driven off without pumping the pre-paid fuel. Somewhere between the cashier and pump, the torrent of thoughts that bounce around in my brain completely eliminates the mind's message to pump the gas.

Frustration boils over on the highway when I have a Homer Simpson "Doh" moment, realizing that somebody is pumping my gas into his or her car. Now I know why cars line up behind me at the pump when there are other pumps open.

****

SOCIAL SKILLS

Amen-Says what comes to mind without considering its impact (4)

Amen-Failure to see others' needs or activities as important (4)

Jasper/Goldberg-My relationships with people are made difficult by my tendency to talk first and think later (Very much)

Jasper/Goldberg-I say things without thinking, and later regret having said them (Quite a lot)

Individuals with ADHD generally have underdeveloped social skills because of their inattention, impulsiveness, and hyperactivity. As children, we do not interact successfully with peers and authority figures. We do not do much better as adults, where a repetitive pattern of broken relationships leads to a large dose of emotional duress. It is easy to comprehend why we struggle in social situations. To interact with others, an individual must be attentive and be able to control impulsive behavior. A detailed self-assessment of my past social skill set reveals an alarming list of deficiencies.

- I had difficulty paying attention to someone who directly spoke to me
- I missed important pieces of information, which gave the appearance that I ignored others
- I was unable to sit still and concentrate at concerts, religious ceremonies, educational events, and socially interactive business engagements
- I spoke with an imperious tone while perched on my soapbox
- I missed social cues and had difficulty understanding verbal undertones
- I shared information that was inappropriate and at times unapologetically crass
- I ended conversations abruptly or completed the other person's sentence before they were finished speaking
- I abruptly changed topics during the middle of conversations

- My opinions were shared in their raw form, without the political correctness that most people deemed socially appropriate

People perceived the aforementioned behaviors as coming from someone who was rude, self-centered, petulant, lazy, uncouth, and a host of other negative personality traits not suitable for print. Friends and enemies regarded me as someone who did not care about the feelings of other people. My lack of social skill development prohibited me from the most rudimentary understanding of what it took to build and maintain relationships. They were the skills I needed to develop early in childhood, so they could have taken root before adulthood.

The most important social skill is oral communication, a skill that was one of my glaring weaknesses. Often times, people had a difficult time understanding my message. They frequently asked me to "slow down." They also addressed me as "mumbles" or told me to "stop mumbling."

My brain transmitted signals so fast that I blurted out things before contemplating the ramification of the message. I said things that were inappropriate in a social setting, especially a formal one that required modesty and etiquette. My solution was to quietly count to ten when I was tempted to make a rude remark. I never reached five because I was too eager to get in my two cents. What people got with my oral communication was an unvarnished view of what went on inside of my head.

I dated a woman two different times during the early nineties. The first time was a rebound relationship for her and we stayed together for a short period. We worked for the same employer about a year later and ended up in a more involved relationship. She had her issues with the brain as well. The clashing of our idiosyncrasies caused immeasurable strife in our dating relationship. The relationship ended after I made one of the more insensitive remarks I have ever made to anyone, let alone someone I was dating.

We were enjoying a few libations at a friend's party, sitting off to the side from the main gaggle of people.

I suddenly blurted out, "You're not as fat as the first time we dated."

The great conveyor belt in my brain moved the thought packages at warp speed without stopping at any of the filtering stations. The second a thought emanated from whatever part of the brain that thoughts emerge from, it hit the conveyor belt and went directly onto my tongue and out of my mouth. Once out my mouth, the thought packages were irrevocably lost and I spent an inordinate amount of time apologizing for what I said. A formal etiquette class would not have slowed down the conveyor belt.

I received an invitation to Cotillion when I was in 7th grade. Cotillion was a voluntary after-school class that strived to strengthen a child's social interaction and decorum skills. Manners? Etiquette? Learning how to interact with girls? Nah, I did not want anything to do with Cotillion. I was more interested in an unruly game of street hockey than developing obligatory social skills.

My parents eventually relented in their insistence that I attend Cotillion. I am sure the etiquette class would not have helped during that phase of my life. In fact, my attendance may have done more harm than good, exacerbating an already troublesome set of social skills. Expulsion would have followed either a profane verbal harangue or aggressive defiance. I would have benefited more from a mentoring approach to develop my social skills.

****

RUNNING AWAY FROM PROBLEMS

Amen-A prisoner of the moment (3)

If Hollywood sanctioned a screenplay on a day in the life of someone with ADHD, I would pull out from my neatly organized brain filing system a day from the first semester of my sixth grade school year. Actually, I would pull out ninety-six hours, starting when the dismissal school bell released its joyful sound on an early autumn afternoon.

I was supposed to spend some extra time after school with Mr. Matheny, who was my sixth grade math and science teacher. He caught me cheating on one of the math block tests. My punishment was to sit for an hour after school and stare at his collection of dissected frogs. Instead of languishing in detention, I impulsively decided at the last minute to attend soccer practice on Thursday afternoon. I knew my decision to attend soccer practice would give Mr. Matheny a good reason to conjure up a more strident punishment by the time Friday's math class rolled around.

I decided to evade punishment by skipping school on Friday. I roamed the neighborhood around North Glendale, hiding among the trees to watch my classmates frolic on the school playground. A surge of adrenaline suppressed my unequivocal fear. Without the benefit of a watch, I still made it home by the usual time of 3:00.

Later that afternoon, I went to our school district's middle school to watch the ninth grade team play football. I strolled around the track without a care in the world when I crossed paths with the last person I expected to see at Nipher Middle School-Mr. Matheny. I will never forget the intonation in his voice when he said, "Where were you today?" He sounded like Lurch from the *Addams Family*. I turned pallid as he lumbered off into the crowd. He had proof I was alive and well. A health excuse for Friday's school absence would not fly on Monday.

The events that followed unraveled at such a tortuously slow place that it is facile to recollect what ensued during the next seventy-two hours.

I spent the rest of the weekend counting down the minutes towards the moment when I was going to answer for my truancy. Instead of confessing and putting an end to an already troublesome situation, I made matters worse by concocting a scheme that ultimately led to one of my more severe parental and teacher punishments.

On Saturday morning, I took my normal position as our team lined up for the weekly soccer game. My body was there, but my head was definitely elsewhere. I missed two wide-open goals and was generally listless on the field. My parents sensed something was wrong and asked if I felt all right. I seized the moment to say I thought I was coming down with something. Mom spent the next two days feeling my forehead and exclaiming, "You don't feel sick."

I was miserable by Sunday night, realizing that within twenty-four hours I would have to account for my poor decisions. We gathered for our weekly Sunday dinner at my aunt and uncle's home. I was hyper-focused on my situation and barely said a word to anyone. That was quite out of character for me, since I usually dominated or tried to intrude upon any conversation that went on during our Sunday dinners. When I got home, I finally came up with a plan that would solve my problem. It just delayed the inevitable.

Early Monday morning, I took a cup of water and slowly poured it into the toilet while making retching sounds. I made the sounds within earshot of mom, who was clearing breakfast dishes off the dining room table. I also pressed a hot towel on my forehead just before she felt my skin for a fever. She let me stay home for a couple of hours before sending me off to school.

I finally entered North Glendale, after walking the Glendale streets for two hours trying to invoke one final scheme. By then, the shit hit the fan because the school contacted mom an hour after my morning departure. She spent the better part of the morning frantically looking for me. Never add worrying your mother to an already long list of punishable offenses.

My parents were steamed. When they realized why I skipped detention on Thursday, they banned me from playing organized soccer for the rest of the year. That was just the opening salvo. Matheny had me for two weeks of after school detention and the other six grade teachers in the rotation made sure that I paid for my transgressions.

****

IRRITATION

I wish my parents banned me from playing soccer for the rest of my life. If enemy combatants ever threatened me with the viewing of non-stop soccer footage, I would immediately cough up the location of my fellow troops.

I used to think the Hispanic announcer was yelling “GGGGOOOOOOAAAAAALLLLL" when calling a soccer match. That was, until I realized he was responding to the question, "Do you want to watch soccer?"

"NNNNNOOOOOOOOOOOOOOO."

The only time I even contemplate soccer is every four years when the sports page features the World Cup. I used to ignore the World Cup altogether until I noticed that more and more Americans were tuned into the matches (I call them games). Even my friends started calling me up to catch a match at a local bar. I would rather watch snails cross a road than be subjected to watching soccer games. To make matters worse, my friends watched the most recent tournament at a restaurant that served cuisine from one of the participating countries. I told them thanks for the invitation, but I had already contracted my annual case of food poisoning.

Later that week while exercising at a local YMCA, I noticed a group of people glued to one of the television monitors. Must be a baseball replay, I thought. I went over and found a World Cup game on the screen. The score was 0-0. I went back to the anaerobic machines, exercised for fifteen minutes, and then returned to the television monitor. The score was still 0-0. Fifteen more minutes of exercise and the score remained 0-0. Gratefully, the game ended 0-0, or so I thought. The scoreless tie was the beginning of two mundane overtime sessions that still produced a 0-0 score.

Breathtaking!

They finally decided the game with a series of kicks where the kicker goes one-on-one against the goalie. The goalie has no defense except for an athletic supporter. Kind of like a gun duel where only one person has a gun.

There is never an opportunity to release pent up tension when the game finishes in a scoreless tie. The fans fight instead, which ends up being the most entertaining aspect of a soccer game. After all the merriment, the fans from the victorious nation riot in the stands and destroy cities in their homeland.

Soccer is not only boring, but the rules are peculiar to say the least. Instead of a clock winding down to signal the end of a half or game, Soccer uses a clock that tick, tick, ticks until it reaches the forty-five minute mark for each half of play. The games never stop at the forty-five-minute mark. The clock keeps ticking to account for every delay in the game. The players keep kicking each other in the nuts until a referee blows a whistle to signal the end of the half or game.

The only pleasure I got from soccer was when I kicked a kid in the shin or nuts. They still do that on the world stage, except for that display of sportsmanship a player receives a color card. The color depends on the severity of the foul. Yellow means bad and red means really bad. The more cards collected by a team (not club), the worse it gets. This is my only explanation for the cards because I still do not understand what they mean.

There will soon be another display of unbridled enthusiasm for the World Cup.

Remember to wake me when it is over.

****

COMMITMENTS

Amen-Avoids group activities (4)

Jasper/Goldberg-Especially in groups, I find it hard to stay focused on what is being said in conversations (quite a lot)

Dependable and reliable are two adjectives that rarely described my character. The two traits are essential in building rapport with people and the cornerstone for establishing any type of relationship, be it with friends, co-workers, or lovers. I never fully understood why I failed to fulfill commitments until I recently realized the answer lies with my aversion to group activities. The vast majority of my unfilled commitments occurred when people counted on me to meet an obligation in a group setting.

I have sent in wedding invitation acceptances and then did not show up, sometimes without the common courtesy to explain why. I have paced around my living quarters on the day of a wedding, anxiously pondering an escape clause in the invitation. I have showered, dabbed on a little cologne, dressed in nice attire, and drove toward the church only to abruptly turn around and head back home. The time I spent at receptions was ephemeral because I stayed until the toast and departed the premises out of a side door once the revelry began.

If it was just weddings, I could probably justify my unreliability by pointing to a number of factors. The groups I have stood up also include volunteer organizations, and they depended on my contributions when they planned their event. I promised to work a three-hour shift at the Salvation Harbor Lights shelter on Christmas day 2005. I showed up with some clothes to donate, gave the clothes to a volunteer, and left the building without even muttering, “Merry Christmas.”

It is not as if I had something better to do, or something more pressing to do. It was the anxiety of being around a large group of people, for whatever reason, that prohibited me from contributing in a group setting. Unreliability has unquestionably hurt my ability to start, grow, and sustain relationships.

It has also caused unmitigated shame.

****

IRRITATION

I have no shame when it comes to stiffing the dentist. I make appointments, sometimes three simultaneously, and I do not even make an effort to call the offices to reschedule or cancel. I know I have a dentist problem when my car has a longer life span than my crown.

I have an irritating sensation that dentists like performing unnecessary procedures on our teeth so they can drain our wallets. I actually had a dentist who wanted to take the roots out of my molars on two separate visits. His slogan should have been "Double the pain, double the dollar."

Dentists like to stick suction tubes, tongue depressors, drills, and scraping objects in our mouths while asking, "So, what have you been up to the past six months?" My favorite question is, "Does it hurt?" No, sticking a sharp, pointy object directly into my tooth nerve does not hurt you stupid son of a bitch.

****

DEFENSIVE

Jasper/Goldberg-I seem to be thin skinned… (Quite a lot)

Psychological testing questions can be pure party entertainment. Just sit around the living room, quaff a few cold ones, and ask inane questions to the rest of the inquisitive participants. A common question asked, usually in the wee hours of the morning was, "If you were an animal, what would you be?" The question is redundant, of course, because at three in the morning we sometimes forget that we are all animals.

I used to think I was the majestic lion, roaming throughout my domain as the official king of the animal world. I have an affinity for bears, because you have to respect a species that gorges to the point of needing a three-month nap. While I despise snakes, the animal I resemble the most is the rattlesnake. If you invade my space or taunt me in any way, I will coil into a pose that is one quick strike away from unleashing verbal venom.

Peers often made fun of my pants length, asking me if I was expecting a flood. My bowl-style haircut was the butt of many jokes. As I grew out of the materialistic obsession with my appearance, I started to lash back at people who commented on my school or work performance. My retort was to denigrate something about them, even if my invective was unrelated to their initial insult. People who analyzed my taste in music or women got an ear-numbing diatribe. When people spoke disagreeably of my opinions, I spit vitriol into their ears.

I tried for years to use self-deprecating humor in order to prevent the esteem destroying critiques. I found that people just piled on after the self-deprecation. I resorted to attacking others first, before they launched their hurtful comments. Many of my disparaging remarks were condescending, when I stood high on my soapbox and talked down to people in a demeaning voice inflection.

My acerbic responses to people, some whom were genuinely trying to help me, have led to the demise of many close relationships. It goes back to the alarm that triggers anger, the bell that sounds the call for the chemicals in my brain to mix in a fomenting cauldron.

My rattle has faded as the years have passed. If you do you hear my rattle, it is time to mosey out of striking range because my fangs will cause irreparable damage to our relationship.

****

FRUSTRATION

The most unpleasant job I had-besides washing dishes-was bagging groceries. Bagging groceries is a monotonous activity for a *normal* person. For someone with ADHD, it was sheer terror staring into the bottom of a bag trying to decide whether to put the jar of mustard or egg carton in first.

****

UNPREDICATABLE

Amen- Mood swings (4)

Jasper/Goldberg-My moods have highs and lows (quite a lot)

I worked with a woman who encapsulated my mood swings by stating, "Ninety-nine percent of the time you're a great guy. But one percent of the time you're a real asshole!"

I come up with explanations for living with ADHD and they involve using metaphors. The telephone operator of years past is a good metaphor for mood swings. Picture her console as the brain, with connecting wires entangled in a seemingly incomprehensible manner. She constantly moves the connecting cables to different open slots on the board and adds more cables to slots as the calls come in; there are so many calls that she cannot keep up. The console overloads and shuts down or, in some cases, catches fire from a spark caused by all of the fury. That was my brain when it reached critical mass. At some point, my brain absorbed so much information that it shut down.

Brain shutdowns generally happened in two distinct settings. The first setting involved taking in instructions, directions, or vast amounts of new information in a short period. My focus was keen at the start. Inevitably, my mind started to wander, I began to fidget, and I impulsively moved about in a random manner. When I came back to the topic, I wished for an abrupt conclusion to the steady stream of information. All of the connecting cables in my brain were shooting out of their respective slots. The loose cables caused a haze to envelope my mind, akin to the visual static seen on our television screens after a station has signed off for the day.

The second way in which my brain shut down was when I became enraged or so acutely disgusted with something or someone that the wires all delivered the same negative message: **meltdown.** Meltdowns usually involved situations where I was receiving criticism or inundated with requests and demands from all angles at the same time. An incident that occurred two years ago provides a prime example.

After three hours of sleep, I begrudgingly showed up for a morning meeting with T.H., Barney Chiselhead, and the other owner of the restaurant. I knew the tone of the meeting was not going to be positive.

Many issues were on the table, but none more pertinent than the asinine way the owners scheduled employees. They wrote the same schedule every week, making the employees responsible for covering or trading shifts. They had a bulletin board full of post-it notes from employees looking for people to cover their respective shifts. I wanted to utilize a system where I controlled the scheduling, changing the shifts week-by-week as employee requests dictated. Their response was, "Fuck them." They did not care how cumbersome it was for the staff, as long as they made scheduling a fifteen-minute exercise in leadership.

I was humiliated for ninety minutes. The two stooges and the third owner expected me to take the verbal beat down and work with a clear conscious and positive attitude. I showed up at the restaurant and the staff immediately confronted me problems, retorts, and infantile demands. I tried dialing up a purveyor to place an order when my mind shut down.

My brain felt like a pouch of vegetables that explodes in microwave. I tried to get some fresh air to quiet the tumult inside of my brain. I got up from the filthy milk crate I was sitting on and glibly told the person next to me that I needed some space. I left to clear my head and regenerate the chemical composition of my brain.

People got tired of the ADHD act. I do have a keen wit and most people find my sense of humor endearing. In order to maintain relationships, it is important to establish consistent and dependable behavior. My sense of humor is irrelevant. Unpredictable was how people ultimately judged me. I was a walking temperamental time bomb.

I have broken off innumerable relationships because of brain meltdowns. If I was around people who knew me well enough, they saw the meltdown coming by the blank look in my eyes and abrupt change in my disposition. When they saw the look, they tried to get as far away from me as possible.

My expression exuded the same type of information a scientist gets from monitoring the gauges of a nuclear reactor. The radiation coils overheat and the gauges display the appropriate warning signs. Sirens wail, lights flash, and if not detected soon enough, the reactor melts down to the core. It was the same thing with my brain. When it melted to the core, the ensuing collateral damage was immense.

****

IRRITATION

I recently canceled my cable service. I do not like to use the hackneyed phrase, "When I was your age," but I remember when the content of cable programming was much more captivating.

ESPN has become nothing more than a sports soap opera. An anchor actually lamented during the week leading up to the Philadelphia-New England Super Bowl that there was no drama to report. He wished Terrell Owens would "do something" to make the news. The sports giant from Bristol, Connecticut runs *TMZ* footage of Tom Brady wearing a foot harness. Jason Taylor receives a ten-minute feature story, not because of his football prowess, but because of his appearances on *Dancing with the Stars.* I guess giving a candid and succinct analysis of a sporting event has passed the late, great ESPN by. They need the same healthy competition that Fox gives CNN.

CNN is nothing more than a platform for promulgating every politically correct viewpoint known to humankind. They used to provide the best coverage of unfolding events. Where is the M and V in MTV?

In the early eighties, CNN, ESPN, MTV, and David Letterman all premiered to rave reviews and surging popularity. The only program that I watch is Letterman because he is true to his roots. I may not be a financial wizard, but I do save fifty bucks a month by not watching the crap on cable television.

****

FRIENDSHIPS

Amen- Trouble sustaining friendships (4)

Amen- Failure to see others' needs or activities as important (3)

Friendship is such a vital part of our connected lives that they named a television show about it called *Friends*. I never took to the show because I cannot relate to the central theme of friendship. My friendship resume is akin to the cycle of a washing machine. Once I run through one cycle of friends, I start another cycle with a disparate group of people.

The move our family made at the end of first grade began an unsettling friendship trend that has lasted a lifetime. From the first day of school, the kids at North Glendale grade school ostracized me from group activities. I was ceaselessly in confrontational situations with my peers and the hyperactive behavior made me an instant outcast.

There was one activity that most of the boys took part in before school and during lunch break. It was an unorganized game of soccer where one side had a huge personnel advantage over the other. I started playing with the dominant team until I noticed some of my teammates moving to the other side of the ball. They did not like my fits of rage after every goal scored against us. I eventually took the side of the "up" team, because we were going against a slight incline. We were also up against superior talent. It was the first time my peers ostracized me because of hyperactivity.

I never became tight with any group of people in high school. I did hang out with a cast of characters just so I could connect to any group in the adolescent social world. They had many common pursuits: hunting, fishing, and *The Grateful Dead*. I was not interested in any of that stuff, but I tagged along when they occasionally invited me out to concerts and for nights of general mischief. Andy Froesel was part of the group. He and I developed a friendship in grade school and it lasted through high school. He was one of the few male friends I ever had that put up with my undiagnosed ADHD.

Andy and I had personalities at the opposite ends of the spectrum. He was self-sufficient in his early teens, cutting grass for people he knew in his neighborhood. He parlayed his entrepreneurial spirit into a thriving lawn care business that he still runs today. I worked with him a couple of times and found mowing lawns to be monotonous. I have always respected Andy's work ethic. He is one of the more responsible and dependable people I have ever met.

We drifted apart when I went away to college. He started cutting my grandmother's lawn in the early nineties and mentioned to her how it would be great "to go out with Don sometime." The sometime came in 1996 at Wayne Gretzky's inaugural game for the St Louis Blues.

A week later, my grandmother remarked that Andy told her I had not changed since high school. He said I was "the same old Don." I did not understand what Andy meant until I found out about ADHD. "The same old Don" was still inattentive, impulsive, and exceedingly hyperactive.

I thought about what Andy said the other day. As traffic came to a halt, I watched a funeral procession make its way into a cemetery. The line of cars was long, yet it was not long enough to deduce that some dignitary had passed away. I mused about my short funeral procession. My immediate family will attend and that is it. The problem with living with undiagnosed ADHD and being "the same old Don" boils down to one simple thing.

I will not have any friends to hold up traffic during my funeral procession.

****

FRUSTRATION

I like to eat fish. I just do not like catching them. Fishing is about sitting still, not making any noise, and waiting interminably for a starved fish to attack a plastic worm. Fishing required patience and I never had any. The only time I went deep-sea fishing turned into a comedy highlight reel because of my impulsive behavior. I kept casting my line into fishing spots that belonged to other people.

I did enjoy the time a friend and I went fishing without bringing our poles. We threw breadcrumbs into the water and then clubbed the fish with huge chunks of wood after they came to the surface.

We called it skull fishing.

"You're not any good in bed!"

-Anonymous

INTIMACY

Amen-Easily distracted during sex, causing frequent breaks or turn-offs during lovemaking (4)

Amen-Trouble with intimacy (4)

Jasper/Goldberg-My thoughts bounce around as if my mind is a pinball machine (Very much)

Rejection comes in all shape and sizes for someone with ADHD. I have taken rejection from friends and family members as often as ultimate fighters receive kicks to the nut sack. Rejection is a common reaction to ADHD. People get sick of being around me.

Clubs and organizations have rejected my membership applications. We all have experienced membership application denials. Credit rejection notices have become wallpaper for my living room. Prospective restaurant industry employers have rejected me so often that they have compiled a form letter just to deny my job application. Women have rejected me for numerous date requests and I understand that comes with the fickle dating game.

A woman's rejection because of lackluster lovemaking skills was not only a slap in the face, it was the most significant reason I have built a wall of isolation. After years of intense anger, I now understand why the anonymous woman made the disparaging remark.

Nevertheless, when I heard the stinging words during a stage of my life when undiagnosed ADHD was like a cancer to me, I completely lost faith in my ability to perform one of the more basic acts known to humanity. When she dropped the lovemaking bombshell on me in 1985, I immediately transformed a relatively stable life into an uncontrolled lifestyle of untenable choices and bad decisions.

ADHD had a more negative impact on intimacy than any other area of my life. I was not cognizant of ADHD's impact on sexual intimacy until I started seeing questions on ADHD surveys that pertained to intimacy. Even when I found out about the ADHD connection to intimacy, my focus was on the condition's money management and relationship impact.

I have always been a passionate person, with what I consider a normal amount of sexual encounters. I effortlessly ran the sexual bases until the turn for home plate. Women have said that I am a great kisser, that my kissing is a real turn on to them. I have always hit a clean single. Second base was there for the taking, especially if I excited a woman by the way I hit the single. Third base involved a little trial and error, but I usually rounded third with momentum towards home plate. Somewhere between third base and home, my ADHD mind took over and I stumbled towards the plate with a perpetually powerful detachment with intimacy. I swung for the fences, but I could not make contact.

I did not attain a sexual relationship that included intercourse until I was out of college. That is right. I popped my cherry after I received my college diploma, making me eligible to be the lead character in the movie *The 40 Year Old Virgin*. At the time, I was relieved when I first did it. I found out later I was not any good at it.

It was not from a lack of education that I waited so long to engage in sexual intercourse. While it is true that the oldest child is Ponce de Leon searching for the fountain of sexual truths, I was around enough people to assimilate bits and pieces of sex education. My parents were reticent about sex. I asked dad about the birds and bees one time and his response was ambiguous at best. The school system might as well have chucked its sex education curriculum, because I never got beyond giggling at all of the female anatomy parts shown in sex education books and films.

When the action got hot and heavy, the racing thoughts that ran through my mind made me incapable of focusing on the one thing that I was trying to do at the time. The thoughts bounced around in my head as if they were an assortment of numbered ping-pong balls moving about inside of a lottery basket. The more intense the physical encounter got, the more my mind exploded with frenetic brain activity.

In the middle of most of my sexually intimate encounters, I simply lost the passion of the moment. The sound of water dripping out of a leaky faucet distracted me. Wondering if I had paid my bills on time drowned my focus. My attention span was more limited than it was in any other facet of my life. My partners became extremely frustrated when I suddenly pulled away as if Mr. Freeze came into the room and fired his ice gun into my veins. After a few distraction incidents, women began calling me a cold fish in the sack.

If it was not distraction inhibiting my ability to perform, the classic ADHD symptom of rushing through things reared its ugly head on numerous occasions. I treated love making at times like it mattered how fast I finished the act, not how much I enjoyed the process that culminated in mutual satisfaction. I wanted to finish as quickly as possible and start on something else. I was concerned only about gratifying myself and selfishly ignored the wants and needs of my partner.

Ironically, the same woman who uttered the words, "You're not any good in bed," was also the one woman whose compassion nurtured me through the lovemaking ritual. That is why it hurt so much to hear the debilitating words come from her. I felt ashamed, embarrassed, and disconnected from intimate contact for years after I heard her comment. For a short time after her ruthless comment, I went on a sex binge to fulfill my selfish desires.

After my sexual conquest phase, subsequent physical encounters abruptly ended when my lack of self-confidence impeded moments of intimacy. I was more concerned about my ability to maintain an erection and ejaculate than I was about being intimate. The racing thoughts that distracted me during lovemaking had changed. The thoughts changed to "I'm going to fail," "I won't be able to satisfy her," and "I'm going to lose my erection at any moment."

I went to see a sex therapist in 1993 and nothing came out of that meeting that confirmed ADHD was the primary reason for my inability to be sexually intimate. When I extensively researched ADHD, I found the link to sexual intimacy and that eased my mind. The revelation, however, did not ease years of frustration, puzzlement, and dejection.

The inability to enjoy the most joyful and free act in life scarred me more than all of the other symptoms of ADHD combined. I hid from intimacy when it came knocking in the form of a new female admirer. I indulged in self-pity and walked around at times with my head lowered so I did not make eye contact with an attractive female. I have contemplated suicide. My choices in life seemed reduced when I could not perform the most basic animal function.

It is sad. It is depressing. It tears me apart to think that misfiring neurons ravaged my ability to have sex. You can take all of the other *normal* behavior like successfully managing money, having a vibrant career, or flourishing in school, and stuff it in a trash receptacle for your class reunions.

The only abnormal aspect of undiagnosed ADHD was the inability to consummate sexual intercourse.

Imagination is more important that knowledge."

-Albert Einstein

EDUCATION

Amen-Short attention span, unless very interested in something (4)

Amen-Tendency to be easily bored; tunes others out (4)

Jasper/Goldberg-At home, work or school, I find my mind wandering from tasks that are uninteresting or difficult (Very much)

My erratic academic record and unmanageable behavioral problems were the obvious signs I had ADHD. I struggled every school year valiantly trying to achieve at a level that met adult expectations.

Distraction prevented me from achieving at a high level. At the core of my inattention was a predilection for daydreaming. Unless I was in gym class, the daydreaming thoughts cascaded the minute I sat down and caused me to miss significant portions of class content. My thoughts ran the spectrum, from wondering what I was going to do after school to how I was going to get even with a kid for stealing my pencil. The grade level or complexity of the subject did not matter. I unfailingly drifted out of most classroom discussions and landed into my own little daydreaming world.

Extraneous stimuli affected my attention span, like a commotion that came from the playground, the noises that came from outside the classroom door, or discrete conversations held by classmates in nearby seats. I loved sitting by the window so I could gaze outside at all of the activity I missed by being ensconced at a desk or cubicle. The end of spring semester was when I consistently started an academic slide. I wanted to be outside playing on a spring day. There were times when teachers could have been lip synching, because I would not have recognized the difference between silence and their classroom lectures.

I firmly believed the inattention abated when I enrolled in the MBA program at the University of Missouri-St. Louis. At the age of thirty-four, I was confident I finally had the discipline, wherewithal, and positive attitude that I sorely lacked during my academic career. I vigorously prepped for the GMAT and psyched myself up with the internal catchphrase, "this time I'll thrive in school." I did not even get by much less thrive.

The first semester was tolerable. I applied myself and completed all of the assignments and projects expected of me. I kept up with homework and even focused at a high level inside of the classroom. My final grades were indicative of the time and effort I put into the coursework. I was confident that I put my lackluster education history behind me. My second semester schedule included an introduction to Management Information Systems. I eagerly entered the classroom on the first day of school and chose a seat behind one of the computer monitors. As customary, I chose a seat in the last row that was on an aisle.

The curriculum entailed a nascent concept called the World Wide Web and a variety of software applications that Microsoft quickly rendered obsolete. I liked the Web so much that I spent the majority of class time going in and out of discussion boards, usually with the intent of offending someone with some type of caustic comment. The instructions about electronic mail were nothing more than puerile exercises for me. I continually sent two women, who sat in front of me, salacious email that included pointed barbs about our professor. They cackled as if we were in second grade again and I had just whispered a wisecrack into their ears.

I also had a difficult time paying attention and integrating myself into group discussions in the other class I took that semester. The course examined the relationship between business and the legal system. Our textbook was the daily edition of the *Wall Street Journal*, which was a cool supplement to the classroom lectures.

The professor was a real jackass. He was the immaculate example of an authoritative jerk who tried to mimic John Houseman's character in *The Paper Chase*. He did not like my tendency to blurt out comments in the middle of his discourses. The students despised me for the way I talked down to them during current event debates.

I assimilated nothing, except for a few terms like hacker and pornography. I should have surrendered to the education system and withdrawn from a program that cost me about one thousand dollars a semester. I inexplicably signed up for one more semester. I dropped out of all three classes, two of which were beyond the deadline to recoup any of my tuition money. My tenure lasted two semesters in the University of Missouri-St. Louis MBA program. The goal to procure a MBA was irrational, given my record of accomplishment in the sausage grinder.

By the age of thirty-four, with my proclivity to underachieve in the sausage grinder firmly established, I decided to hang up the backpack and seek knowledge through unconventional methods.

****

School was the perfect setting for my ADHD to flourish.

It all started with having to sit still for the entire length of a class. The desks in grade school were so unwieldy that I could barely squeeze into a seat. I raised desks with my legs and waddled around the classroom like a pregnant goose, much to the amusement of my classmates and chagrin of my teachers. I became restless within minutes after a class began, passing time by engaging in activities that disrupted class like shooting spitballs or throwing objects at other kids. The biggest problem with my behavior was it seemed there was not a punishment severe enough to curtail it.

Prior to enrolling in middle school, after-school detention usually meant sweeping the hallways and taking out the trash. My decision to disrupt class depended on a teacher's reputation or my experience with their reprimands. Most teachers did not even want to deal with me for another hour after school, so they made me sit outside the classroom after a disruptive episode. I spent so much time outside of my second grade classroom that I told classmates I was brushing up on my hall monitor skills.

I rejoiced when a teacher said we were going to watch a film. I was especially elated when the film started and the teacher left the classroom after admonishing us to stay in our seats. I disrupted the film by throwing objects at the video screen, blurting out answers to the film's questions, making lewd noises, and involving other kids in my schemes. In fourth grade, I spent the duration of one film dropping wet paper towels from our third floor window. I still see the children fleeing from my paper bombs.

My favorite tactic during a film was to raid lunch bags. I lowered myself and crawled under the protection of a darkened room to the area where we kept our lunches. I loved to torment one kid in particular. His mother packed him squishy things like bananas and PBJ sandwiches, so I tore into his bag and smashed the shit out of those items. I also took big bites out of his sandwich, making sure I left large enough tooth impressions for him to see. Thankfully, Gil Grissom and his team of crime scene investigators were not around to match my tooth marks to the sandwiches.

None of the after-school punishments had an official term until 7th grade, the first year when teachers slapped a seventh hour on to my school day. They were the hour spent after school to answer for disruptive behavior. I collected multiple seventh hours on the same day. By the time I got my third seventh hour, I sarcastically informed the teacher "I'm already spoken for." I set a record for seventh hours in Mr. Essmeyer's math class. He handed me fifty-nine of them over a nine-month period. We became acquainted with each other over the course of the school year.

An amazing thing happened. The three components of ADHD waned during Mr. Essmeyer's seventh hour. At first, I sat and counted the minutes until I was free to leave. Mr. Essmeyer eventually incorporated learning into my seventh hours. He realized I was more productive when I was alone and my attention was riveted on him.

Mr. Essmeyer ceased issuing me 7th hours towards the end of the school year. His after-school punishments turned into offers to review the math material. My grades improved rapidly when I received the one-on-one focused learning I was not getting when I blew spitballs in class.

****

IRRITATION

I cannot sit still or stand long enough for a photograph. The agitation of having to listen to someone implore me to smile or position myself in some superficial manner usually leads me to form some type of goofy facial expression. I appear in school photographs as if I want to explode out of the sitting position and grab the photographer's throat.

****

I was confused about the story of the tortoise and the hare. How could a reptile, with a cumbersome shell enveloping its body, make it to the finish line before the swift hare? I did not buy it. Teachers repeatedly told me the story when I was a young child. I never understood the metaphor meant to take my time, check my work, and hand in a carefully crafted assignment or completed test.

The propensity to rush through things hurt the quality of my work. I never proofread tests, projects, or homework assignments. My goal was finishing first in the academic dash. I never colored inside of coloring book figures or cut paper in a straight line. My clay-molding project in sixth grade was so hideous that I threw it out of a third floor window in disgust. I then ripped off another kid's project that won third prize in our art class competition. I gave the ashtray to dad on Father's Day.

I have in my possession an abundance of art from when I was in pre-school until I stopped taking art classes in 6th grade. The prevailing theme of my work was the way I drew or painted pictures. The pictures look like I had only twenty seconds to complete them before heading to the bomb shelter for a tornado drill.

Artistic Mess

I rushed through school projects and assignments like I have rushed through life. Part of the reason I rushed through projects was my obdurate desire to be the first one done. Mostly, I rushed through projects because of an ADHD mind that pushed me to finish anything I started as fast as I could. I was not concerned about quality. I stopped enrolling in typical male classes like shop and electronics because my work habits were so shoddy. I got a D in shop instead of an F because either the teacher had a big heart, or he realized that trying to get me to slow down was an invitation for him to take an early retirement. He moved me onward in the sausage grinder.

I rarely read the directions or instructions that accompanied tests. It makes me wonder what my test scores would have been if I had slowed down, read the directions, and concentrated on each question. My level of intelligence belied all of the poor test scores. I cannot locate my IQ score in the sundry of personal artifacts I have collected throughout the years, so all I have to go on are the online IQ tests I have taken over the past two years. My scores range from 128 to 141, a range that states I am gifted or a borderline genius. The scores may not be indicative of my true IQ. I tore through the IQ tests like any other test put in front of me.

My level of intelligence is not commensurate with my mediocre academic record. Educators gave me many labels, most notably the infuriating label of chronic underachiever.

****

"Physical evidence," Gil Grissom said on *CSI*," always leads you to the truth."

An ADHD diagnosis does not include physical evidence. The diagnosis relies on anecdotal descriptions of an ADHDer's condition. The evidence that ultimately leads us to the truth about ADHD lies within the wiring of our brains. Until then, I have to settle for the current system of soft evidence.

The most conclusive soft evidence of my ADHD is in a plastic pouch that contains all of my secondary education report cards. A review of the report cards verifies my erratic academic performances. My grade point averages fluctuated like the stock market during periods of over speculation. Not only did my performances radically change between semesters during the same academic year, they also started out strong and then finished weak or vice versa during the same semester.

Sophomore year of college is an excellent example of my grade fluctuation. Living in a fraternity house for the first time caused a partying spree unmatched during my academic career. I had to scramble during finals just to pull out a 2.2 GPA during the fall semester. Under pressure from the home front, I posted a strong 3.3 in the spring semester to assuage my parents' concern. Nevertheless, the 3.3 average was well below the mark I was at just two weeks before finals. Another weak spring semester finish due to my mind wandering towards the disturbances outside of classroom windows.

My academic performances depended on the ability to focus, my interest level in the class, and the impulsive decisions I made on how to spend my time. I vacillated so much that I consistently achieved a high A on one test, followed by a low D on the next. The grade fluctuations must have driven my parents to the point of inexorable bewilderment, not to mention what it did to my instructors.

Our elementary school report cards not only included a letter grade designation, they also included an effort number grade listed directly next to the letter grade. I occasionally received a number grade at least one level lower than my letter grade, which was an indication I was not reaching my full potential. On the left side of the report card were a list of personality traits and work habits. If the teacher checked any of the categories, then I needed to work on that specific area in order to improve my academic record.

Throughout elementary school, my teachers regularly checked the categories of "lacks self-discipline," "neatness," "independent work habits," "inattentiveness," and "proofreading." My 4th grade teacher was so frustrated that he gave me multiple checkmarks in the categories that needed improvement. You can see Mr. Young's tension by the way he dug small holes into certain categories, as if he let out a huge frustration roar when he made his marks. He even added small editorials to some categories, including the independent work habits category where he wrote with obvious angst, "Too fast!" My 2nd grade report card is almost a carbon copy of 4th grade, without the editorials added to the checkmarks.

I consistently brought home marked up report cards during every elementary school year except for the fifth grade. Mrs. Ogles was an engaging teacher whose radiant smile and positive energy put me at ease and made class a little more bearable. More importantly, her teaching style mitigated my ADHD symptoms and improved my academic performance.

We constantly moved about the classroom during class sessions by participating in education drills like spelling bees and math speed competitions. I thrived in a classroom setting that required spelling words or computing math problems on the chalkboard. We met in groups to work on projects and she made it a point to call on every member of the class during her lectures. Mrs. Ogles did not force me to sit in a desk for any considerable length of time. I did not have to calm my shaking legs and itinerant nature because the class was set up to be interactive. I was excited to go to school in 5th grade, the only year of my academic life that my pulse reverberated in a positive manner.

The way Mrs. Ogles taught should have been the model that promoted ADHD education. The problem is nobody took the time or had the hard data to confirm I had ADHD. The condition was not the talk show glamour condition back when I was drudging up blemished report cards. Someone had to notice the A's and B's with outstanding effort numbers I received in Mrs. Ogles 5th grade class. Someone had to take note that not one checkmark was placed in any personality or work habit category. I followed directions, paid attention to the curriculum, and did not blurt out answers before my turn.

****

FRUSTRATION

I cringed the first time a teacher handed me a semester long project. It happened in high school, when my 10th grade English teacher handed us an incredibly detailed writing project to analyze John Steinbeck's *Grapes of Wrath*. After about forty pages into the novel, my summation was the people were poor and pissed off. I put the book down, never again to open it and analyze the story, characters, or metaphors that supposedly leaped out of the book for all to see.

Procrastination is a frustrating behavior. I procrastinated on any semester long project that a teacher handed out on the first day of class. If I had homework due tomorrow, it was done by tomorrow. But three, four, five months down the road? There were quarter draw nights to enjoy at the West End and girls to chase up and down the hallway. There was always something better to do because I had time, lots of time.

I wrote a letter to my Public Administration (my college major) advisor that informed him I would not be submitting a project for a class he taught, begging him in essence for a D in the class so I could graduate. I got the D, but I did not know why I could not start lengthy and involved projects. I now know why: I never comprehended how satisfying instant gratification influenced my future academic performance.

****

I could have averted some of my inattention problems. I never sat at the front of a class unless the teacher was using an alphabetized seating chart and the letters PO put me in the front row. I always surveyed the classroom layout on the first day and immediately looked at the back row, where I found an assortment of burnouts and behavioral problems. I chose the back row anyway and sat through entire class sessions assimilating absolutely nothing from the class discussion. It did not help that the malcontents sitting beside me were distractions as well.

I started a novel approach to absorb college class lectures. I implored or paid fellow students to take notes for me while I sat through the same class. When the class was over, I compared my notes with those of the person who helped me.

Not only were my notes incomprehensible due to poor handwriting, they were also fragmentary, with important parts of the lecture missing from the notebook. If a teacher listed the succession of presidents, I got George Washington as the first, but missed the next five until I wrote down Andrew Jackson. I could not even get the instructions right for completing homework assignments. I either incorrectly transcribed the instructions or did not remember to write them down. I figured out class attendance was not necessary if my notes were to be neatly written and organized for my review. Why bother going to class when I was not absorbing the material?

I first took the truancy route in high school. I did not skip entire school days, just a class here and a class there when I felt like a stroll to the convenience store or spending an hour in Kirkwood Park. On some days, I showed up for the third class. On other days, I left after the third class. School attendance was a whimsical merry-go-round.

I consistently skipped college classes, especially the ones that had hordes of students packed into an auditorium. My favorite declaration on the first day of class was, "Most of your grade is based on what is in your textbook." I knew after the first day of class that I needed a Rand McNally atlas to find my way back to the classroom so I could take the final. The only college classes I attended on a regular basis were the ones where instructors used attendance as the main criterion for assigning a grade.

I fought the brutal Des Moines winter mornings on my way to class. The winds cut palpable lines across my face as I muttered obscenities at Mother Nature. Des Moines was a brutal place in the winter, where the artic blast crossed an unencumbered farmland landscape straight into an icy soul. After twenty minutes of frozen purgatory, I walked in from the cold and towards the room where I would waste fifty to ninety minutes of my life. Right before making the last turn towards the room, I abruptly made an about-face and headed outside towards the warm bed in my apartment.

I gave the valiant college effort to fight undiagnosed ADHD, but I acquiesced to the reality of my symptoms. I was fortunate to devise a system in order to make it through the sausage grinder. The note-takers preserved my academic record.

****

We utilize a variety of sausages in varied ways. We have pork sausage, beef sausage, and something called Chorizo. We use sausage in our spaghetti sauce, on top of pizzas, and between toasted garlic buns. I like sausage with pasta and will occasionally dabble in a slathered up barbecue sausage sandwich. My least favorite is education sausage. Not the crap they call food in the cafeteria, but the absurd process of grinding students through the same educational routine.

Diversity underscores the political correctness movement. The diversity mantra is a sanctimonious plea to ensure that our places of employment, universities, and communities reflect the diverse nature of our culture. Ironically, the education system lacks diversity. The education system expects every student to go through the same inane process, regardless of ability, acumen, or interests. The people who sit behind their office desks at higher learning institutions fail to recognize that the first place we need diversity is in the manner in which we teach our children.

Students who have ADHD are one segment of the student population that requires specialized accommodations in order to thrive in an educational environment. I do not mean sending them off to another building for kids with disabilities. Children and adolescents with ADHD need an environment that allays the debilitating effects of classroom distraction. They need focused attention from a teacher or a tutor. I would have benefited more from one-on-one teaching instead of herded into classrooms with twenty other students.

Why do we continue to shove the generic education system down the throats of children who may succeed under a different regimen? I have mentioned why I did so well in Mrs. Ogles' fifth grade class. The class was vibrant and her instructions were laser sharp. While it was not a pure one-on-one environment, it was close enough for me to engage in the learning process. Mom was the quintessential home school instructor, having been a teacher before giving up her profession in order to raise three children. My sister-in-law followed the same teaching path. Her oldest child is now in the grinder after flourishing in home-based education.

Why did I have to endure a year of physics when I have not used any of the information in the thirty years since I took it? My physics teacher once asked the class how fast a rock was falling if it had so much mass and that much acceleration. I told the classmate sitting next to me, "Who the fuck cares! It is going to hurt like hell when it hits you on the head." I could have used the three years of high school to pursue my interests, like writing and political science. The same requirements applied to every student, regardless of our interest or acumen in the subject matter.

I am not sure how it works today in the classroom except schools need metal detectors to screen kids before they enter the building. From reading about the hyper-competitive nature of college entrance examinations, it seems like nothing has changed. The main difference between contemporary education and my school experience is the amount of prescription drugs shoved down the throats of children. The education hierarchy is creating an army of mindless zombies. I strongly urge parents who have ADHD children, especially those with strong distraction and hyperactivity components, to consider home schooling or at least a more intimate environment for your child to learn.

I always tell corporate recruiters that receiving a college degree is the most significant achievement of my life. I had to make many creative adaptations in order to keep my head above water at Drake University. Once I saw that classroom inattention could cost me a shot at a degree, I came up with ways to compensate for the distraction component of ADHD. Nobody understood how difficult it was to earn my college degree.

College Degree

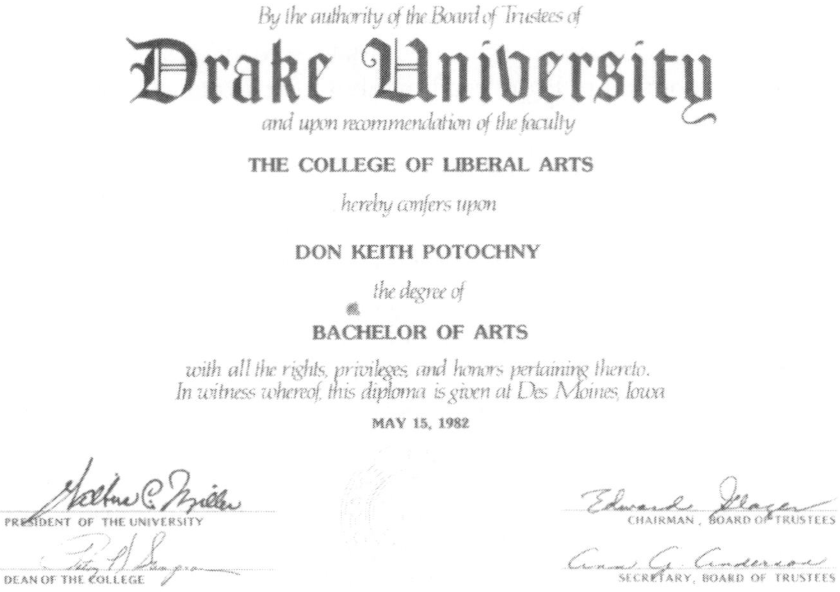

By the authority of the Board of Trustees of

Drake University

and upon recommendation of the faculty

THE COLLEGE OF LIBERAL ARTS

hereby confers upon

DON KEITH POTOCHNY

the degree of

BACHELOR OF ARTS

with all the rights, privileges, and honors pertaining thereto.
In witness whereof, this diploma is given at Des Moines, Iowa

MAY 15, 1982

PRESIDENT OF THE UNIVERSITY

CHAIRMAN, BOARD OF TRUSTEES

DEAN OF THE COLLEGE

SECRETARY, BOARD OF TRUSTEES

After the futile attempt to procure a MBA, I realized my most prolific teacher is the computer because I control the flow and content of information. High schools promote interactive learning and of course, there are universities that provide curriculum over the Internet. I find the new curriculum to be a welcome departure from the mundane and mostly worthless time I spent in the classroom.

I learn Spanish via CDROM discs. I am developing Excel skills by completing textbook chapters at a rate that is commensurate with my attention span. I absorb the morning news from the Internet. I am no longer part of a consortium of students trying to learn at the same time. I learn best from one other person or in an interactive environment at my own pace.

Higher learning "experts" want diversity. Try diversifying the methodology you devise to teach our children. Otherwise, I will take a toasted garlic bun for my next education sausage sandwich.

****

IRRITATION

I am sick of hearing the elitist term diversity. The diversity movement is the quintessential double standard imposed by those far removed from reality, perched in their corporate human resource departments and college universities. One of ADHD's appealing traits is questioning the status quo, to offer a contrarian point of view. To the scholars at institutions of higher learning, diversity is not about disparate points of view, but about skin color, gender, and sexual orientation.

Corporate human resource departments and college administrators forget about age diversity. Americans are a society that shovels anyone over fifty into a retirement trash heap and then tries to dump them into an area where they cannot make an impact on our culture. The wanton disrespect of our elders will change when the baby boomers take over the age discrimination debate.

Age diversity will resonate on college campuses and in corporate human resource departments for the next twenty years.

"Success is the ability to go from one failure to another with no loss of enthusiasm."

-Sir Winston Churchill

CAREER

Amen-Poor listening skills (4)

Amen-Easily distracted, tendency to drift away (4)

I thought a college degree gave me instant access to any company that recruited on the Drake campus. I shunned input from the career counseling office and went in search for the first professional job on my own. I created my first resume, wrote my own cover letters, and prepared for interviews without seeking advice from anyone who was familiar with the job search process. The first interview during my senior year of college was with upstart retailer Wal Mart.

The interview was a veritable disaster. I had no idea about the types of questions the recruiter planned to ask me. My resume was incoherent and included superfluous information. I left the interview more confused than ever about the job search process. My self-esteem was low following the embarrassing interview performance in front of a company I thought was beneath my intellect and self-professed superior academic credentials.

Liberty Mutual requested an interview after my Wal Mart fiasco. They flew me to Chicago to discuss a career opportunity over lunch. I did not follow interview protocol in an open social setting. I smoked during the interview and even ordered a beer that I left untouched after I perceived the recruiter's disapproval. My organizational skills at the time were weak and it showed by my lack of interview preparation. I mistakenly assumed that any company flying me, Mr. Big Shot, to Chicago had an interest in my background and credentials. I flew back to Des Moines mystified by my first two interview performances.

My interviews were doomed before the recruiter asked the first question. I wore disheveled clothes or attire that was inappropriate for someone trying to exude a professional image. My legs moved in the same motion that a cyclist uses when he negotiates the steep inclines of the Tour de France. My shoulders slumped and I rarely gave a recruiter eye contact. My eyes darted towards every object that piqued my interest.

The recruiters who did not make up their minds quickly did so after the initial perfunctory questions. I did not comprehend the implications of a question. I also blurted out questions before recruiters finished with their sentence. During one interview, the recruiter started to ask, "Where do you …" and I finished his question with, "…want to be in five years?" I smiled as he slowly recoiled from his position and sternly said, "No. Where do you see yourself with our company in a year?"

My answers to interview questions were rambling discourses that had nothing to do with the question asked. I answered interview questions in a speech format. The speeches were pontificating editorials on unrelated topics. For most of my interviews, I had to ramble on since my interview preparation was abysmal.

I continually demonstrated during interviews that I was an impulsive person. Contemporary personality tests expose people who exhibit similar behaviors. For the first ten years that I interviewed for jobs, it was up to the interviewer to discern whether I was mature and stable enough to warrant a job offer. The verdict was usually a resounding no.

I finally polished my interviewing technique by assiduously preparing myself for potential questions and thoroughly researching company information. I was knowledgeable about restaurant management topics and calmly communicated my expertise, sans the leg shaking and pen tapping. The inclination to rush through interviews also waned, as I looked forward to an equal exchange of information with a potential employer.

After I became adept selling myself during face-to-face interviews, companies decided to cut back on recruiting expenses and conduct initial interviews over the phone. If my mind wandered when I was in a face-to-face interview, it certainly raced like a hamster cage wheel when a recruiter interviewed me over the phone.

I needed to meet an interviewer in person because I could not tell over the phone when they were about to complete a question. I loathed phone interviews so much that I did one in the nude. The interview went well, but that was because the female recruiter who interviewed me had just enough sensuality in her voice to grab my attention.

****

FRUSTRATION

I abhor talking on the telephone. I have no idea what the other person is doing on the other end of the line. People who call me would be surprised at some of the faces and gestures that I make when I am on the phone with them. I stand over my answering machine and listen while someone leaves a message. Sometimes I pick up; sometimes I do not. My golden rule is a phone conversation should never last longer than the time it takes for me to meet with someone in person.

If you live down the street, our phone call will last less than one minute.

****

Amen-Frequent, impulsive job changes (3)

Jasper/Goldberg-I make quick decisions without thinking about their possible bad results (Quite a lot)

The General Manager seemed impressed with my background after scrutinizing my resume and asking me a few of the same questions I have heard over the past twenty-five years.

“I like what you bring to the table, Don. You have energy, enthusiasm, and a lot of knowledge about the restaurant industry. But your resume indicates there are some red flags with your job history,” he said.

I had to bite my lip so I did not laugh at his statement, because the reality is there are not red flags on my resume. My resume is one big white flag, essentially a piece of paper that screams, “I know I can’t keep a job, but could you give me one more chance?” There are so many holes in my resume that I have worn copies of it as a hairnet. If forced to produce a factual resume starting with my first job, I would provide a document longer than the Dead Sea scrolls and more confusing than reading a federal tax instruction booklet.

Most prospective employers did not even bother to ask for a resume after reading my job application. They have routinely discarded my applications because the person reading it could not decipher the mess that I put on paper. I filled out applications too fast, making numerous mistakes like putting my name on the Social Security line. Not many employers want to speak with someone who cannot follow simple directions. I finally asked to take applications home so I could take my time and neatly proffer my qualifications.

Pope's Cafeteria was where I filled out my first job application and it was my introduction to the working world. I was the pot scrubber, the employee in the chain of command who pried chunks of lasagna out of chafing pans until my elbow required Tommy John surgery. Black & Decker should have developed a power drill to extricate the crap that was super-glued to the pans. I immediately hated the job because not only did scrubbing pots suck, but I also had the pleasure of working for my first asshole boss. I never claimed to be a human resource specialist, but I assumed any job that entailed chiseling the remnants out of a buffet chafing dish required an empathic supervisor.

I decided to get even with my boss after an impulsive ADHD light bulb lit up one night while I was on a trash run. I went back inside and stuffed as many of the dirty pots and pans as I could into a trash can. I then clandestinely went out the back door and dumped all of hardware into a dumpster. I told dad that I quit the job because it was taking time away from my studies, which impressed him because he was concerned about my academic diligence. Pope's Cafeteria was the beginning of a trend that has spanned three decades.

ADHD experts claim frustration is the number one reason for impetuous job-hopping. I did not have the patience to work for or with a bunch of uncaring, selfish people. Frustration poisoned the workplace after an employer passed me over for a promotion or did not recognize me for putting in extra effort. When I truly felt unappreciated or neglected, I walked out unannounced or I did not show up for my next shift. The no-call, no-show section of any training manual should read "The Don Potochny method of quitting."

I had a constant need for stimulation and demanded new challenges on a regular basis. If a job did not provide increasing levels of responsibility, frustration mounted until I eventually created a void in the work schedule. If I decided to hang on a little longer, I directed my vindictiveness towards the employer.

I got so disgusted with the my lack of progression at a major restaurant chain that on the day I quit, I poured bottle after bottle of high end booze down the sink before I clocked out for the last time. In another fit of impulsive anger, I quit a bartending job during a busy Friday night happy hour. I drove home, took a shower, and drove back to the same commercial center to start working for a competitor.

I gave the obligatory two-week notice to employers early in my career, until I realized a two-week notice was just a ploy for the employer to find a replacement before the culmination of two weeks. Therefore, I became king of the instantaneous job resignation. I have gone to work, pulled up into the parking lot, and then suddenly driven off for an episode of no-call, no-show. I have gone to bed at night angry about a shift, only to awake in a more foreboding mood that hastened another no-call, no-show.

Like many people with ADHD, I have experienced self-doubt for most of my life. The self-doubt started in childhood and carried over into my adult professional life. I have always prejudged new encounters on negative past experiences. The thought of not reaching my professional potential or disappointing yet another manager haunts me every time I begin a new job. I wish I could wipe my sordid professional record clean and start over with a blank piece of paper.

****

Early into my junior year of high school, I met for the first time with a career counselor to discuss my vocational aspirations. This was a futile session for me because I did not know what I was going to do after school on any given day, much less what I had in mind for my future. My first meeting with the career guru entailed the completion of personality profiles. It was a meaningless process because even Albert Einstein could never have constructed a lucid profile for me.

Occupational counselors delineated my strengths and weaknesses. They then tried to match my profile with a career. The list of potential occupations for me was long. The restaurant industry never made it on the list that depicted occupations commensurate with my personality strengths, skill level, and occupational interests. An early diagnosis of ADHD may have prevented the inordinate amount time I wasted with career advisors.

The most comprehensive career profile test I took in high school spit out three possible occupations for me: forest ranger, social worker, and public administrator. I must have scored well on all of the questions about service. My profiles consistently churned out pieces of paper that said I was a caring individual, which eliminated me from becoming part of Dick Cheney's staff.

My career picture became more muddled in college. The career development office scheduled me for interviews with Wal-Mart, Liberty Mutual, and the Des Moines public school district. I befuddled career counselors at Drake to the extent that I expected them to put out a "Gone to lunch" sign on their office door when they knew I had an appointment.

I chose careers like parents choose Halloween costumes for their children. Instead of changing my career aspirations once a year, I changed them two or three times a month. I have aspired to be a human resource specialist, an attorney, a private investigator, an energy analyst, a commodities trader, an urban planner, a National Park tour guide, a radio talk show host, and a teacher in Korea.

The last jolt of insanity came when I received a packet in the mail that promoted the virtues of teaching in Korea. I filled out all of the paperwork, including a detailed essay on why I wanted to teach overseas. I sent back my application and waited a few weeks for a response. The response I got was, "Do you know Korean?" After I spent time preparing for a teaching job in Korea, I missed the only prerequisite that was clearly printed on the application.

I did discover that I reviled desk jobs. I worked briefly as an intern for an Iowa state agency, shuffling papers and acting as if I had impulsion behind my daily purpose. The job was monotonous. My constantly shifting priorities and inability to finish projects was an embarrassment. Sitting behind a desk eight hours a day recounted the exasperating classroom experiences from my childhood, when my legs incessantly shook, and my mind wandered the vast and sparsely decorated landscape that surrounded me. My experience with the Iowa Office for Planning and Programming eliminated one occupation. Nevertheless, I faced the intractable dilemma of selecting the right career.

I was fortunate to have found the restaurant industry, after an extremely frustrating stint as a Yellow Pages sales representative. The restaurant industry was the perfect match for me. The work was unpredictable and the multi-tasking allowed my distraction, impulsiveness, and hyperactivity-especially hyperactivity- to accentuate instead of hinder my performance.

There were some aspects of restaurant employment, however, that inhibited my vertical career ascension. I miserably failed in management training programs because of my daydreaming mind. I flunked corporate training sessions because of hyperactivity.

One of the biggest challenges that someone with ADHD will face is to find a career that fits their personality. Career coaches may help, but a person with ADHD needs to be honest in self-assessments that take inventory of strengths and weaknesses. It all boils down to what we like to do, just like the *normals*. Figure out what you are good at and what sustains your interest. Never play the silly adult game that asks the question, "What do you want to be when you grow up?" Do not capitulate to other people's perceptions of what constitutes a meaningful career.

****

FRUSTRATION

I found out about my fear of heights the first time I went up in the Gateway Arch. I took a quick glance down and immediately felt queasy. Royal Gorge in Colorado made my head spin. The Sears Tower almost made me vomit a fine dining dinner all over my date.

I thought flying would exacerbate my fear of heights. Once the plane lifts off the ground, I do not feel any symptoms while looking out at the vast horizon. I am not sure why I do not have a physical reaction to being 30,000 feet up in the air.

I do know I hate every other element of flying. There is nowhere to go. I cannot sit still for thirty minutes, much less three hours. I cannot run away from the unwelcome stranger who decides to strike up a frivolous conversation. My seat assignment cards have an invisible S, designating that I get to sit next to someone who stinks. I always seem to get the seat next to Mr. Cesspool.

"If you think nobody cares if you're alive, try missing a couple of car payments"

Anonymous

MONEY MANAGEMENT

Money management is a foreign concept for someone with ADHD. We forget when the car payment or mortgage is due. We bounce checks and neglect to pay our bills on time. We do not save for the future, because the future is now. We are unable to save for big-ticket items like vacations, computers, or home video systems. Retirement plans are nothing more than a financial mirage. Our nemesis is the credit card. We barely make ends meet or we do not earn enough for survival.

Dad was a good role model for fiscal discipline. He overcame many obstacles in order to accrue the wealth he has today. He valiantly tried, up until I reached the age of thirty-eight, to instruct me on the value of money. I do not blame money tribulations on my upbringing.

Dad taught me every aspect of money, starting with my first bank account as a young child. The concept of interest was a nebulous theory that only showed results on paper. Cash flow was nothing more than a term that described the rate money left my wallet. "Save it for a rainy day" was replaced in my vernacular by "Better spend what I've got before the sun goes down."

Inattention was the main factor in my inability to curtail spending and accumulate cash for a rainy day. I found finance and money related college courses to be boring. My mind continuously wandered, always coming back the supreme money issue of the day: fifty-cent beer pitcher specials at the West End Lounge. At least I had some concept of value.

The scatter-brained reality that is ADHD caused some embarrassing money mismanagement situations. I have withdrawn money from ATM machines and then walked away without taking the money out of the cash slot. I have left money in grocery store self-checkout slots because I hastily took the groceries, but not the change due to me. Even if I remembered to reach down and grab the cash, I left some of the bagged items on the checkout line, not realizing my indiscretion until I got home and muttered a profanity laced monologue.

Money mismanagement has impacted my life more than any other element of ADHD except for the quagmire known as sexual intimacy. When I scraped the bottom of the financial barrel, I walked a perilous line that divided destitution and solvency. Somehow, I have always shown the resiliency to rebound from a financial hit.

I see the homeless struggling to carry their only possessions to the next park bench that offers solace. I have been precariously close to that lifestyle, resorting to begging and living off the streets. Towards the end of my Chicago nightmare, I collected fallen coins in order to amass enough money to buy a lousy burrito. When I have stumbled in the material world, I have always had the abiding support of my family and for that, I am eternally grateful.

Oil and water; Donald Trump and Rosie O'Donnell; Meth-heads and paint thinner; Dick Cheney and the truth; ADHD and money management. They are all incompatible.

Money, so they say, I have none because I pissed it away.

****

Amen-Poor financial management (4)

Jasper/Goldberg-I make quick decisions without thinking enough about their possible bad results (Very much)

I attribute money mismanagement to the introduction of credit cards into my financial world. I was completely oblivious to the credit card payment option until I graduated college and received offers from credit card companies.

I had no clue about the minutiae of credit cards. I did not read the directions for anything, much less a wordy legal credit card document. Because of my flippant disregard for reading service agreements, I failed to recognize the key feature of an American Express card: no revolving credit line.

The American Express card was an extra five hundred dollars to spend, which was the limit set on my first card. Within five days of activating the American Express card, I took my girlfriend out for an expensive dinner, bought my friends rounds of drinks, purchased some overly hyped clothes, and wasted two hundred dollars on a Des Moines hooker. I reached the credit limit after one week and received a bill about three weeks after that. I owed over five hundred dollars due within ten days on a bartending job that barely allowed me to keep up with living expenses.

I called American Express to complain and the customer service representative asked if I read the agreement before I signed it.

"Of course I did," I tersely replied.

"Then you must know," the customer service representative said, "that you pay off the entire balance at the end of each month."

I told her I did not have the money and she flatly stated my days with American Express were over. I cut up the card and stiffed my first credit card account, starting a string of defaults with banks and credit card companies. I was unaware of the default ramifications because I did not see my first credit report until five years after my Chicago adventure. The American Express debacle was the first blemish on my credit record

A couple of weeks after the American Express default, I told a friend about what I did. He laughed and said I should have applied for a MasterCard, since they had a revolving credit policy. I did not know what my friend meant about a revolving credit card, but I got one nonetheless and started my own revolving credit card policy: default on one card, throw it out, and then get another.

Credit cards were a way for me to make purchases when I did not have the cash to do so. When I did not have the cash to buy a cashmere coat from Carson Pirie Scott, I used their credit card. When I did not have enough money to gas up my car, I reached into my wallet and used a Texaco card. Sears was kind enough to send me two credit cards at the same time. I exceeded the limit on both cards during one Christmas shopping spree. My relatives got some pricey gifts that year.

I only need to provide one explanation to financial advisors so they can understand my lack of financial expertise. When I paid for a group dinner with a credit card, I thought I made money on the transaction by asking each person at the table to pay me cash.

****

FRUSTRATION

I never read the fine print on anything. Long-winded legalese documents lost my attention immediately after the greeting of

"Dear Sir." I referred to an owner's manual only after the product broke down. I read the instructions of a board or video game only after incorrectly playing it multiple times.

My mind wandered, I wanted immediate satisfaction, and I did not have the patience to read small print documents.

****

My first bank account was a doggy bank. I placed all of the coins that I earned through odd jobs and allowances inside of a semi-plush, dog-shaped container. The problem was there was not much of a rattling sound, since the coins I placed in the doggy bank quickly found their way to the inside lining of my pants pocket. Gary's doggy bank was always full of coins and I helped myself to his stash when he was not around to catch me in the act. We also had a family doggy bank that was on the top shelf of a bedroom closet. The dog had a smile on his face because he was replete with silver half-dollar coins. The smile receded when I reached my grubby hands into the bank to snare coins, which was my introduction to John F. Kennedy.

Mom occasionally handed me five dimes to buy five packs of baseball cards. She implored me to open one pack of cards a day in order to stretch the money she gave me. That was like placing five lines of cocaine in front of an addict and telling him to snort one line an hour. I opened every pack before I got home, feverishly tearing off the packaging to see if I got my favorite player. When I was disappointed with the collection of players, I ran upstairs to pinch some dimes out of my brother's doggy bank. There was no reason to check my doggy bank because it was empty.

Things did not get any better when I opened my first real bank account. Dad tried to explain the ledger concept for tracking my savings account, but the account invariably had zeros in the balance column. The first bank account of mine to hit four digits was the one I started after college. By then, I somewhat comprehended the value of saving money through an interest bearing account and my balance slowly grew to over $1000.

I took the $1000 to Chicago where I opened an account that started out as a savings account, but quickly turned into a cocaine binge account. Four years later, I started another savings account in St. Louis. I resolved to diligently save money and not touch any of it unless I needed some cash for an emergency. My first DUI was the money emergency and my account emptied into an attorney's Caribbean cruise account.

I have somewhat controlled my impulsive spending, but that does not mean I have become an astute shopper. I never price compare or use coupons at grocery stores. The final tab is incessantly higher than what I plan to spend. I buy clothes straight off the rack without trying them on. The purchasing mistakes exacerbate when I discard the sales receipts. I am stuck with clothes that do not fit.

Financial management was one of the Boy Scout merit badges required for achieving Eagle Scout. How I got someone to sign off on that merit badge is beyond me. I probably used an ADHD coping mechanism to cover for my financial awareness shortcomings, like cheating my way through the work or forging the document that signified I completed the tasks required for the merit badge. Scout leaders should have ripped the financial management merit badge off my scouting vest and tossed it onto a Times Beach dioxin covered back road.

****

FRUSTRATION

Friends stopped inviting me to play games like *Monopoly* or *Trivial Pursuit* after they saw how I behaved. In addition to being a sore loser, I had little patience for people who took their time making decisions on a property purchase or trivia question. I inadvertently blurted out *Trivial Pursuit* answers before the person gave their response. I won more games for other *Trivial Pursuit* teams than I won for mine.

I played board games by myself as a kid, banished to isolated disrepute due to my ADHD behavior. Women did invite me to play naked *Twister* when I was in college.

I definitely took my time playing naked *Twister*.

****

Seven months after my visit with Dr. Kia, I signed up for three boxes of Girl Scout cookies. The little girl who sold me the boxes said she needed the money up front. It did not occur to me at the time that I had always paid for the cookies when delivered to me in person. Six weeks went by and no cookies. The precocious little girl who pocketed my money to buy a Spice Girls CD swindled me. I am not sure if ADHD had anything to do with the little girl stiffing me on the cookies.

I did have a keen sense of what goes around comes around.

"I don't know what I may appear to the world; but to myself I have been only like a boy playing on the sea shore and diverting himself and then finding a smoother pebble or a prettier shell while the greater ocean of truth lay all undiscovered before me."

-Isaac Newton

SPORTS AND GAMES

Parents generally believe that organized sports will help their ADHD child burn off excess energy. Organized sports participation is different than running around in the school playground. Organized sports require concentration on the rules of the game and strategy execution.

Above average physical skills were not enough to compensate for my wandering mind. I had a strong arm in baseball that helped me in the outfield and on the pitching mound. I eventually developed the leaping ability to slam-dunk a basketball. I had the quickness and agility to run circles around defenders when I played wide receiver in pickup and intramural football games. My reflexes made me the darling of pickup hockey games as a tall, yet nimble goaltender.

One sport confounded me.

Golf taunts someone with ADHD. The sport demands supreme patience and concentration. Dad tried to impart his passion and wisdom of the game, but I balked at his exhortation to hit the ball right-handed and the coaching seminars went downhill from there. He told me to bend my knees, stay down on the ball, and take a nice, easy swing. I could accomplish one of the three coaching tips, but not all three in their proper order. Other players constantly admonished me to take my time when errant shots led to profane outbursts. I believed golf success was finishing a round in less than four hours.

Golf pissed me off like no other activity because it seemed effortless to stand over a ball and whack it hundreds of yards down an open stretch of nature. I broke clubs after bad shots, unremittingly cursed God, and tore up pristine sections of fairways due to my tumultuous temper.

I never had the potential to get a scholarship for golf, but I did for baseball and basketball. Now I understand that ADHD held me back. The pundits are right. Most of the success one achieves in sports is due to an authoritative mental edge.

I never had a sporting chance.

****

Amen- Trouble listening carefully to directions (4)

Jasper/Goldberg- I am unable to stop daydreaming (Moderately)

Jasper/Goldberg-Especially in groups, I find it hard to stay focused on what is being said in conversations (Quite a lot)

I heard the mild roar from the crowd swell into a fever pitch. I looked around and realized that the throng of spectators, teammates, and parents were screaming at me to look up and catch the fly ball. It was too late. By the time I looked up, the ball was on a rapid descent until it smashed into my right eye. I was so proud of the shiner that when I got home from the little league game, I immediately ran over to Becky Duggan's house to show her my tough guy look.

The outfield was a tough position to play when my mind wandered. There was rarely any action for a Little League outfielder, so I stood in an upright position and daydreamed. I constantly looked over my shoulder at the developing events that occurred during other games. The typical penalty for not concentrating on the game was chasing down balls that went over my head.

In high school, I was always the player who the coach asked, “How many outs are there?” I had a one in four chance of guessing the correct number of outs. Make that a one in three chance, because even I was astute enough to realize there were three outs when the team on the field collectively jogged into their dugout.

I joked about my inattention until one game when a line drive miraculously sailed through a six-inch opening in a dugout fence and slammed into my left jaw. The jolt was so violent that my retainer embedded into my tongue. The steady hand of a teammate’s parent extricated the retainer. Three glasses of milk per day prevented what should have been a shattered jaw.

Basketball also required concentration. The plays were intricate and changed on a moment’s notice, either at the discretion of the coach yelling from the sidelines or from the point guard holding up fingers. Teammates always chided me for my glazed eyes, mocking me with the label of “airhead.” Some went as far to insinuate that I was “fried.” They joked that I was high on marijuana because I could not absorb the coach’s chalkboard session. The irony of their pot reference was I concentrated better in a competitive sporting environment after I smoked marijuana. It is too bad I did not know about my pot remedy when I was in high school.

Even when I stayed focused, impatience and hyperactive energy diminished my performance. I always swung at the first pitch in baseball. Coaches on the other team noticed my glaring weakness and started instructing their pitchers to throw junk out of the strike zone. They knew I would wildly swing at anything that was within two feet of home plate. My coaches beseeched me to work the count when I pitched, but I ignored their pleas and threw consecutive fastballs in an attempt to get a quick strikeout.

I launched basketball shots from positions that were almost impossible to make. When a situation called for more restraint, I treated a basketball as if it was a fiery hot piece of coal that needed to be out of my hands as quickly as possible. Coaches instructed my teammates to keep the ball away from me. If that strategy did not work, they sat my impetuous ass on the bench until the game was over.

I spent a lot of time riding the pine at all levels of sports competition.

****

"Potochny! If you try one more free throw underhanded, you'll be running wind sprints until you puke."

I turned my head and saw the grim expression on my coach's face, gave him a little smirk, and proceeded to shoot the next free throw attempt underhanded. I saw Rick Berry shoot free throws that way and I wanted to emulate his high percentage rate at the charity stripe. I defied my coach's admonishment and shot the free throw the way *I* saw fit. I ran wind sprints until the coach relented and sent me home for the day. I did not puke, but I did dry heave with my body slumped over a locker room urinal.

The great Denver Miller was the basketball coach who made me run the wind sprints. Coach Miller set the national standard for high school coaches, shattering the all-time record for wins during his era. He was renowned for his suffocating full court pressure defense and creative fast break playbook.

Coach Miller also taught algebra, where he spent time during tests or quizzes drawing up plays for the next practice or game. I saw this first hand because not only was I part of his basketball team, I was also a student in his first hour honors algebra class.

Coach Miller was passionate about teaching basketball and algebra. When his rope of patience reached its end, he stormed out of practice or the classroom with his face a beet red. He then calmed down with a cigarette. I only exasperated him during basketball practice; I made it a point to curtail my excessive behavior in the classroom. I think it helped that I sat in the front row where I knew he could detect my wandering mind.

I was a physically gifted basketball player and Denver Miller knew that. That is why he never, for the last cigarette in his crumpled pack, understood why I underachieved under his tutelage. My defiance was not the only behavior that raised his dander. I could not fulfill my obligations under his intricate offensive schemes that required impeccable timing. I preferred freelancing on offense, moving myself into an open space on the court and screaming for the ball. Coach Miller threw up his arms in exasperation over the hyperactive way I played defense. I never stayed in my zone position and I carelessly tried to make steals in a man-to-man. Basketball was over stimulating, sometimes leading me to commit aggressive fouls or talk back to the officials.

Sadly, Denver Miller retired after my junior year. My progression under Coach Miller was enough to give me a shot at starting during my senior year. Though I practiced with the first unit for about a week, I received the biggest shock of my young life when Coach Meyer erased my name from the locker room chalkboard. I was so devastated that I walked with my head down. I gave up on sports, school, friends, and extra curricular activities, living for the first time in my life a hermit's existence. I started hearing on a more consistent basis the phrase, "You're not reaching your full potential." I felt like an unmitigated failure and did not have a clue as to what was causing my mental lapses. The technical aspect of sports perplexed me.

I also failed to follow simple instructions from my coaches. On two occasions, I did not hear the coach instruct us to wear our full uniforms to the next practice. I showed up to a little league practice game in street clothes-baseball undershirt, jeans, and tennis shoes. The other players wore their full uniforms. I thought someone conspired to make me look bad until the coach asked, "Didn't you listen to what I told you yesterday?" In high school, I showed up for the team photo day in a t-shirt, blue jeans, and red jacket.

****

Rule breaking was my favorite sport. I learned how to bend or obliterate rules in childhood when I played the neighborhood games of *Kick the Can*, *Manhunt,* and *Capture the Flag*.

Kick the Can was a game where a kid sat on an empty coffee can, covered his eyes, and counted to fifty while the other kids went to hide. After counting to fifty, the kid on the can became the hunter. He had to find and tag a kid before another kid ran in to kick the can. Cheating in this game was facile. I made sure that my fingers were apart so I could see where the kids were hiding. I then came up with a plan to tag the kid who seemed the easiest to catch.

Manhunt entailed a scenario where a group of older kids gave a limited number of younger kids five minutes to run away and hide. When the five minutes were up, the horde of older kids began looking for any of the younger kids who were hiding and, if they caught one, performed some type of infantile punishment like tying the poor soul to a tree. We were supposed to stay within a certain boundary in our neighborhood during *Manhunt*, but I ran as far away as I could to avoid capture. Sometimes, I ended up a couple of miles away from home.

In *Capture the Flag*, the most important rule was that at least a portion of the flag had to be visible in order to make the game competitive. I always stuffed the flag into the ground and covered it with dirt or I used my height to put the flag as high up into a tree as possible. I enjoyed playing the game at my house, where all it took was simple cheating to capture the flag. I stood inside and watched where the other team hid it.

I never liked to be constrained by someone else's boundaries or rules. I took rule breaking and cheating into organized sports, which got me into trouble with coaches at all levels of competition. Cheating was a way to get one up on the competition, to get an edge towards the ultimate goal of victory. I admire Bill Belichick for taking the art of cheating to another level.

Two incidents left an indelible impression, albeit a negative one, on two of my coaches. In grade school, I learned the art of tripping basketball opponents when they tried to fight through a screen. During one game, my coach caught me tripping an opponent who was driving for a lay up. He took me aside and gave me the type of tongue lashing that I usually got from my parents. I did not play as often the rest of the season, which was the first time I clearly saw the ramifications of my conduct in organized sports.

The most dramatic event, the one that I still replay in my head to this very day, happened during a high school baseball practice. I made a wager with the team's best hitter that I would strike him out on three straight pitches. The only stipulation was he had to swing at the pitches if they were near the strike zone.

I took the ball behind the mound, turned my back to the plate, and added a little advantage to my side of the wager. I stuck a tack between the two seams at their closest point on the ball. I then turned around and whiffed Geoff Morehead on three straight breaking balls that broke so hard it looked like I threw a wiffle ball. After the third strike, a booming voice came from the dugout with the demand, “let me see that Goddamn ball.”

I shuddered when Denver Miller came out and looked at the ball. He threw it back to me and went back to the dugout in a huff. The tack was missing. I knew he at least saw the hole where the tack made an impression on the ball. He may have taken the tack out before tossing the ball back to me. I never got into another game that season and I wonder to this day if cheating in front of Denver Miller cost me a spot on the varsity basketball team during my senior year.

****

IRRITATION

People who smoke while they pump gas are the biggest assholes on the face of the earth. I believe thinning the herd is a good thing in an over populated world.

Do I have to be included in some asshole’s desire to meet his maker?

"You're only given a little spark of madness. You mustn't lose it."

-Robin Williams

SELF MEDICATION

Amen-Tendency towards addictions like food, drugs and alcohol (4)

Jasper/Goldberg-My mind gets so cluttered that it is hard for it to function (Very much)

ADHD appears to be a function of two brain neurotransmitters that stimulate or repress brain activity. The brain must be adequately stimulated in order to pay attention and maintain focus. On the other hand, the brain requires suppression in order to have apposite impulse control. Scientific research indicates that adults with ADHD may have only ten to twenty-five percent of the two neurotransmitters found in normal brain activity.

Many ADHD medical professionals prescribe medication for their clients in order to enhance neurotransmitter activity. Dr. Kia certainly used the prescription drug remedy when he was ready to shove Ritalin down my throat the minute I walked into his office. Besides what clinicians like Dr. Kia pompously claim, there is still disagreement within the scientific community about the efficacy or even safety of ADHD drug prescriptions.

I arrived at my ADHD revelation too late in life for a Ritalin prescription and then sent on my way as another mark on some psychologist's drug ledger. I already took the initiative to self-medicate with a variety of drugs, including caffeine, tobacco, alcohol, marijuana, cocaine, and mushrooms. I never understood why I turned to drugs until I found out about ADHD and researched the topic from A to Z. Researchers claim self-medication is a common trait among people who have ADHD. People who have ADHD self-medicate in order to suppress or fire up parts of the brain that are not functioning in a normal manner. Self-medication was how I adapted to the neurotransmitter deficiency.

Dr. Kia should have been more perspicacious when he proposed his drug remedy. I needed a stimulant like Ritalin when my mind raced in grade school. I needed Ritalin to comprehend what the coach was trying to inculcate during high school basketball practices. I needed an ADHD prescribed drug to soothe impulsiveness when I obliterated my life savings. I could have used a prescription drug to subdue my wandering mind during moments of sexual intimacy.

But then again, who is to say I would not have abused ADHD drugs as so many people are doing today? Would I have been more responsible with a prescribed drug than an illicit one? My track record indicates the answer is no.

Self-medication can lead to drug abuse and addiction. Most prescription narcotics carry the same abuse and addiction risk. Some prescription drugs inflict more long-term damage than provide short-term medicinal benefits. I always get a good chuckle when I watch an advertisement for a prescription drug that lists the benefits of taking the drug, followed by a longer disclaimer that delineates the side effects. A prescription drug may alleviate arthritis pain, but it can also cause hot flashes, pounding headaches, and explosive diarrhea.

Marijuana helped slow down my brain and control most of the ADHD symptoms without the addiction potential and negative side effects of Ritalin. If self-medication is an abomination, then so be it. The ADHD medical establishment is hypocritical for denouncing self-medication while writing us prescriptions for addictive and sometimes life threatening chemicals.

I do not indulge in cocaine anymore, since it put me on the grim reaper's doorstep. Mushrooms are a poison and the resultant effect is a multiple day recovery period; the clearing of my mental closet is not worth the physical drain of mushrooms. I have not smoked marijuana in over two years. Not only have I put my binge drinking days behind me, I have also ceased using alcohol as a crutch to help me fall asleep. Tobacco and caffeine are the only drugs I consistently use to combat the haze that sometimes envelopes my mind. I have significantly cut back on both of them.

I made it forty-four years before I found about ADHD. I devised a self-medication regimen that has not killed me yet. I do not advocate the way I coped with the wildly firing neurotransmitters in my brain. I am only explaining how I dealt with the impact of undiagnosed ADHD.

Save any pompous lectures for the pharmaceutical industry.

****

Caffeine

Rise and shine is not an adage that I follow. I rise all right, but my temperament out of bed is not even close to a shine. The early bird gets the worm after a full pot of coffee.

I did not drink coffee until my early twenties, when I frantically sought a way to rev up my internal motor after a night of drinking and debauchery. I start my day with a bowl of cereal, multi-purpose vitamin, and pot of coffee. Coffee is not the only beverage I drink for the caffeine effect. I drink tea as well, usually when I am at work and need a boost for my indolent mind.

Caffeine is a calling card to the racing neurons inside of my brain to calm down and channel a little bit of the chemical energy into concentration. Caffeine allows me to focus on priority tasks. The jolt prevents the invasion of multiple thoughts that shorten my attention span.

Tobacco

I did not start smoking cigarettes until I was twenty-four, which is at the end of the statistical curve for when people start to smoke. Most people commence with the filthy habit in their teens, induced by advertisements that portrays smoking as chic behavior. Peer pressure is another factor that determines if a teen will start smoking. Neither advertisements nor peer pressure swayed me. I thought someone who smoked looked cool.

When I was in my early teens, I snuck cigarettes out of dad's cartons and feigned inhaling the lit cancer sticks. He caught me one day lighting up in my bedroom. My punishment was to inhale a couple of cigarettes down to the filter. I gagged on the cigarettes and vowed never to try another one again.

When I worked in restaurants and hung out with people who smoked, I slowly picked up the habit until I bought packs on my own instead of mooching or pilfering smokes from others. I liked the Vantage and Winston brands. I was not fond of Marlboros because I thought the Marlboro man looked like the cowboy from *The Village People*.

I did not attribute the effects of smoking to the anxiety release that most people claimed, but I did sense a discernible difference in my brain activity. What I noticed about a cigarette was that it kicked out extraneous thoughts. Unaware of ADHD,

I still understood that tobacco had an effect on my rapidly moving mind. Researchers agree, discovering that ADHDers use tobacco as a form of self-medication.

I do not smoke a lot, at most fifteen cigarettes a day unless I am engaged in an alcohol bender. Even in my wild days, I rarely smoked more than a pack per day. I often go eight hours or more into my day before I light up, certainly not the image of a bedraggled soul rolling out of bed and lighting up a square before turning on the coffee pot. Around the eight-hour mark, I start to lose focus and the clutter becomes unbearable. After taking a few puffs off a square, the fog that permeates by brain begins to dissipate.

I have tried to quit smoking a few times. Before the expected physical withdrawals, I experienced a scatterbrain feeling that made me feel like I was living in a dream world. I became overly hyperactive when I tried to quit smoking. People who knew me commented that I was more hyperactive than usual.

Tobacco is the one self-medication crutch I wish that I never tried. The long-term health implications are not worth the temporary cleansing of my brain.

****

FRUSTRATION

Tobacco calms my brain when I am frustrated with a project that involves either assembling a product or fixing car problems.

I do not think cigarettes would have calmed my nerves when I worked on model airplanes. All of my peers spent time with their fathers or on their own constructing model airplanes and military vehicles. I never read the directions. I just went at it until the plane looked like a wounded bird.

Cigarettes did come in handy when I set delayed fused M-80s in my friend's model airplanes and ran away to safety amid the sound of large explosions.

****

Alcohol

I cannot enumerate the times when alcohol caused me to lose grip with reality and cross into a different dimension. I have calmly sat on a bar stool while quietly talking about the weather. The next minute, as if a little gremlin inside of my brain turned on a switch, I changed into the quintessential drunk who was full of antagonistic intentions. Alcohol consumption brought me to my knees in tears and caused me to carry out destructive thoughts at the snap of the finger.

Even though it is a depressant, alcohol also lowers inhibitions. The reduced inhibition accentuated my impulsive and hyperactive behavior. Alcohol took my wound up and reckless nature when I was sober and turned into a machine of utter chaos. ADHD is a formidable obstacle to overcome while trying to develop and maintain relationships. Throw alcohol into the mix and you have what one researcher calls the phenomenon of putting out fires with gasoline.

Alcohol is the supreme self-medication drug, used by millions to drown their sorrows, heighten celebratory events, or make them forget the lousy day that they just had. As a member of the restaurant industry, I have witnessed alcohol's repugnant effect on hundreds of people. I know alcohol destroys relationships, health, and finances. People should never consume alcohol when they are agitated, depressed, or pissed off at the world. I got so disgusted with the behavior of drinkers that I stopped working as a bartender.

I did not stop drinking.

I used alcohol to douse the firestorm inside of my head. A perfect example of self-medication happened after I impulsively quit my first job out of college and crawled inside of a Black Velvet bottle. I was so wound up after finishing the bottle that I made a couple of phone calls in a desperate cry for help. I was fortunate to have someone who cared enough about me to intervene and settle me down.

Alcohol had an unpredictable affect on my disposition. I drank with the best of them, even men much larger who drank on a full stomach. I could down sixteen beers over a five hour period and walk home whistling a tune I heard on the bar jukebox. The next time I went out, I unleashed a verbal harangue on a complete stranger before touching the lip of my sixth beer bottle.

I started drinking alcohol when I was sixteen. My first binge came on an overnight church youth fellowship outing when a friend and I each downed a six-pack of Busch and a few shots of Jack Daniels. I awoke the next morning, not only in trouble with the youth leader, but also wondering how I contracted the flu. My parents were informed about the church drinking incident, but they refrained from punishing me because they were not sure if the story was true. They found out soon enough when I came home late one Saturday night and vomited all over the toilet in their bathroom. I did not raise the lid to deposit the night's worth of Miller pony boys.

As I got older, I found alcohol to be a sleep remedy for those restless nights when my mind was doing a Jane Fonda aerobics workout. I also drank to self-medicate away the miserable and empty feelings I had of loneliness, isolation, and abandonment. The fact that I am in relatively good health after all of my drinking years says less of my exercise routine than of my good fortune.

Besides the toll alcohol has taken on my relationships and finances, it has also gotten me into trouble with the long arm of the law. I received my first DUI in 1989, at a time when the penalty for such an offense was a drained savings account. I did not lose my license, even though the cop gave me six ancillary citations that included reckless driving, speeding, and refusing to pull over when signaled by a police officer.

Eight years later, a Des Peres police officer pulled me over at three in the morning. I went through a variety of sobriety tests while the officer tried to find one that would give him probable cause for whipping out the breath analyzer. He found it when I tried to walk a straight line in my cowboy boots. I could not walk a straight line in my bare feet sober, much less in a pair of snakeskins. I quit drinking three hours prior to leaving a party because I understood the ramifications of another DUI. I was sleepy and must have dosed off a bit before the cop pulled me over. I measured right at the legal level of intoxication and lost my driving privileges for one year.

Contrary to the spoon-filled crap that we heard in high school, alcohol is ***the*** gateway drug. It is the gateway to bad decisions, lost tempers, and ruined relationships. It is the gateway to abuse of other drugs like cocaine, amphetamines, and heroin. It is the gateway to divorce court and the unemployment line. Alcohol's deleterious effect significantly impacts the life of someone with a normal functioning brain.

Imagine what is does to someone who has ADHD.

****

FRUSTRATION/IRRITATION

In the eight years between my two DUIs, the vultures in the legal profession and Mothers Against Drunk Driving (MADD) found a way to create a system that pays off the school debts of law school graduates, while lining the pockets of an obtuse organization that claims to be an advocate for the elimination of drunk driving.

DUIs are one of the few legal violations in this country where guilt usurps the judicial process. When you call an attorney, the glee in his or her voice is manifest over the phone because he or she has just hit the DUI jackpot. MADD sanctioned weekend intervention programs might as well be called a DUI offender's Guantanamo Bay.

Lowering the blood alcohol limit is not the answer. Involving the hospitality industry in the formulation of a real action plan that emphasizes and rewards interdiction is the way to reduce the incidence of drinking and driving.

****

Marijuana

I was dissatisfied the first time I smoked pot. There was no feeling of the high that I anticipated. I tried it again two weeks later prior to a jazz band concert. I was amazed at the feeling I had as I sat in the back row waiting to lay down some chops. My racing mind abated and the restless movements I made in the chair came to a sudden halt. I gave the best music performance of my life.

I smoked marijuana on a regular basis because of the calming influence it had on me. My daily routine in college began with four to six bongs and a Pink Floyd song. I was less distracted and more at ease in my seat. The leg shaking stopped. The urge to bolt the classroom disappeared. Pot did not completely stifle my hyperactive behavior. My friends observed that I was the most hyperactive marijuana smoker they had ever met.

Marijuana helped me perform in college intramural sports. I did not display the histrionics that were normally associated with my style of play. Everything slowed down for me when I smoked pot. I focused on the moment, though I still freelanced with my routes as a wide receiver.

The first time I smoked weed was the first time I used a drug for self-medication. I smoked it eights years before I picked up the tobacco habit. I was changing bong water six years before I started using cocaine. I rolled my first joint a full year before I drank a cup of coffee.

There is a reason for the term medicinal marijuana. Pot stilled my restless soul in social settings. It helped me stay quiet during church sermons. People remarked about my calm behavior, but I was too stoned to assimilate their praise. My only thoughts were on easing my insatiable appetite. Marijuana gave me an incurable case of the munchies.

Cocaine

Researchers often compare Ritalin to cocaine. Both drugs sharpen concentration levels, but they also present the potential for addiction. Dr. Kia made the cocaine-Ritalin analogy during our initial consultation after he asked about my cocaine usage history. What I failed to mention to him, or he failed to extract from me, was I abused cocaine to the extent that my life was headed down the road to perdition.

Cocaine initially was the best antidote for my ADHD. I liked the way it logically sorted out the thoughts that exploded inside of my head. It did not make me physically wired, just mentally connected to whatever I needed to be connected to at the time. I took cocaine while I was completely sober, usually on the job where it enhanced my concentration level.

I gained a tremendous amount of confidence in social settings when I used cocaine. I felt more comfortable in conversations and my already quick wit became rocket fast, entertaining people with humor and insight. People compared my monologues to the spontaneous and at times incomprehensible ones of Robin Williams. Some of the great comedians of my era battled cocaine addiction because they relied on the drug to give them an edge while they were on stage.

Then it got ugly. I started buying large quantities of cocaine while I was drinking, usually at an obscene hour of the night when I should have been asleep. Self-medicating with cocaine to increase my mental acuity became abusing cocaine to ease the emotional pain. Cocaine is the most abject thing a person with ADHD can put into their body, which is why I am skeptical of those who claim Ritalin and its family of narcotic stimulants are the remedy for mitigating ADHD symptoms.

Mushrooms

Mushrooms were the one drug that cleansed the mental closet, depositing all of my cluttered thoughts on the wayside and giving me access to a straight line of reasoning. They lifted the persistent fog that engulfed my thought process. They also drained me like no other drug; it took me days to rebound from the hallucinogen. Their self-medication purpose came in the clarity in which I saw my life and the answers I found when I peeled the layers away from my brain.

"Dreams never hurt anybody if you keep working right behind the dreams to make as much of them become real as you can."

-Frank W. Woolworth

SLEEP AND DREAMS

ADHD's impact on sleep is a burgeoning field of study for the scientific community. Some experts claim up to eighty percent of people with ADHD have difficulty sleeping. The most common ADHD related sleep problem is the inability to fall asleep. One study showed people with ADHD vary from the average time it takes to fall asleep by as much as two hours. Many people who have ADHD also report they often wake up during the night. Once wide-awake, they have difficulty falling back to sleep.

There are varieties of reasons for the slumber troubles, most of which have directly influenced my attempt for a restful night of uninterrupted sleep. Even when I am physically exhausted, the brain fails to follow my body's lead and continues to move at a feverish pace. At times, my brain suddenly stops on one thought and the obdurate thought prevents me from clearing my mind long enough to fall asleep.

Disruptive sleep causes psychological problems. General fatigue leads to added distraction, impulsive, and hyperactive symptoms. Fatigue also leads to health issues, including the body's inability to fend of viral and bacteria infections. ADHD's impact on my sleep is immense and closely mimics the research recently released to the ADHD community.

The one area that calls for more research is the impact that dreams have on someone with ADHD. A nebulous concept at best, dreams are tough to interpret for those who have a normal functioning brain. For someone with ADHD, the brain activity during a dream sequence is like an Independence Day fireworks explosion.

****

Amen-Difficulties falling asleep, may be due to too many thoughts at night (4)

Jasper/Goldberg-My thoughts bounce around as if my mind is a pinball machine (Very much)

I envy the people who can kick off their shoes, lay back in their chair with a good book, and unwind after a long and eventful day. In preparation for a good night's sleep, they have the ability to make the transition from being on the go all day to falling into a state of somnolence. My transition to sleep takes longer. The transition involves the impossible task of slowing down the ping-pong balls that ricochet inside of my brain.

I have always told people- particularly my family- that I soundly sleep on most nights. I do, except the process of getting to deep sleep takes time. My parents should be cognizant of my inability to fall asleep. When I was a child, I stomped around in the bedroom directly above theirs. My frustration boiled over because another night had come and I was the only one on our block still awake. I valiantly tried to count sheep, but never made it into double digits because extraneous thoughts bumped the sheep out of the counting line.

I stumbled upon a solution to my sleep woes when I started using a vaporizer to clear my nasal passages. The soothing noise from the vaporizer relaxed me. A superfluity of thoughts or the maniacal one thought did not assail me. I realized the same phenomenon occurred during the hot months of the year when a fan produced the same effect as a vaporizer. A fan always hums when I turn in for the night or take a nap. During the cold months, I point the fan away from me so the white noise can continue to soothe my restless soul.

There were times when a fan could not overcome my tendency to toss and turn in bed as if my body was churning butter. Instead of working off the excess mental energy, I drank alcohol to tame the brain's tempest. I knew alcohol was a counterproductive remedy, but I still used it as a sleep aid during moments of desperation. I started using alcohol to fall asleep while I was in college, usually as a last resort when I rolled around in my bed the night before a big test. A few years later, I turned to over the counter remedies like Unisom. I have unfailingly taken Unisom for the past fifteen years.

I am difficult to arouse after I fall into deep sleep. Not even a tornado siren that is blaring from three hundred feet away can stir me while I lay in dreamland.

****

IRRITATION

Is it asking too much for municipalities to synchronize their traffic signals? In an era when we are trying to conserve energy, you would think someone who got a Public Administration degree could figure out a way to make driving a more fluid motion. I wonder if city leaders take a course in college called "How to piss off the taxpayer."

****

Yesterday was a bad day, Mary. Everybody has a bad day now and then. I guess it boils down to how I handle a bad day, brush myself off, and move on with unbridled optimism towards the next day. I woke up pissed off and carried the sentiment into every activity throughout the day. I went to bed the night before completely devoid of any internal negativity. My pissed off disposition was due to whatever unfolded inside of my head while I slept another night away.

Dreams complicate my life. I have a keen intellect, colorful imagination, and a brain wired differently than those considered normal. I wonder how all three of the combustible ingredients affect my sleep. I do not mean the regeneration of blood cells and muscle tissue. I mean the dreaming phase of sleep, the part of my sleep in which outrageously inexplicable movies have unfolded during every night of my life.

Dreams are a phenomenon we will never fully comprehend. Researchers can attach as many brain monitoring devices as they want, but they will never be able to unlock and interpret what goes on in our subconscious while we sleep. I would like to be part of a sleep study that focuses on brain waves and dream interpretation. I cannot see myself trying to fall asleep with electrodes attached to my head. A fan emanating its beautiful white noise would help.

The dream research I have come across centers around Freudian references. I do not need a PhD to tell me the reason why I wake up with a stiff penis. The breadth of my sexual subconscious is a mystery. Some mysteries should remain unexplained.

I am intrigued, like most people, about what our brain does as we renew ourselves in deep sleep. How do the neurobiological differences in an ADHDer's brain affect the dream sequence? Are ADHDers, because of neurobiological differences and a generally high intellect, able to presage the future through their dreams? I know how some situations will unfold in my life because I dream of the future with clairvoyant clarity. I also have the quintessential dreams we read about in science publications. I have flying dreams, fleeing dreams, and episodic dreams where someone I have not seen in years suddenly pops into one my overnight movies.

Dreams affect me in more ways than just molding my daily temperament. There is not anything more distressing than my tendency to abruptly change course and pursue a different plan of action after I wake up in the morning. I fall asleep the night before starting a new job, only to awake with a completely different vision of my employment aspirations. My impulsiveness begins the minute the alarm goes off and the mental movie stops. Whatever I dream about reveals a new set of ideas for the beginning of a new day.

I wake up on some days so anxious that I feel like I have little time to accomplish daily tasks. There are days when I wake up completely exhausted, my mind numb from another night of brain neuron misfires. My bed looks like I wrestled with it throughout the night while immersed in another subconscious thriller. If my ADHD mind moves at a rapid fire pace while I am awake, imagine what my subconscious does when I drift into somnolent rapture.

Yesterday, I had another full-length dream about my Chicago assault. It has been the same dream since the fateful day in 1988, when I had the left side of my face sliced open while I slept. The dream used to be a frequent companion of my slumber, sometimes playing out on consecutive evenings in the same exact manner.

I do not recall anything in the dream until the moment right before someone violently strikes me as I lay in bed. I see the face of the perpetrator, but I cannot remember the face from the dream. Something gets lost between my recognition in deep sleep and the moment that I suddenly sit up in bed.

I no longer have frequent dreams about the Chicago assault. Yesterday was the first time I had the dream in over a year. The dream still provokes a horrendous start to my day. Because I intensely dwell on the dream, I cannot concentrate on anything but the elusive face that has haunted me for the past twenty years.

"Whether you believe you can or believe you can't, you're absolutely right."

-Henry Ford

UNFINISHED BUSINESS

For someone who stumbles through life with the mental imbroglio called ADHD, it all boils down to waking up each morning and tackling the day with a stubborn persistence. A number of ADHD experts mention tenacity and resiliency as the two traits most often associated with those who have ADHD. The perceived failures, disappointments, and hurtful labels bestowed upon us by uninformed friends, family, and employers builds a tenacious spirit inside of us. Tenacity allows us to integrate into a society that places materialistic possessions above spiritual gifts.

One of the more eloquent ADHD experts who mention tenacity is Dr. Edward M. Hallowell, the co-author of two wildly popular books about ADHD. Hallowell takes a more balanced analytical approach than most of his peers. He insists ADHD is not a debilitating disorder. He also forewarns those who have the condition to understand the symptom ramifications. He emphasizes that ADHD's positive attributes allows an ADHDer to triumph over failure. Much of the failure is a long trail of unfinished business.

Hallowell makes an astute observation that links ADHD with unfinished business. He points out that people with ADHD "have difficulty turning great ideas into significant action." Another way of putting it is ADHDers do not finish projects that take time, concentration, and effort.

My life has been full of stalled projects, incomplete assignments, and broken promises. As a pattern of unfinished business developed early in my life, people became incredulous when I promised to take action or start a project that required detailed attentiveness. The growing list of unfinished business created skepticism.

My mind sprouts new ideas like a fertile field that nurtures perennial crops. The mental crops reach fruition and are ready to for implementation into a grand plan of action. Most of the mental crops wither under extreme inattention, impulsiveness, and hyperactivity. I could devote an entire book to the number of ideas I have hatched and let fade in the fertile field that is my brain.

I hope writing this book is not another piece of unfinished business.

****

Amen-Starting projects but not finishing them, poor follow through (4)

Amen-Enthusiastic beginnings but poor endings (3)

Jasper/Goldberg-I have trouble planning in what order to do a series of tasks or activities (Quite a lot)

Decreased worldwide demand hit farmers hard during the deep recession of the early eighties. An absurd federal agricultural policy imperiled farmer income. My brainstorm was to collect a percentage of tip income and matching business donations in the Court Avenue entertainment district of Des Moines. I planned to donate all of the proceeds to a group devoted to farmer aid. My idea came before the Farm Aid concerts that became hip in the mid-eighties. I was ahead of the idea curve with my brainchild.

The problem was I conceived a complex idea that required dedication, planning, and follow through. I received enthusiastic support from the employees and restaurant owners who worked in the Court Avenue district. I contacted a friend at the Iowa State capital who had strong political connections. He was impressed with my plan and asked one simple question: "How are you going to pull this off?"

The word got around that I was planning a fundraiser for the farming community. Friends and associates stopped me on the street to ask, "How is the farmer project going?" Restaurant workers and patrons were visibly disappointed when I told them the project stalled due to a lack of support. My declaration was an outright lie. The project had support from the beginning. I just could not logically sequence the tasks necessary to organize and pull off the event. I had an idea (point A) to help a group of farmers (point F), but I had no clue about how to progress through points B, C, D and E. I quit working on the project.

I came up with a more profit-oriented idea in the early nineties. My fertile brain came up with a board game called *Rush Hour.* The game's premise centered on the hundreds of scenarios we face driving to and from work snarled in bumper-to-bumper traffic. I came up with the game's initial look and wrote out hundreds of ideas on cards that depicted the twists and turns of navigating rush hour traffic. I sketched the outline of the board and filled in most of the spaces where the game's players would take turns moving their quasi automobiles. I researched the patent process and wrote a detailed description of the game that I planned to submit along with the patent application.

Then one day, I stopped working on the game. There was not a compelling reason for putting the *Rush Hour* project into a deep mental freeze. The decision to quit in the middle of the project was strictly impulsive. Something else provoked the mental roots that captured my capricious focus and strangled the exigency to finish the project. I hit the proverbial mental wall and could not knock down the barriers that precluded me from advancing the idea. I did start a Web site dedicated to restaurant management issues shortly after dropping the ball on *Rush Hour*. The Web site is still under construction.

One prominent accomplishment in my life has required a few years of patience and untiring perseverance. I became an Eagle Scout when I was fifteen, a monumental achievement for someone who was unlikely to finish a project or task. I proudly display the vest that has all of my neatly sewn merit badges. I listed Eagle Scout as a resume accomplishment until a recruiter told me the achievement was not impressive enough to promote on an employment resume.

I beg to differ.

****

IRRITATION

We have worked with them. They have worked for me: the employee who starts with, "I know this a bad time, BUT…"

If you know it is a bad time, then why the fuck are you bothering me? Are you such a self-centered asshole that you are unable to wait for a good time to push your overweening personal agenda up my ass?

If you are a manager of anything, get rid of anyone who acts like that. They are nothing but selfish, negative ingrates. Show them the door and push them into the competition's open arms.

Is it too much to start with, "When is a good time to…?" My answer may vary from 20 minutes to 20 hours to 20 days to never. At least you showed some common courtesy.

****

1994.

I did not envision the sweeping political changes engendered by the Republican revolution. I was too damn busy. One of the classic signs of ADHD is a frantic lifestyle, starting one project and then becoming deeply involved with another. In 1994, I exhibited the classic symptoms of ADHD that coalesced to destroy friendships, eviscerate academic dreams, and create turmoil with occupational responsibilities.

A group of friends I first met after moving back from Chicago finally accepted me into their tight-knit circle. One was an aspiring lawyer who decided to run for a seat on the St. Louis County Council. He asked me to be his Campaign Treasurer, the person in charge of maintaining an accurate snapshot of campaign finances and filing quarterly financial statements with the State of Missouri.

His request for help impressed me. I deemed it an opportunity to network with some influential people in the St. Louis community. My title was mostly perfunctory, as a more prominent member of the community became the official Campaign Treasurer title that appeared on all of the campaign literature and stationary. I was responsible for the details of managing the campaign's finances. If I failed to file financial documents within the designated period, the candidate certainly would have faced negative publicity for the remainder of the campaign

The candidate offered me the campaign position in January 1994. By early spring, I was involved with the U.S.

Olympic Festival as a volunteer coordinator, immersed in a MBA program at the University of Missouri-St Louis, and trying to make financial ends meet as a bartender. I looked at my schedule and compared it to the candidate's hectic time constraints. Here was a full time, second year law student trying to become a member of an influential governing body. He was already a City Council member, so his plate was full. My schedule seemed light by comparison.

I thought I could juggle the multiple responsibilities. The first to fall was the bartending job. I hated the company and decided to walk away after a dreadful shift. I never called the company to inform them of my resignation. Like most jobs, I did not show up again. I moved on to another bartending gig that lasted less than six months. I pulled another no-call, no-show so I could start working at a popular sports bar in St. Louis County.

The Olympic Festival was a bore because my role was to enter volunteers into an archaic database system. I fell behind inputting the names because of my indifference. On a stormy spring day, I stopped inputting names, turned off my computer, and never participated in another Olympic Festival activity. I did not call them either.

I stayed on top of most of the campaign responsibilities. A quarterly report-filing deadline almost flew under my distracted radar. I noticed my oversight on the day of the filing. I hastily did the numbers, neatly wrote the report, and drove ninety miles to Jefferson City to beat the closing time of 5:00. I then drove another 120 miles to work. It was another frenetic day in the life of an ADHDer.

Work was a playground because we all knew the business was going under. Every night after work, we decided to accelerate the business' decline by drinking an excessive amount of booze with a large group of invited guests. I was not living the lifestyle of someone who had academic and professional obligations, a pattern that persisted throughout my life. I chose immediate gratification over balancing the campaign books or working on a project for a Management Information Systems class.

By October of 1994, I ceased putting any effort into the campaign. The campaign's energy diminished and I noticed odd receipts in the campaign treasury folder. The incumbent obliterated our campaign on Election Day. He rode the tail wind of the Republican revolution.

There were some hard feelings after the campaign, which came to the surface on election night. One embittered campaign worker called to scream at me after I stumbled home from the election night party. I obviously alienated some members of the tight-knit group.

I had the thankless job of filing the last campaign report. I could not account for half of the expenses from the final filing period because there was not any proof in the form of paper receipts. I quit in frustration, leaving a note for the candidate explaining my reasons for an abrupt departure. I left him with the task of figuring out the financial mess at a time when he was cramming for law school finals. Our relationship was not the same after the campaign, although he was nice enough to represent me during my second DUI offense in 1997.

1994 was going to be my breakout year, a year when I established myself as a credible player in the real world. I squandered everything, including my bank account. As the holiday season approached, I was broke and worn down from the previous eleven months of myopia.

A completely new set of ADHD symptoms came to the surface after the election. The symptoms were more egregious than the ones that occurred during the Republican revolution of 1994.

"Do not follow where the path may lead...Go instead where there is no path and leave a trail."

-Robert Frost

PHYSICAL REPERCUSSIONS

What came first: the chicken or the egg?

The debate is the fundamental question that keeps evolutionists and creationists entrenched in the middle of our heated culture war. The chicken and egg puzzle is appropriate for analyzing the ADHD condition, with a slight twist. Do early life head injuries cause ADHD or does ADHD lead to a higher incidence of accidents, some of which cause head injuries?

Researchers have spent years trying to determine the causes of ADHD. Technology has enabled some scientists to conclude ADHD is a neurobiological phenomenon. The disagreement between scientists, however, stems from whether the neurobiological cause is chemical or structural. Chemical imbalances explain a genetic root cause, while brain structure deviations emanate from a series of head injuries.

The head injuries that I sustained at an early age might have exacerbated my ADHD by either altering the structural composition of my brain or impinging the progress of neurobiological development. I received three significant head injuries-from what I remember-before the age of twelve. Each of the three head injuries was serious enough to have caused a concussion.

I did not talk much about the head injuries during my session with Dr. Kia. The only physical attribution he made to ADHD was his insistence that people with ADHD are more likely to have allergies. I have not come across any declarations by other medical experts about ADHD and allergies. Maybe Dr. Kia was trying to get me hooked on Ritalin and a powerful decongestant.

****

The brain is analogous to the CPU of a computer system. A CPU coordinates an intricate system of commands. If a CPU falls from a two-foot high desk, the impact will probably shake loose of the few connected wires, causing a variety of problems with the computer's operation.

I recently knocked over my computer and subsequently had trouble connecting to the Internet. A cable popped loose from the CPU and that prevented the computer from dialing up Internet access. Head injuries affect the brain in a similar manner. I have received some strong blows to the head that may prohibit me from having neurotransmitter access.

I was barely three years old when I tumbled down a flight of escalator stairs at a local Famous Barr. Mom was holding my hand as we reached the top of an escalator flight. I suddenly pulled away from her and tried to get to the top of the escalator on my own. I lost my balance and fell backwards down the flight of escalator stairs until I rolled over at the bottom. My head hit at least one of the jagged stair edges, giving me a deep gash that required stitches to close the wound.

I still have a knot on the back of my head from the tumble down the escalator. I vaguely remember the fall, but I unmistakably recall how I felt as I stared at the ceiling from my bed. The doctor wrapped my head with a dressing that secured the bandage and protected the stitches. The intense throbbing felt like my most recent Super Bowl hangover. Mom does not discuss the Famous Barr tumble because she was probably so traumatized that she filed the incident deep into her subconscious.

About two months after tumbling down the escalator, I came up with the anti- ballistic missile code that hastened the fall of the Soviet Union.

Anti-ballistic Missile Code

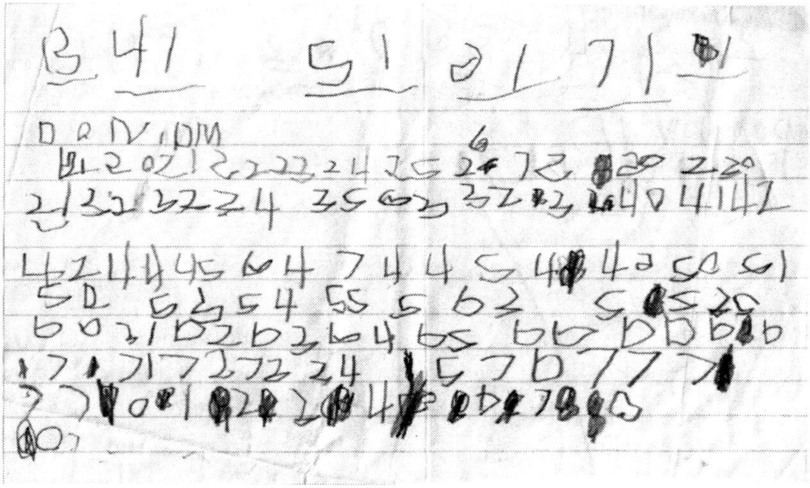

Three years later, I decided to emulate Evel Knievel. I tried some simple bicycle ramp stunts at home before deciding to try a more difficult jump at my uncle's residence in Pasadena, Texas. I missed the landing ramp and flew forward off my bike. My face slammed into the pavement in front of his house.

A local hospital treated me and I stayed bedridden until the following morning. I spent the next three days shaking off the lingering effects of a concussion. The same day the hospital released me, the entire family went to a baseball game at the Houston Astrodome. I vividly remember throwing up into a box of popcorn and did not realize until years later that nausea is a conspicuous symptom of concussions.

My third concussion happened six years later during a neighborhood football game. I am not sure if Chuck Blum meant to, but he delivered a knee shot to the base of my temple. I aimlessly wandered home from North Glendale grade school. Dad's easy chair was where I remained in a stupor for the rest of the afternoon. Before the daze receded, I had a difficult time remembering what day it was or whose house I sat in.

I have received other blows to the head that may have resulted in a concussion. I hit my head on the side of a brick porch while trying to fly like Batman. An intruder struck the side of my face with a thick soda bottle when I lived in Chicago. I put my head through a North Glendale classroom window. A classmate threw a rock from about 100 feet that struck me on the top of my head. The rock split open a large section of my scalp. The two times a high velocity baseball nailed me in the head did not help my brain's wiring system. The innumerable violent collisions I had playing sports added more chaos to an already jumbled CPU.

I speculate if my head injuries disrupted the delicate neurobiological balance within my brain. I wonder which blow to the head augmented my ADHD symptoms to a category 5 mental hurricane. Either way, I know I have a delicate situation inside of my head. I just do not know what came first, the chicken or the egg.

****

FRUSTRATION

Sermons are the most exasperating element of a church service. The Bible is ripe with metaphors and parables, and I have a hard time staying focused on the Pastor's message. I usually depart church with the thoughts, "Jesus did what?", and "God is where?"

****

Amen-Coordination difficulties (4)

I do not define coordination in terms of athletic prowess because I had physical gifts that included dexterity and balance. My coordination problems happened far removed from the fields of organized sports and the courts of neighborhood pickup games.

Mom always pleaded with us to refrain from talking when our mouths were full. She should have pleaded with us to keep our eyes on a steaming pot pie. In college, I turned my head towards a commotion going on in our apartment while simultaneously sticking my fork into a chicken pot pie. I moved the pot pie off the table and onto my lap, searing the inner portion of my thigh about one-half of an inch away from my manhood and the family jewels. The burn was so severe that blisters instantly appeared. I went to the hospital for some curative pot pie treatment.

I have a history of doing stupid things. I do not know how many car hoods have crashed into the back of my head because I did not properly secure them in the hood notch. I do not know how many times I have burned myself by touching objects such as griddles and frying pans. While I was cleaning the roof of a restaurant, I stepped on a plastic light unit and crashed through the material onto the concrete sidewalk about twelve feet below. Luckily, I landed on my ass and no bones were broken. I fell off a ledge and onto a stack of pallets while stocking items at a Des Moines grocery store. I am not sure if

ADHD was the culprit because I was drinking the store's beer prior to my flight.

To my credit, I never swallowed any of the poisons stocked in the family cabinet or ingested any medication that was not prescribed for me. The skull and cross bones insignia on toxins back in the day was more than enough to deter me from going in that direction. I was also very methodical when I crossed a street, looking both ways to make sure I was clear of oncoming vehicles. My parents and grandparents were proud of me for looking both ways. They were also shocked I finally did something without impulsively taking action.

****

I found out about allergies the same way I discovered ADHD. I caught a segment on the Discovery Channel that prompted me to dial up my old friend Google.com. Like ADHD, I went forty years before figuring out that the sneezing, coughing, and watery eyes were the direct result of allergic reactions.

Allergic reactions overwhelm my sinuses throughout the year. Spring is my favorite season, but I endure the bee's pollination of everything living with fits of sneezing and wheezing that makes me ponder destroying a hive or two. The pollen gets so severe in the St Louis region that on some mornings, there is so much of it that meteorologists should detail the pollen count as they do snowfall: by the inches of caked yellow shit that blanket our cars. Ragweed pollen makes its annual visit to my respiratory system in late August, sometimes blowing in from places hundreds of miles away.

Rain alleviates pollen allergies, but it also raises the mold count. My mold allergy usually runs year round, but it really hits hard during the growing season when the temperature is constantly above thirty-two degrees. Mold hits me like a cold, with a bloated head feeling that lasts longer than pollen allergies. Mold is the reason I take daily doses of Clariton.

The colder, drier months in St. Louis should offer a reprieve from allergies. Instead, the dry weather causes my dog's skin to flake, giving me the honor of inhaling dog dander throughout the winter months. The dander is so prevalent that it looks like someone sprinkled powdered sugar on Jasper's back.

What does all of this seemingly irrelevant allergy information have to with ADHD? You have to ask Dr. Kia, because he is the only medical professional I have come across that has made the ADHD-allergy connection. I still do not understand the correlation between ADHD and allergies. ADHD is a neurobiological condition. Allergies affect the respiratory system. When I contracted a sinus infection due to a strikingly severe allergy season, I went to see an ear, nose, and throat specialist, not a neurosurgeon.

The allergy assertion by Dr. Kia prompted my suspicion of his dubious claims. It became clear to me Dr. Kia was reaching beyond logic and entering into the vagaries of ADHD theory. Specious conjecture is one of the reasons why some people do not take ADHD seriously (see Montel Williams).

I am sure if I told Dr. Kia I had herpes, he would have said, "Well, most people with ADHD have herpes." He would have then sent me on my way to fill a prescription for treating herpes and ADHD.

"When I get real bored, I like to drive downtown and get a great parking spot, then sit in my car and count how many people ask me if I'm leaving."

-Steven Wright

THRILLS

Boredom is my constant companion. It lurks in every classroom, on every job, and at any event where a group of people listens to a designated speaker. Boredom does not give any advance warning of its presence. It is a spontaneous sensation that creates an indelible need for immediate gratification.

I can be content working on a crossword puzzle when all of a sudden boredom appears like a lightning bolt and transports me to a local sports bar. I proofread the text for a commentary submission when boredom takes me away for a boisterous night on the town. I can be leading a training seminar at work when boredom pushes me out the door to apply down the street with a competitor.

Scientific researchers promulgate the neurobiological causes of ADHD, confining their arcane explanations to neurotransmitter activity. They are missing an integral link between the brain and ADHD. The link is boredom. A vault that houses boredom quietly resides in the deep reaches of the brain. In a normal brain, the vault securely prevents boredom from permeating the thought process. In an ADHDer's brain, the vault is forced open as boredom gains control and ignites the fireworks known as impulsiveness.

When boredom escapes from the vault inside of an ADHDer's brain, what ensues is a veritable smorgasbord of thrill seeking behavior. The thrill can be jumping on a slow moving train for a few hundred feet. The thrill can be taking all of the cash we have on hand to play blackjack at the local casino. The thrill can be performing bicycle stunts similar to the ones we see daredevils attempt on their motorcycles.

Boredom is the fourth component of ADHD. Most people experience a foretaste of boredom. ADHDers handle boredom differently than the *normals*. As in every other aspect of an ADHDer's life, our response to boredom is grandiose. Instead of letting boredom runs its course, we immediately embrace it by abruptly changing course to engage in a thrill seeking activity.

****

FRUSTRATION

My grandmother introduced me to jigsaw puzzles before I stepped inside of a school. I was frustrated the instant she dumped 500 pieces onto a table and enthusiastically said, "This is going to be fun, Don!" I went through with the torture of trying to find the pieces that fit, my hands trembling in anger every time I found two pieces that met with resistance.

We eventually finished one puzzle, but I did not get a sense of achievement by completing the picturesque scene staring me in the face. Mom likes to work on jigsaw puzzles. As a subtle reminder of another activity that I cannot see to its end, she hangs the puzzles on a wall that exalts her due diligence.

I stopped getting jigsaw puzzles as Christmas gifts when I was overhead muttering, "That's why they invented goddamn cameras!" The penitence for my sins will be to work on jigsaw puzzles as the fires of Hades surround me. The only jigsaw puzzle I want to solve is meshing the multitude of pieces that form the meaning of my life.

****

Amen-Frequent search for high stimulation (bungee jumping, gambling, race track) (4)

I have completed over a dozen professionally certified ADHD surveys and checklists. Every self-assessment scale or test I took included a question about thrill seeking.

Gambling has been my most consistent thrill seeking behavior. I started playing cards with a gang of study hall malefactors while I was in high school and continued to play with the same group outside of the school environs until I moved to Chicago. When I lived in Chicago, my poker playing stakes reached new heights. The games were for substantially more money and the players were the best that I have ever played against. My heart pulsated every time a member of our poker ensemble summoned me for a game of cards. I felt the blood rush through my body.

I also bet on baseball games while I lived in Chicago, which was my introduction to the nameless bookie system. I always discerned my Chicago bookie's glee when I called, as if he anticipated his next audio system purchase with the number seventy-one windfall. I never understood the simple premise of baseball gambling was about the starting pitchers. I should have asked Pete Rose for advice.

Sports gambling teased my boredom. I bet on a whim, usually when I was in the middle of serving six tables at a busy Chicago eatery. The American Express card verification phone kept me in contact with my bookie. While the people in my section needed immediate attention, I called my bookie for the latest odds on the evening slate. After placing bets, I called a sports hotline every five minutes for updated scores.

Football became my favorite sport to bet on, but the urge to place Sunday bets abated over the past few years. I did well at football, but I became puzzled by my pattern of betting. I did not like the habit of trying to make up for early game losses by doubling my wagers on the late games. Sometimes, I did not have a reason for placing bets. I placed bets just so I could feel the adrenaline rush.

The general theme of my gambling was I never lost more money than I could afford, which was not much. The thrifty principle changed when the casino boats came to St Louis and I started gambling rent and other bill money at the blackjack table. I never took the time to learn blackjack until it sucked hundreds of dollars out of my pocket. I once tried to hit on seventeen in Las Vegas. Everyone from the pit boss to the players looked at me with unequivocal disdain. After minutes of consultation, I got the green light and hit a four.

Vegas.

The first time I sauntered into a casino, the bells, whistles, chimes, and intermittent roars from the tables of people playing games of chance overwhelmed me. All of the frenzied activity occurred simultaneously, overloading the part of my brain that was in charge of filtering sensory messages. If there is an archetypal place that pushes all of the ADHD buttons, that place is Las Vegas.

Instant hits to the pocketbook spoiled my first few trips to Vegas. I was a human magnet pulled towards every game of chance. I couldn't get off the plane at McCarran Airport fast enough to drop coins into the slot machines that were strategically placed next to the exit ramps. When I got to the hotel, I played five slot machines at once and then went from table to table trying to score a huge win until all I had left was enough money to splurge on a buffet. When I drove into Vegas from Los Angeles, I received an instantaneous adrenaline jolt when I reached the last plateau on Interstate 15 before the descent into Sin City.

As I got older, I began formulating a Vegas strategy. I only placed bets in the sports book and avoided the other distractions that surrounded me. I stopped bouncing between the roulette, craps, and blackjack tables. I refrained from filling slot machines with loose change and dollar bills as if I was filling a deep hole with cement. Of course, there have been ADHD moments of weakness, like the time when I was so drunk I broke the handle off a slot machine. I enjoy Vegas for the sports betting, which at worst is a $100 per game beat down over a three-hour period. I can lose that in twenty minutes playing the other distractions.

Horseracing is the most subdued version of gaming. The track is appealing because it drains my pocketbook at a slower rate than blackjack and other sporting events. Nevertheless, there are distractions that compete with live racing.

I became the gambling Tasmanian devil once I walked into a betting parlor and saw televisions broadcasting races from across the country. An impulsive frenzy came over me, as I bet on six simultaneous races and lost each one within a matter of a few seconds. The racetrack became a place of leisure once I learned to slow down my gambling pace. I place a bet or two every twenty minutes.

Slowing the pace has helped me in Vegas and at the track. The thrill may be gone, but I leave Vegas and the track with some cash. When the impulsive meter is completely empty, I leave with more cash than I had when I walked through the door.

****

FRUSTRATION

I will never be a good poker player. I can read people well, but I show non-verbal cues after looking at my cards. Above all, I am an impatient player, frustrated by slow play, players who talk too much, and players who ask, "What's wild?" Impatience leads to impulsive decisions that cause my once tall chip stack to dwindle into IOUs.

****

My first and only watch was a birthday gift from my parents. Within days, the watch was a mangled mess after I unsuccessfully tried to complete a difficult bike stunt. Mom took the watch for repair. I proudly wore my new watch when I tried another jump on the bicycle. Once again, I fell a bit short and the watch looked about as bad as my scraped up body. Mom was peeved after the second incident. She warned me not to attempt another bicycle jump.

I ignored mom's warning and tried to make a third jump. This time, I made the second ramp but crashed into a parked car because I could not control the landing of the bicycle. I was a mess. My legs and arms bled profusely as I scurried into the house for some first aid. What I got instead was a loud harangue and two weeks worth of punishment from mom. I have never worn a watch since that day. Because my arm is devoid of a time keeping device, I have developed the uncanny talent of discerning time during any hour of the day.

My ramp jumping days ended after I landed on my face in Galveston. After the last ramp stunt, I did wheelies like the other kids and found the activity to be boring. In order to recapture the thrill, I took my bike and sped down the slopes of hilltops trying to dodge trees, boulders, and other barriers placed in my path by Mother Nature. I called it bike skiing.

While I have never jumped at the last moment to avoid an oncoming train, I have outrun trains on trestles and hitched rides on a train or two heading to who knows where. The only reason I worked at Six Flags over Mid-America was to enjoy the free park ride privileges after work. The most thrilling ride at that time was the Screaming Eagle rollercoaster, and I rode it repeatedly until I got blurred vision. If it was not for my fear of heights, I would have tried bungee jumping and sky diving.

I have securely locked the boredom vault. I rarely get the urge to participate in activities that titillate my senses. I have become interested in storm chasing because violent thunderstorms and other potentially calamitous weather events give me an adrenaline rush. Weather's fury has always revved up my internal motor and added a few extra heartbeats that palpitate within my chest.

Thrill seekers are ebullient when they live on the edge, pushing the ordinary societal imposed boundaries out into a new sphere of comprehension. Thrill seeking is what motivates our greatest inventors, explorers, and entrepreneurs.

"The reasonable man adapts himself to the world; the unreasonable man persists in trying to adapt the world to himself. Therefore, all progress depends on the unreasonable man."

-George Bernard Shaw

CALMING INFLUENCES

Dr. Kia failed to ask relevant questions during our sixty-minute session. The first and most germane question should have been, "What do you want to get out of this process, Don?"

The second question Dr. Kia should have asked was, "Is there any environment that calms you and allows you to focus?" The second question might have established a more subdued behavior pattern when I was in certain environments. I had to ask the question instead of a registered professional, which leads me to believe the ADHD diagnostic process is flawed.

The answer to the environment question is a resonant yes. Certain environments eradicate the clutter that bounces around in my head. They slow down my thought process, thus reducing or completely expunging the components of distraction, impulsiveness, and hyperactivity. Instead of emphasizing how people with ADHD melt down, maybe we should explore the environments that are calming influences on their tumultuous minds.

Long before I knew about ADHD, I marveled at how long distance driving calmed my mind. Hyperactivity should pose a problem for someone with ADHD who drives long distances. I do get restless, but it is because I need to relieve myself or grab a bite to eat. When I drive long distances, my mind slows down and previously muddled thoughts become revelations.

The open road is just one example of a calming influence on my ADHD.

****

FRUSTRATION

I have always been an impatient driver. There is nothing more frustrating than traffic. The unexpected logjams on our nation's roadways make my blood boil. Unlike long distance driving where my movement is unrestricted, idling in the middle of traffic brings my ADHD caldron to a boil.

I start muttering, swearing, and beating my fists on the steering wheel. I try to be cute by moving in and out of lanes, looking for the one lane that is moving at a faster pace than the other lanes. Impulsiveness usually leads to picking the slowest lane, as my muttering, swearing, and beating my fists on the steering wheel reaches a crescendo. I do like the perplexed stares that I get from other drivers.

****

Jasper/Goldberg- I am almost always on the go (Quite a lot)

An environment that produces a calming influence is one that decelerates my mental and physical activity. It supersedes the urge to be on the go, the one that brings the ADHD motor to a standstill. It takes a special place for my internal motor to shut down. When I come across such a place, I want to stay there until the end of my days. The ocean is such a place.

Family excursions introduced me to the ocean when I was a young child. While impressed by the ocean's beauty and enormity, I was too preoccupied with mundane childhood activities like building sand castles and collecting seashells to appreciate what lay before me. I did not like swimming in the ocean because the salt water ran up my nose and into my mouth. In addition, I deplored the jagged fragments strewn along the beach that caused an uncomfortable and sometimes skin breaking pain on my shoeless feet. I preferred the floating plastic duck in the motel swimming pool.

It was not until I visited family in California that I realized how much of an impact the ocean has on my ADHD. Sections along the Southern California coast provide a tranquil sanctuary. The Newport Beach stretch of the Pacific Ocean puts me in a trance that I long for on a daily basis.

I sit on the pier and gaze into the Pacific Ocean. The mystical vast realm stops the ping-pong balls from rattling inside of my head. An aura of calm is omnipresent. I force myself to leave the pier and head back to the car.

Where I Slow Down

The ocean gently knocks at my mind's door. I let it enter where it melodiously touches all five of my senses. I taste the trenchant saltwater. I feel the ocean spray a fine mist upon my face. I hear the sea gulls and occasionally the distant mating calls from forlorn whales. I smell the wind bring a variety of flavors from all parts of the world. In the most surreal manipulation of my senses, I see a sun like no other sun that I have ever seen illuminate the grainy dusk sky as it sets over Catalina Island.

When I leave the ocean, I slowly walk away and take a number of turns to look back at it one more time. I reflect on what is on the other side of the vastness. I wonder if another day will arrive when I see a horizon that stills my restless soul. The ocean is my friend. The ocean is my confidant.

The ocean is where I conquer ADHD.

****

I love wide-open spaces of any kind. The Arizona-California-Nevada stretch of desert has the same impact as the ocean. The summer blazing inferno and winter howling wind limits my time gazing out into the horizon. Mountains are an excellent place to view wide-open spaces, if I can stand the permafrost that encases my body.

I found a peculiar place to sit and calm ADHD besides Mother Nature's spiritual havens. The railroad tracks, especially ones with long stretches of an open view, have always been a place where I seek refuge from my crazy, mixed up world. My grandmother and I used to walk the tracks by her house on the way to the grocery store. She taught me how to place my ear on a track and listen for the high-pitched vibration that signaled a train's arrival.

I have walked for hours on railroad tracks to seek solutions for my seemingly intractable problems. Before every school year, I wandered along the railroad tracks by my home pumping myself up for another school year with the mantra, "This year is going to be different." The sound of a pending locomotive was the signal to make the long trek home. While I have not solved all of my ADHD issues on the railroad tracks of America, I have found the miles upon miles of laid steel to be my refuge from the chaotic world that I try to leave behind.

My fascination with trains and railroad tracks came from a pioneering television show. *The Wild Wild West* was the first television show that I sat through without fidgeting, squirming, or getting up from my seat to start another activity. For five years, I came home from grade and middle school to spend two hours watching *The Wild Wild West* and *The Three Stooges*. My parents did not object to the ritual since it was the only two hours during my childhood and adolescent years when I was calm and quiet.

I have always been on the go since I exploded out of the womb. Long before the advent of political correctness and the absurd "No Child Left Behind" gibberish, I spent my time in school running around and burning off excess energy. We frolicked before and after school in the playground. We also had two lengthy recesses, a half hour to play after lunch, and a daily dose of gym that lasted one hour.

Political correctness did not intrude inside of the school walls. We played dodge ball in gym and in any other venue where adults allowed us to play. The only thing that ever kept me from playing outside was inclement weather. Even during inclement weather, I headed straight to the basement to play some type of physically demanding game. We were allowed to display our exuberance without being scolded or having our physical release curtailed by some whacked out school psychologist. Instead of shoving Ritalin down our children's throats, try getting them off their collective asses and have them engage in some physical activity.

I found out in 1998 that a structured exercise program alleviates all three ADHD components. After a workout, I lose the desire for impulsive behavior and I move about in a more composed manner. My regular dedication to exercise helped ease the rampant running around in circles that best described my life. Whether it is walking, biking, or lifting weights, I owe my slow transformation over the past ten years to a consistent exercise regimen.

****

FRUSTRATION

One of the more maddening rites of passage is the asinine process we know and love as jury duty. The judicial system should never call someone who has ADHD for jury duty. There should be big black letters that spell out ADHD on the prospective juror roll.

I understand the justice system's version of supply and demand. There are too many crooks in the system to match with the supply of law-abiding citizens. My experience as a violent crime victim excused me from serving on jury duty in 2001. I thought the wizards down at the Jury Supervisor's office permanently deleted my name from their database. I thought wrong.

I received my latest summons about a month before I started a new job. After a number of calls to the supervisor's office and requests of help from contacts who work in the judicial system, I found my tired ass downtown on a beautiful Monday morning waiting for the signal to serve or enjoy the rest of the day. I went in front of a hardship judge to plead my case, but he obviously had not worked out breakfast from his digestive system. His disgust grew discordant after he noticed my three previous attempts to get out of jury duty.

"You will serve this week, Mr. Protawcknee," he sternly advised.

I waited for him to give me the civic duty speech, but he just waved his arm in a dismissive motion. At least he could have correctly pronounced my last name. I went back for day two of judicial boredom and waited until the call came to serve in a jury pool. Once again, a judge dismissed me from a criminal case. I dropped a couple of names and described my assault; I knew crime victims had the upper hand for jury duty excuses. Nonetheless, they wasted my time and prevented me from working a new job that demanded my presence.

To the Jury Supervisor:

We need a system in this country that employs professional jurors to hear court cases, not ordinary lay people who are ill equipped to understand the mind boggling legal jargon that comes out of the mouths of attorneys and judges. If a courtroom is full of professionals, why must untrained novices assume the most important position in the courtroom? The simple answer is attorneys would lose about half of the reasons for their existence, since law school devotes time to curriculum that teaches aspiring lawyers how to get convoluted legal terms across to knuckleheads like you and me.

The next time you summon me for jury duty, I will assert that ADHD prohibits me from fulfilling my civic duty. What court wants someone who has a short attention span and is easily distracted sitting in judgment of someone? I envision the Judge giving directions or the attorneys giving their opening statements. After the interminable mind-numbing nonsense, my only response would be, "HUH?"

The most tortuous aspect of jury duty would be to sit in a closed room and try to reach a consensus with eleven other people who base their analysis on the latest *CSI* episode. My mind would wander and my hyperactivity would have me pacing the room like a caged tiger before I impulsively blurt out, "When are you stupid motherfuckers going to make up your minds?"

The jury system in this country needs a major overhaul. After all, would you want your fate determined by twelve people who are too stupid to get out of jury duty?

"What counts is not necessarily the size of the dog in the fight-it's the size of the fight in the dog."

-Dwight D. Eisenhower

THE JASPER EFFECT

Fear and anxiety broadsided me when I moved into an apartment in 1999. For the first time in ten years, the prospect of living alone became reality. Living alone can bring on bouts of loneliness and boredom. This time, fear and anxiety overshadowed my typical loneliness and boredom companions. A violent assault not only left a fifty-five stitch scar on the left side of my face, it also left an ineffaceable scar on my emotional state.

I felt vulnerable and spent the first month in my new apartment staying up as late as I could to avoid any late night surprises. When I finally grew weary and headed off to bed, I compulsively checked every door and window until I secured all of the possible avenues for entry. My scrupulous behavior resulted from the lingering effects of Post Traumatic Stress Disorder (PTSD). Many victims of violent crime experience PTSD symptoms, as well as those traumatized in combat or law enforcement situations

Compounding my vulnerability were two incidents that occurred sixteen days apart when I lived in the central west end of St. Louis. Each time I came home from a draining day of work to find the apartment ransacked. The thief ripped off many of my valuables the first time. The same thief made sure he finished cleaning out my possessions the second time. He even ripped off my set of left-handed golf clubs. I moved out without fulfilling a large portion of my lease obligation, vowing I would never live alone again.

The two intrusions exacerbated my vulnerability to violent crime, even though the effects of my Chicago assault had somewhat diminished. My solution to mollify the anxiety was to get a dog that would ensure my safety inside of the apartment. I have always liked dogs and feel that my affinity for them, along with some providence, allows them to feel comfortable around me.

My family did not raise dogs when I lived at home. They told us we were not responsible enough to handle the responsibility. Once I left the nest, dogs became a part of our family and they were a shared responsibility between my parents and brothers. My parents were right about my lack of responsibility and that played a factor in my decision to refrain from getting a dog. By July 1999, I did not care if I was responsible enough to care for a dog. I was not sleeping well at night, constantly looking out the windows for potential intruders.

I methodically researched the entire spectrum of dog topics before making a decision. The strategy seemed to work. I acquired information over the Internet and solicited advice from family members. All of the careful planning went out the window when I got out of bed one morning with the hyper-focused mindset to bring home a dog. I headed off to a local Pets Mart in search of my new best friend.

****

Every Saturday, a local Pets Mart hosted an organization that presented all of its adoptable pets to the public. As I entered the store, I reminded myself to take my time, peruse the aisle of dogs, and ask many questions. Before I went up to the first dog,

I became infatuated with a puppy that wagged his tail as he stretched his slight frame over the cage that held him. I walked over to his cage and he almost jumped over the fenced enclosure into my outstretched arms.

I asked the handler about the puppy. She said the dog's name was Jasper and that the dog directly next to his cage chewed his ear. I walked over to the offending dog and whispered, "Maybe someone would take you home if you weren't such an asshole." I turned around and told the woman I wanted to take Jasper to his new home. I completed Jasper's adoption paperwork in fifteen minutes. The shelter did not have much information on Jasper's past, a period of nearly five months where he lived in a condominium. I did not care. I came to find a best friend and I found one.

Three days later, I picked Jasper up at the animal hospital. The veterinarian staff gave him a going away present the day before; they neutered my puppy. He did not respond to my effusive greeting and barely acknowledged my presence when we walked out to the car. He sat in the back seat of my car with a look of total disdain, as if I was the one culpable for the loss of his doghood. Would you like having your nuts sliced and then handed over to a complete stranger? Besides convincing Jasper that I was not the neutering culprit, I also had to nurse his chewed up ear with a daily dose of antibiotics and skin medication.

Now that I had a Border Collie-Labrador Retriever mix in my house, I thought it was an opportune time to research the breed. Another quirk with ADHD was that I improperly sequenced events, especially when it came to a product purchase or selection of a canine companion. I should have researched the mixed breed before bringing Jasper into my home. My mind also rapidly processed what I had to do in order to ease Jasper into his new home. He appeared emaciated from a lack of regular feedings.

Jasper was a handful from the start. He chewed everything in sight and dug holes in the backyard as if he was storing a dinosaur bone. I did not put Jasper in a cage while I was at work, as recommended by numerous dog experts. I quickly found out that leaving Jasper to waltz around the apartment was a bad idea. I came home one night to find a couch destroyed and a set of stereo speakers clawed so thoroughly that Jasper must have been sending a message to me. I decided his message was, "I'll teach that fucker to leave me alone for such a long time."

I was stern when I showed my disapproval. I raised my voice and started punishing him for bad behavior. The chewing and digging continued to the point when I contemplated giving him up for another dog. Giving up on Jasper would have been another in a long line of failed relationships, this one with a perfectly fit and loving dog.

One night before heading to bed, I walked passed Jasper as he slept by the bedroom door. He convulsed and whimpered in his sleep, so I crouched down to calm him. I brought over my blanket and spent the rest of the night sleeping by his side. I realized that screaming at the playful puppy might have aggravated an already fragile emotional state. I vowed to do whatever it took, regardless if it meant spending more time and money, to eliminate the digging in the backyard and the chewing of my compact discs.

I decided to spend as much time as possible with Jasper, teaching him commands and coaching him to walk in step with me. I nourished him to a healthy weight and gave him unconditional love. However, he never barked! I desperately needed a dog that alerted me to any intruder who was attempting to come into the house while I slept.

During the first winter with Jasper, I stayed up until dawn or when I was tired enough to drift into deep sleep. I vividly remember when I first heard Jasper bark; it was sweet music to my ears. I finally had an alarm system, but more importantly, I had a friend that took me as I am. I realized that Jasper was more than a dog living in my home.

Support dogs train to assist the seeing and physically disadvantaged. Jasper became my support dog for ADHD.

****

IRRITATION

People have a tendency to spoil their dogs. Dogs are clad in sweaters, walking briskly with their owners through municipal parks. Their owners feed them a steady diet of human food. The attachment between humans and dogs has gotten so strange that people (rich people) are cloning their dog so they can bring an exact replica into their homes.

I become irritated when I witness people who treat their dogs better than they treat people. My skin crawls when I run into a dog owner on the street and they tell me their dog's name. I have met dogs with the names of Jack, Mike, Megan, and Lucy. What is next? That I run into a family who introduces me to their children Fido and Spot?

****

Jasper is now ten years old and the past nine and a half years have been, for the most part, the most tranquil of my life. He is the quintessential guardian of the household, barking to alert me when anyone approaches the front door. He is so protective that he shows downright animus towards any other person or dog that he feels is an imminent threat. He is aggressive enough to spear a Rottweiler down a ravine. He forced a larger Chow to give the dog version of "No Mas" during an altercation. Yet, he is gentle enough to be beloved by everyone in the neighborhood and almost every dog he meets on the street.

Jasper has brought out the positive ADHD traits of creativity and thinking outside of conventional wisdom. I do not use a leash when I walk him. I exclusively use verbal commands, some of which mix in small phrases of profanity that he recognizes as a signal to follow the walking plan. I receive perplexed stares from people everyday when I curtly tell Jasper to "Get the fuck off their lawn!" However, I also receive accolades for having one of the few dogs in the canine world that walks without any physical restraint.

Dogs are excellent companions, but I highly recommend that people with ADHD seriously consider man's best friend. Routine is what we need and routine is how a dog thrives. Jasper's most profound impact has been my transition to a life based on routine and not impulsive actions.

Once I brought Jasper into my home, I stopped staying out after work to chase the next line of cocaine or hit of pot. I had a new regimen, one that ensured that I was home in time to let him enjoy the backyard. The routine included walking him at a vigorous pace through the park while he hunted down squirrels with uncanny precision. Jasper's favorite part of the routine was when I filled his food bowl at the same time every evening.

I let him outside every morning for an hour after I finish breakfast. He gets two lengthy walks and at least two more excursions outside where he loves to roll in the grass. He knows it is time for a walk when I take the leash off the kitchen shelf.

He also knows its time for a walk when he hears the toilet paper roll before I flush the toilet.

I have heard derisive comments from people concerning my care for Jasper. They just do not get it, even after I explain in detail why Jasper means so much to me. When I tell people I cannot go out after work because I need to walk the dog, they usually laugh and openly question why my dog is worthy of such attention.

T.H. never understood my dedication to Jasper. He chastised me for leaving work for short periods so I could walk Jasper. He never understood why I spent more time with my dog than he did with his children. He should have looked into the bottom of the empty pint glasses he amassed after deciding that staying at his restaurants and drinking was more important than being at home with his family.

Sleep medications do not have the same impact as Jasper. The Jasper effect enhanced my mental and physical health.

Jasper

RUNAWAY
BRAIN

"Humility is not putting yourself down or denying your strengths. Rather, it is being honest about your weaknesses."

-Pastor Rick Warren
The Purpose Driven Life

Brain imaging studies find that low levels of the neurotransmitter Norepinephrine causes distraction. The inattentive aspect of ADHD is generally harmless, unless you fail to pay attention to road directions and find yourself at the corner of Crack and Freebase Avenues. On the other hand, low levels of the neurotransmitter Dopamine causes the brain to become over stimulated and roar like a crackling bonfire. Dopamine is necessary to repress stimulation that causes impulsiveness and the myriad behavioral problems that are the result of hyperactivity.

The restaurant business has its share of foibles that affect impulsiveness and hyperactivity. One foible is the incongruous work schedule. I was consistently accustomed to the idiotic practice of closing a night shift and then coming back on less than five hours of sleep to open a restaurant for the subsequent day shift. After the day shift, I immediately turned in for a much-needed nap. I was not in bed for more than a minute before my mind heated up and slowly picked up speed until it was crackling like a bonfire. The previous twenty-fours altered the neurotransmitter composition in my brain.

During the last year I worked at the old Busch Stadium, I came home after a couple of nine-hour shifts within a twenty-four hour period and tried to take a nap. It was the day before my birthday and I thought about my plans for a celebration. I realized I did not have any. I started to panic, which caused the first piece of mental kindling to catch fire. My mind picked up speed until it resembled the trailing car lights we see in videos. The thoughts raced so fast that I detected electrical charges running through my body.

My mind raced every day of grade school, every day of high school, every day of college, and every day of my working life for roughly twenty years. People who think they know me have absolutely no idea how difficult it was to achieve anything with the Indy 500 zooming around inside of my head. The racing became sporadic about seven years ago and has recently grinded to a halt.

I came up with a list of four situations when my runaway brain was at the height of its power: the first day, automobiles, stealing, and sporting events. I cannot explain why I was so wound up when confronted with those situations. I just know there was a mechanism somewhere in my brain that released the call: Gentleman, start your engine.

"When one door closes another door opens; but we often look so long and so regretfully upon the closed door, that we do not see the ones which open for us."

-Alexander Graham Bell

THE FIRST DAY

Amen-An internal sense of anxiety or nervousness (3)

Amen-Frequent feeling of demoralization or that things won't work out for you (4)

Jasper/Goldberg-I easily become upset (Quite a lot)

I was petrified when I entered Mt. Pleasant grade school for the first day of kindergarten. The trepidation stemmed from a venue where everything was unfamiliar to me. The kids, adults, school boundaries, and social parameters all made me nervous. By the age of five, I knew that I was different from my peers and was not sure if I fit into the new thing called school. I soon found out it was not just kindergarten; it was the first day of every new school year.

Ironically, I was unhappy after the final day of each school year. I wanted to continue with my daily dose of mischief and tomfoolery. After three months of social freedom and high-pitched chicanery, I was once again anxious because I loathed sitting behind a desk and shuffled around the sausage grinder. I knew on the first day of school the reproaches of "Take your time," "Sit in your seat, Donald!", and "What's wrong with you?" would flow out of my peer's and teacher's mouths faster than a Dick Cheney narration about Iraq's weapons of mass destruction.

I thought about the first day of school on my birthday. School did not even enter into my thought process until I blew out the last of the candles on my birthday cake. While I sat in front of the family and opened presents, my mind hyper-focused on beginning another nine months of academic drudgery. The apprehension alarm went off every year on August 7, a full month before I entered the halls that I loathed.

I was most apprehensive before my first year at Nipher Junior High. Nipher was an integrated middle school that included kids from the predominantly African American Mecham Park neighborhood. I was coming from a lily-white grade school without any experience interacting with African Americans, except on the baseball field and basketball court. Nipher had such a bad reputation that it caused unadulterated fear in white kids when they heard on the street that Nipher was referred to as Knifer.

ADHD preserved my personal safety on the first day of seventh grade and every day thereafter. My African American peers thought I was crazy and word got around not to "fuck with that white boy." My kinship with John Chambers, Ray Taylor, and Phillip Williams made the first day of subsequent school years easier to take. The friendships did not erase the trepidation of a milestone first day. I was twisted up inside on Labor Day 1975, a mere twenty-four hours before my first day of high school.

I am still apprehensive before the first day of anything. I never understood why until I found out about ADHD. Now it makes sense to me. The first day is when I meet new acquaintances. It is a day when I have to control the ADHD components in order to fit into a new social network. It is a day when I ruminate about past mistakes. The first day is when I ponder my abysmal performance record.

For years, I was unsuccessful being the new kid in town. My ADHD traits boiled over the moment I set forth into any first day endeavor, alienating those who were supposed to work with me in a social, educational, or professional milieu. I have consciously compensated for the ADHD flaws by slowly integrating my personality into new environments. I recently heard, “I didn’t know you are like that,” months after getting past the gut wrenching first day.

My incredible apprehension was the primary reason why I did not show up for the first day of work. The prevailing theme was whether the employees and management would accept me into the new environment. The secondary theme was how long it would take me to implode and walk off the job. It was only a matter of time before I detonated without any advanced warning.

I have driven to the first day of a new job, pulled into the parking lot, and then instantly high-tailed it back to the comfort of home. I have sat in my car frozen in time, my mind about to explode with foreboding thoughts of another first day. Recently, another new job brought another first day. I got out of my car, opened up the trunk, gathered my work clothes, and headed for the front door. I then abruptly turned around, hastily threw my clothes in the trunk, and sat in the front seat shaking at the knees and wiping the sweat from my brow. I completed the sequence five times before I finally entered the building.

If any of the new co-workers witnessed my actions, they must have wondered what kind of nutcase was about to start his first day.

****

IRRITATION

The six-class ritual of teachers mispronouncing my last name augmented my revulsion for the first day of school. Some teachers attempted a respectful pronunciation of my last name. Others stammered and stuttered until they muttered an incomprehensive word unrelated to my last name. To make matters worse, students in the class chimed in with their snickering and snide remarks. The teachers who frequently butchered my last name were English teachers, the same teachers who were supposed to instruct me on the concept of phonetics.

****

During every summer hiatus from the sausage grinder, my parents sent me packing for an extended period on a church or scouting related excursion.

I ridiculed the homesick kids, while I felt the same kind of loneliness that was a telltale sign of being homesick. But I was not homesick. I welcomed the chance to leave home for the freelancing world of surrogate adult supervision. Another first day caused the empty pit in my stomach, another episode in which I was going to meet a bunch of new people and try to adapt to an unfamiliar environment.

My parents sent me off one summer to attend a seven-day long leadership camp for seasoned members of the Boy Scouts. Eight campers comprised my patrol; eight people whom I never met in my life. The first day was complete hell. I thought about packing up my stuff and hitchhiking back to St Louis. Another kid in our patrol was also having a tough time. He visibly shook and, like rats at a cheese party, the rest of the kids in our patrol made his untenable situation worse by nibbling away at his self-confidence. They also pulled pranks like stuffing his sleeping bag full of mud and hiding his scout uniform.

I empathized with him and tried to be the good guy. It was first time I assumed the good guy role in a similar situation. We started hanging out together during the course of the week. The teasing and pranks ceased after I had a classic ADHD outburst. The other members of the patrol left my new friend alone for the rest of the week. I realized that in order to mitigate my own first day demons, I needed to find other people who experienced similar, though unrelated feelings of loneliness.

Mike Chaney, the kid I befriended at the Junior Leader Training Camp, remembered me for my kindness. He sat directly in front of me during our high school band class. On the first day of school, he turned around and thanked me for my altruism during the summer leadership camp. About twenty minutes later, I blew a trombone's worth of saliva onto the back of his head.

****

I wonder if my difficulty with first days started when I had a difficult time making the move from our first home to a Glendale, Missouri neighborhood. Every day was a first day. There was the first day to meet neighbors. There was the first day of Indian Guides. I clearly remember my first day at Glendale Presbyterian Church. The Sunday school teacher introduced me to the entire class. I soiled my underwear in God's house. I became comfortable after the disappearance of first days while I lived in our first home. The first days resurfaced on a daily basis after our family moved to Glendale.

I cannot live like that anymore, which is why I lean more on God. In times of weakness and doubt, I turned to God and the scriptures for inspiration and guidance. I need to keep the faith that the first day will eventually turn into the first year, the second year, and maybe I will even be around for a tenth anniversary. I have not celebrated many anniversaries with anyone or any organization, which is why I should have cherished the one-month anniversaries I established with each of my girlfriends.

The first day of school regularly appears in a dream. All I can see are feet as they slowly make their way down a Glendale sidewalk. The feet approach the school's front door on a gloomy winter day. The door slowly opens to the sight of an empty hallway. The eerie calm heightens the apprehension. I hear panting as classroom doors open that lead into empty rooms. A commotion comes from one of the classrooms. Through the keyhole, I see children laughing at a boy who is shaking in his chair.

I am the boy in the chair.

"The brain is a wonderful organ. It starts the moment you get up in the morning and does not stop until you get into the office."

-Robert Frost

ANOTHER CAR BITES THE DUST

Mr. Frost was correct to some extent. The brain is a wonderful organ. It starts the instant I wake up in the morning and does not stop until I am around an automobile.

My automobile incompetence encompassed virtually every car ownership topic. I failed at purchasing cars. I failed at driving cars. I failed at maintaining cars, even the basic type of care that is second nature to most people.

Owner's manuals were nothing more than a clump of paper that took too much room in the glove compartment. Some of my owner's manuals never saw daylight from inside the glove compartment. I guessed about how much air the tires needed. I replenished the oil until it poured over the side of the engine. I checked fluid levels about as often as Dick Cheney checks his speeches for veracity.

My ADHD mind had neither the capacity nor the patience to understand the basics of auto mechanics. Dad tried to explain the mechanics of a car engine, about how all of the parts were coordinated to perform as a finely tuned machine. My mind wandered towards two thoughts: "This car will get me some action" and "I don't care how it works, as long as it works."

I took car maintenance for granted, never abiding by the dealer specified maintenance schedule. Oil changes only took place after black smoke billowed from under the hood.

Incessant squealing sounds meant the tires needed air. I filled the wiper fluid when I could not see between all of the bird splattering on the front windshield.

Car discussions were tiresome. Up until the time of early adulthood, males talk about two things: sports and cars. I have always been knowledgeable about sports. Talking about cars was like trying to understand Russian at a caviar festival.

I faked car expertise by nodding my head in affirmation or adding innocuous comments like, "Yea, that engine really cooks." I could not tell the difference between a 350 or a 450 engine, except one must have been larger by the designated number. I could not identify a Camaro or Trans Am until I was in college. When a peer tried to explain how a car engine operated or why a certain model accelerated to sixty miles per hour in five seconds, I was completely lost because my brain refused to channel the information that made talking about cars an interesting subject.

Most of my adolescent peers noticed I was disinterested in cars and they eventually left me out of activities that involved them, unless the activity was drinking beer and chasing women. My lack of auto mechanic interest had negative social implications. My lack of car comprehension hurt my ability to establish male peer relationships.

I regarded cars as functional entities, a necessary pain in the ass that was my mode of transportation to a job. A car was something that permitted me to bring home groceries or to go out on a date. I never looked at a car as something to disassemble and then put back together.

The inability to form a common bond with my peers hurt my self-esteem. Understanding ADHD has helped me cope with the years of perplexing self-doubt. I have improved my car care skills, learning a little more each time I purchase one. Nevertheless, I will never be able to have a discourse with anyone about cars. When someone mentions the capacity of a specific engine, I quickly change the topic to, "Man, how about those Boston Celtics!"

My parents handed me down my first car at the age of seventeen. I was in heaven. I had the one thing I coveted since I first saw my peers swing into the high school parking lot with their respective rides. The car allowed me to play hooky. It allowed me to go out to McDonald's for lunch or drive around and smoke a joint with one of my friends.

Mom and dad said the car was mine as long as I maintained my grades. They said nothing about maintaining the car. I avoided learning about how to take care of cars until years after I hitched up behind the wheel of the first one. Since I lived at home, dad was scrupulous in his care for *my* car. He valiantly tried to impart his wisdom into my headstrong mind. I never listened to his words of wisdom.

An antiquated orange Datsun became my ride just before sophomore year of college. The car was a bad idea that I made worse when I let some of my fraternity brothers borrow it to do laundry. They brought back the orange Datsun with a huge dent on the rear quarter panel (Hah! I do know some car lingo). I contemplated what I was going to tell my parents and decided that lying to them was the solution. It only took me a few minutes to come up with a lie before my fraternity brothers and I piled into the Datsun for a drinking binge at the West End Lounge.

My ADHD nemesis distraction got the best of me when I made a trip from St. Louis to Des Moines. I pulled over for some gasoline in Hannibal, Missouri and noticed steam coming out from under the hood of the Datsun. Bemused, I propped up the hood and saw the entire engine engulfed in white smoke. I looked around for a minute and then decided to venture a glance under the car. A greenish liquid dripped from the radiator onto the pavement. Upon closer examination, I saw the cap from the bottom of the radiator was missing.

Before I left St. Louis, I drained the radiator and flushed out the impurities with cold water. I then replenished the radiator with fresh antifreeze fluid. But I neglected to seal the maintenance deal because I forgot the most important step: to replace the cap after adding the new antifreeze. The car probably produced steam the entire ninety miles to Hannibal and I was oblivious to it because my mind was anywhere but on the task of driving the car.

I stuffed some toilet paper into the radiator drain, filled the radiator with water, and headed onward to Des Moines.

****

FRUSTRATION

When I drive, I want to get from point A to point B as fast as possible. I do not want anything or anyone to slow me down. I become frustrated on interstate highways when I am stuck behind someone who is in the far left lane going at or below the speed limit.

I speed by them with a grimace that melts the skin off a mannequin.

****

I thought a car purchase was like shopping for produce. Look at a few models, pick out a color I liked, touch the car, and off I would go. I quickly found out that one of the more odious tasks for someone with ADHD is participating in the car purchasing process.

My high school and college cars were hand-me-down clunkers that merely provided transportation. I never had to buy a car until it was time to get serious about life and purchase one before I started my first post-college job. I wanted to purchase a higher end model for my imminent move back to Des Moines.

Dad volunteered to help me with my first car purchase. The most important step in the car buying process was the research phase. Dad utilized the annual *Consumer Reports* car buyer's guide as a standard for selecting potential car lots to visit. I thought we would pull up into a lot, survey the inventory, and then walk into the dealership and state, "We'll take that one." We would pay the man and drive off in a matter of fifteen minutes

Before we met the first sales representative, dad said that we were going to haggle with him over the price. I thought the sticker on the car was the price we paid, just like the sticker on a box of cereal. Dad and the sales representative went back and forth, with the sales representative leaving the room at times to consult with his finance manager. Dad kept saying, "We have to be patient, son." I just wanted to pay the sales representative and get the hell out of Dodge, or in this case Honda.

We never made it past the haggling stage on the first day. We visited eight lots until we finally headed home to discuss what we saw. I stopped paying attention after the second lot, so I had no idea about the remaining six prospects. Dad took notes and compared them to the *Consumer Reports* guide. He then made his list of the top three choices, all of which we planned to look over with more scrutiny the next day. The next day came and my impatience was at its apex. We went back to the Honda dealer to haggle some more with the smarmy sales representative.

You could see the scorn in dad's eyes. The sales representative walked in from the showroom, looking like he had just awakened from a hangover induced nap. Dad asked questions about a used Honda Civic. We drove around, discussed the car, and went back to the lot where Dad started haggling with the sales representative. Once again, the sales representative had to check with the finance manager. I wondered if the finance manager was The Wizard of Oz, a portentous man who hid behind his desk and bellowed, "Go back and make them pay what we want!"

Armed with *Consumer Reports*, dad wore down the seasoned haggler from Honda until he got fairly close to the price that he wanted. Unfortunately, I learned absolutely nothing from dad during my first car buying experience. One of life's greatest lessons unfolded in front of me. All I got out of the lesson was that I hated the car buying process.

My first car purchase was a white Honda Civic that had a manual transmission. I stayed on top of the maintenance until I decided to attach a packed U-Haul and make a 300 mile relocation drive to Chicago. The car broke down after two months because of negligence (I thought cars took care of themselves, as people do). I could not afford the exorbitant repair bill and, after adding over twenty-five outstanding parking violations to the financial equation, I decided to discard the Civic on a side street without getting one measly cent for it.

I did not tell dad about the Civic for two years, when the normal toll of obsolescence gave me a compelling reason for not having the car anymore. I also told him I could not afford to pay him back for the loan that he co-signed with me.

The relationship with my father was never the same.

****

I have gone on two other car-buying missions with dad, each time when I was in my ripe thirties.

I needed dad to co-sign a loan since my credit was abhorrent. The first car we bought together was a Chevy Corsica. I paid off the loan to dad in two years, exactly the amount of the loan term. The second car was a newer model Chevy Cavalier, which cost more and demanded more of my attention. Dad felt I was ready for more responsibility, which made me feel good that I finally earned his trust with such an immense burden at the age of thirty-four.

I crashed the blue Cavalier into a condominium mailbox about six months later, totaling the car and owing about three years on the loan. An insurance company would have reimbursed me for the Cavalier's total loss, but I did not carry any automobile insurance. I should have carried car and ADHD insurance.

I went out the next day to a used car dealer. I test drove ***one*** car and told the business manager I wanted it. I did not haggle, negotiate, or follow dad's measured advice for buying a car. I bought one in thirty minutes. It took awhile to get a loan because my credit sucked, but the finance manager called my new employer and then approved one for me. I put down $2000 on the car and drove off with an overpriced hunk of shit.

Now I owed money on two cars, but I did not care because I was driving again. The car lasted eight months until the engine burned out from overuse as a courier vehicle. The genius of ADHD was using my own car on a job that accumulated 200 miles of daily urban abuse. By the winter of 1997-98, I did not have access to a car and owed on two of them. It took me awhile to climb out of that hole, but I started driving again when I paid for older car models with cash.

Scrupulous defined my research. The first two cash purchases culminated after I methodically researched each car prospect. I took more time than I had in the past deciding on which car to buy. My methodical purchasing pattern changed in 2001 after a clunker I had for two years finally conked out. I did not research the first car I bought and it died less than a month after I bought it. I think the man who sold it knowingly screwed me.

The second car I bought was in response to a classified advertisement. I went to the owner's home and looked at the car for about ninety seconds. There was a huge pool of water on the passenger side floorboard. The owner claimed that she left the windows open the night before and it rained inside of the car. I did not recollect any rain from the night before. It might have rained in her neighborhood, which was twenty miles from where I lived.

I bought her story and bought the car. About a month later, the car died on my way home from a festive Thanksgiving dinner and I was back to square one. I pissed away two cars and over 4000 dollars in less than two months. Moreover, I still owed money on two car loans, including a loan that ended up being the second time I stiffed dad. I eventually paid off one of the car loans because for the first time in my life, I received a letter that mentioned the words lien and garnishment. The letter was much preferable to the cold shoulder that I got from dad.

I paid an exorbitant price for a weekly car rental. The lot I leased from had the slogan, "We cater to desperate people like you!" I used the leasing service until I slowly regained my footing on sound financial ground.

The car buying process has become more ADHD friendly with the advent of the Internet. I bought a decent Ford Escort that lasted over two years until I was involved in an accident that destroyed the car. After the Escort buying process, I felt confident that I finally discarded the car purchasing demons of my past. I was thorough, patient, and asked many questions before settling on the Escort. I even haggled on the price. Dad would have jumped for joy when I told him I finally fulfilled a loan obligation on a loan that I signed without anyone's help.

Soon thereafter, I reverted to my spontaneous ways and made another ill-advised car purchase.

****

IRRITATION

I lived in a neighborhood where people parked their cars on a narrow two-way street. Nothing irritated me more than walking outside to find my car sandwiched tight between two other cars.

There were times when my neighbor insisted on pulling up to within six inches of my car. He had open space on both sides of the street to park, yet he chose to invade my parking space. I felt like backing into his car and breaking out his front headlights. He was lucky I was not twenty years younger and in the midst of full-blown ADHD.

****

During our session, Dr. Kia wanted to know about my driving history. He was referring to my driving record, not my pathetic history of purchasing and maintaining cars. After I went through a lengthy list of infractions and accidents, Dr. Kia inferred that ADHD might have contributed to my driving problems. The overly taut doctor was finally making some sense.

I recounted seventeen moving violations (now at eighteen), five accidents (now at six) and two DUIs (forever at two) that had an additional six moving violations tacked on for good measure. Including the complete destruction of my last car, the accidents that I have been involved in were either preventable or explicitly my fault.

I operated an automobile as if I was roaring around the last turn en route to a Daytona 500 victory. Police officers handed me moving violations as often as Dick Cheney's staff receives federal warrants. At the height of my recklessness, I received two speeding tickets within a twenty-four hour period from the same officer who hid under the same overpass on Interstate 44. The second time he wrote me a ticket he smugly said, "You would think you would have learned your lesson yesterday." Yes officer, I did. I remembered my lesson up until about five minutes before you stopped me. Daydreaming kicked in and I only thought about how I was not going to pay the first ticket.

I am a menace on the road. I put myself and other drivers at risk with impatient maneuvers, like weaving in and out of traffic on a busy highway. I always drive faster than the speed limit, regardless if I am on an open stretch of highway or a curving back road. Thank goodness for doughnut shops.

For reasons that perplex me, I enter into some of my most intense daydreaming when I motor down the road. The only thing that nudges me out of my own little world is a near miss. I slam on the brakes to avoid a rear end collision or swerve to miss cars after I run a red light. The closest I came to biting the big one was when I ran off Interstate 70 outside of Kansas City and ended up missing a concrete structure in the median.

The ultimate impact of reckless driving is the drain on my bank account. Whether it is the cost of the DUI extortion, the fines I pay for moving violations and parking tickets, or the sky-high rates I fork over for insurance, ADHD inspired driving has inexorably depleted my finances. Someday a municipal government will consider me for beatification in one of their sanctified chambers.

Maybe now people who think they know me will understand why I take public transportation. It simplifies my life, saves me money, and keeps other people out of harm's way.

"I dwell in possibilities."

-Emily Dickinson

ASSOCIATIVE CONDITIONS

Amen-Trouble with authority (4)

The most fascinating aspect of writing a book about living with undiagnosed ADHD was the seemingly everlasting research process. Like a cave explorer who finds new rock formations, I discovered new information about ADHD every time I logged onto the internet or met someone with the condition. Each day that I explored the ADHD research maze opened the door to new possibilities.

The most profound discovery I made centered on the concomitant conditions of ADHD. Some of the more prevalent ones are depression, anxiety, tics, and behavioral problems. The associative conditions present the scientific community with a dilemma: is ADHD the cause of associative conditions or are associative conditions a result of distinctive brain phenomenon. It appears most of the associative conditions (co-morbidity in medical slang) are directly related to ADHD.

All of the nascent information about ADHD is a bit overwhelming. After combing the information labyrinth, I came across three associative conditions of ADHD that were consistent with my behavior up until about ten years ago. The three associative conditions are oppositional defiance disorder (ODD), conduct disorder (CD), and obsessive compulsive disorder (OCD). I will leave a diagnosis up to the experts as they scrutinize some of the stories I have told up to this point, and as they analyze additional anecdotal evidence that I present in the remaining chapters.

ODD and CD are considered Disruptive Behavioral Disorders. ODD refers to a recurrent pattern of negative, defiant, disobedient, and hostile behavior towards an authority figure. The essential feature of CD is a repetitive and persistent pattern of behavior in which an individual violates the basic rights of others and ignores age appropriate norms. The basic difference between ODD and CD is symptom severity. ODD is the milder version of the two, but it can change into CD with advancing age.

Children under the age of twelve who do not display ODD or CD behavior receive the milder inattention-only diagnosis of ADHD. The impulsiveness and hyperactivity that is characteristic of ADHD's stronger version increases the risk for the kind of conflict interactions that promote the development of Disruptive Behavior Disorders.

Like ADHD, ODD and CD require professional intervention at an early age. ODD and CD symptom treatment must commence immediately after a diagnosis. Both conditions are difficult to treat the longer they persist. Educators and counselors never assessed me for any type of behavioral disorder when I was a child, so I can only deduce from current diagnostic criteria if I qualified for additional acronyms. I easily exceeded the minimum checklist requirements for an ODD and CD diagnosis when I was a child, adolescent, and young adult.

I have been unabashedly anti-authority my entire life. I relentlessly contested adult authority by actively defying their requests or rules. I screwed with adults when I was a child because I felt my peers were not mentally in my league when it came to implementing deviant schemes. That concisely is ODD.

CD is graduating into the next level of bad behavior. I have demonstrated aggressive vindictiveness towards people, caused destruction of property, and committed many acts of theft and deception. I have avoided time in juvenile detention or adult incarceration because of cunning and deception. ADHD and associative conditions may have gotten me in trouble, but the same attributes helped me devise strategies to avoid punishment. I always talked my way out of the more serious accusations.

Picture a hurricane that makes landfall. The storm itself produces strong winds, heavy rains, and a storm surge. Tornadoes can be unleashed on the outer bands of the hurricane as associative and active parts of the storm. ADHD is the eye of a hurricane that produces the storm surge of impulsiveness, the heavy rains of distraction, and the high winds of hyperactivity. I am beginning to realize that behavioral problems were my tornadoes.

I am not sure about OCD. I experienced Post Traumatic Stress Disorder (PTSD) symptoms that occurred after a violent assault. I exhibited OCD type behavior, particularly when it came to obsessively checking every conceivable entry into my residences. The nightly ritual used to take up to thirty minutes of my time. I like things placed in a certain order and I do have an above average collection of neatly stacked personal items laid out across my office. Moreover, I inaugurated the ritual of checking water faucets in my apartment after leaving one on in my brother's condominium

ODD, CD, OCD, and PTSD; add those letters to ADHD and I have a winning combination for a game of *Scrabble*. The more I learn about ADHD and all of the supplementary topics, the more I realize that a bunch of acronyms will encapsulate my life.

****

FRUSTRATION/IRRITATION

Frustration-Trying to figure out which of the ADHD information is valid

Irritation-Knowing that some of the ADHD information is complete bullshit

"It's not stealing if they don't know it's missing"

-Anonymous

THOU SHALL NOT STEAL

I did not like church and not because I abhorred the religious dogma that was preached every Sunday. I disliked church because I already endured five days in a classroom. Church attendance gave me a sixth day, with an hour of Sunday school followed by an excruciatingly tedious hour-long service that included a twenty-minute sermon by the Pastor. Impulsiveness and hyperactivity ruled my world on Sundays.

I squirmed in the pews while the man behind the podium lip-synched another parable or biblical story. I always sat between some combination of my parents and grandparents, so one of them could gently calm my indefatigable leg movement. If that did not work, they kept me occupied by giving me a pencil and paper to write down all fifty state capitals. I barely got anything out of church because either my mind wandered or a crying infant distracted me.

I did memorize the Ten Commandments and a few prayers that we all stood up for and said in unison. I have obeyed most of the commandments. I have not murdered. I have not committed adultery. I do not work on the Sabbath; I watch football. I do not covet my neighbor's wife, unless you consider the married couple who lived three blocks away to be my neighbors. I certainly do not worship false idols like baseball players.

If God grades commandment obedience on a curve, I should be waiting at the pearly gates with a healthy eighty percent score. God will take me to task, however, for repeatedly breaking his commandment that forewarns, "Thou shall not steal." God will add a few more days in purgatory for stealing inside of his house of worship.

I began to enjoy the adult version of church when I saw an opportunity for some easy cash. My parents usually gave me an envelope to place in the offering basket, which I did for a while until an ADHD light bulb came on and the devil appeared on my shoulder. I used a magician's sleight of hand when it was my turn for the offering, slowly placing my hand in the basket and then pulling it out with the money envelope crumpled under my clenched fist. I took the money envelope to the local soda fountain where I bought root beet floats. The counter clerk eventually greeted me by my first name: Gary.

After awhile, I was bored with the envelope scheme and decided to up the theft ante. I took dollar bills out of the basket in addition to keeping the envelope that my parents gave me. With adults surrounding me, I furtively put the money under my leg and waited until we all stood for a hymn before stuffing the loot into one of my pockets.

After church service, adults queried me about what I assimilated the previous hour. They asked me about Jesus and I replied that he healed someone. My parents often asked, "What did you get out of church today, Don?" My replies touched on the basic biblical interpretations of kindness, mercy, tolerance, and hope. My answer changed when my peers asked the same question.

Clint Reed asked me one Sunday as I was leaving Glendale Presbyterian Church, "What did you get out of church today, Stash?"

My answer was, "about $3.50."

****

Amen- Lying or stealing on impulse (4+)

The Hostess cherry fruit pie had a subliminal message of **steal me**. I stared at the fruit pie for what seemed like minutes, while fumbling with the loose change in my pocket. I looked around to see if anyone was looking my way. When I thought the coast was clear, I stuffed the fruit pie under my shirt and headed out the door.

Once I got outside, I briskly walked down Sappington Road until I stopped to cross the street. I cut through the police station parking lot, which was only four houses down from where I lived. A uniformed officer came out of the station and called for me. "Oh, shit," I thought, as he came up and told me the store clerk called about a little boy shoplifting a Hostess fruit pie.

"What's under your shirt?" he ominously asked.

I stammered a bit before replying, "Nothing."

He then asked me to lift my shirt and lo and behold, there was a Hostess fruit pie. A big lump descended my throat.

The officer gave me the standard stealing is wrong lecture and tried to embarrass me into unrestrained shame. He took the fruit pie and sternly advised me to tell my parents when I got home, because he promised he would call them later in the evening to inform them of my depravity.

I walked away while playing out a number of scenarios in my head. The ping-pong balls rattled until I finally decided upon scenario number seventy-nine, which was to make a beeline to my room and not tell my parents anything. I called the police officer's bluff and won the fruit pie poker match. He never called my parents.

I made two vows after the Hostess fruit pie escapade. I was not going to steal from Brownie's, the Glendale mom and pop grocery store where I stole the fruit pie. The second vow was more important: nobody would catch me stealing again. Emboldened by the Hostess fruit pie incident, I waged a stealing campaign against another Glendale convenience store owned by an ornery old man.

The man had a small bar that was adjacent to his store. He and his embittered male friends sat at the bar every weekday afternoon, washing down stale pretzels with lukewarm draft beer and telling old army stories laden with bursts of profanity. A group of kids usually went over to his store after school let out. By then, he was pie-eyed and one mean son of a bitch. We usually mocked him as he staggered from behind the counter to chase us out the back door.

I created a plan to get even with the owner. On a beautiful spring day, the usual suspects entered his store and began running up and down the aisles. Some members of our posse diverted his attention by causing a ruckus at the front cash register. Clint Reed and I went in through the back door and absconded with potato chip bags and cases of soda. We ran down the street giggling about how we outsmarted the drunken old man.

****

Mental health experts define kleptomania as a persistent neurotic impulse to steal without an economic motive. My motive to steal was usually not about economic benefit. I stole to get even with an employer. I stole because of the challenge. I stole for the same reason that Sir Edmund Hillary stated after a newspaper reporter asked him why he climbed Mount Everest: "Because it's there!"

At North Glendale, I took any bike I wanted during lunch break and rode it to the same soda fountain I frequented after Sunday church service. The cherry sodas and ham sandwiches hit the spot. If I stayed on site for lunch and did not like what mom packed, I surreptitiously went to the coat closet where all the other lunches were stored. After rummaging through crumpled brown bags, I usually found a ham and cheese sandwich to steal. I did not even leave my sandwich in return. As a cub scout, I plundered our den mother's dry storage cabinet, taking an assortment of sweet delights like cookies and donuts. I did not eat what I took. I just ran out the front door chuckling about my exploits while discarding what I took down the sewer drain.

Golf courses were premium locations for thievery. Every fifteen minutes or so, a foursome hit shots from the 13th tee at the Westborough Country Club. Most of the tee shots rolled up and over a small hill where the foursome could not see two young boys crawling out of the woods to steal their balls. We made a spring ritual out of stealing Westborough member's golf balls. When we really felt like screwing with the adults, we showed up at the pro shop hours later to sell their balls to other club members. Money was not our primary motive. We got more satisfaction from hiding in the woods and listening to the befuddled inquisitions as the members looked for their golf balls. George and I were Beavis and Butthead before the MTV era.

I do not recollect exactly when, but there was a defining moment when I realized I had a gift, albeit an illegal one. My schemes to steal became more elaborate and less impulsive. By the time I reached the age of sixteen, I devised theft schemes in order to get even with someone or some organization.

****

FRUSTRATION

In 2006, the federal government gave an automatic six-month extension for taxpayers to file their 2005 returns. Maybe the rocket scientists in Washington finally realized they created a genuine tax imbroglio. The tax code so full of lawyer gibberish that even patient and diligent tax filers have to resort to using an expert in order to complete the paperwork. For someone with ADHD, thumbing through the arcane booklets and following the circuitous directions is a protracted nightmare.

I spent an inordinate amount of time in 2006 figuring out my taxes, only to have the IRS respond three weeks later that my tax handiwork was incorrect. They even provided me with the exact number that I owed them. If the IRS already knows our net tax, they should save us the trouble and send a bill or refund check without all of the hair pulling bullshit.

Congress enacted the federal income tax about 100 years ago. A growing number of taxpayers claim that the federal income tax is unconstitutional. Taxpayers should also call it stealing.

The federal government reminds me of a school bully who takes other children's lunch money and spends it on a bogus candy bar.

****

My parents opened a savings account for my brother when he was fourteen. He was not old enough to drive, so my parents had to accompany him to the bank when he made a transaction. However, I was old enough to drive. I got a hold of my brother's bank account number and filled out a generic withdrawal statement for thirty dollars. After practicing his signature until it looked almost identical to his rendition, I drove up to the bank's far right drive thru lane and made a withdrawal out of his account. The teller did not ask me any questions and she even waved to me as I drove off. I had no shame. I felt no remorse. I ripped off my own brother and all I felt was exhilaration.

I took the thrill of stealing to the next level when I worked at a local amusement park. During the summer break before my first year of college, I was responsible for a shooting gallery operation. Park guests deposited coins into machines that let them fire fifteen shots at slow moving targets. My daily tasks included making sure we had enough change on hand and to secure the money we took in until the end of the day.

I came back to work the following year, only to find out the suits demoted me to the warehouse. I blamed the new shooting gallery supervisor for my demotion and silently vowed to get even with him. I kept a copy of the money cabinet key. There was no way the suits were stupid enough to keep the same lock on the money cabinet. There was only one way to find out and that was to devise a plan to break into the cabinet.

The amusement park did not have identification scanners back in the day. We never had to sign in when we came to work. We just flashed our photo identification to the guard. Without having to worry about a paper trail, I came in early on a day off and hid up in the attic above the shooting gallery. Employees, including the supervisor, showed up about an hour after I arrived. I stayed completely still and quiet for almost three hours, which to this day is my personal ADHD best for not opening my mouth or moving my feet.

At lunch break, the supervisor locked the main door and went out the back for a bite to eat. There were still employees out in the gallery, but they did not have access to the money cabinet area. I came down the attic ladder, quickly opened the cabinet, and took every cent that was in the box. I snuck out the back door and slithered through areas of the park packed with people. My heart pounded, but it was not pounding because of fear. I got an adrenaline rush stealing the ninety-four dollars and seventeen cents.

After the amusement park episode, stealing became a habitual and pervasive part of my life. I mainly pilfered in college to derive economic benefit, like raiding the local grocery store for food and paper goods. An older man once chased me down a steep wooded embankment after I ripped off his store. I shouted obscenities at him while dropping packs of bologna and cheese.

I ripped off my own fraternity by embezzling from a house sinking fund account, giving new meaning to the term "sinking." I skimmed off the revenue derived from a Drake Relays hat-selling scheme I was in charge of during my last semester. Even Multiple Sclerosis was not sacrosanct. A fellow fraternity member and I kept all of the pledge money we were supposed to hand over for our annual MS fundraiser. Before the advent of technologically advanced security measures, I was able to wear three shirts under my own and walk out of department stores. I sold the polo shirts to others on Greek street.

I thought once I received my college degree, all of the impulsive behavior would miraculously disappear and my proclivity to steal would subside. I was wrong. Once I began my trek through the restaurant industry, I realized that I had an opportunity to steal during every shift that I worked. The first bartending job I had enlightened me to how easy it was to dip into the owner's bottom line. My mentor taught me how to dilute a batch of margaritas and steal the profits.

I used my observation skills and knowledge of every skimming trick in the book as a secret shopper, a job where I observed and reported any theft that occurred behind a bar. I only wrote negative reports on the bartenders or servers who blatantly embezzled, like the bartender at a restaurant who stuffed all of his ill-gotten booty into a margarita glass by the cash register.

The secret shopper company instructed me on one of my missions to observe a bartender who worked for a national chain. The bartender who the company instructed me to observe was yours truly.

****

As I was leaving a grocery store the other day, I spotted a man who was sitting handcuffed on the pavement. Security and store personnel surrounded him while conjuring up an appropriate punishment. He probably was caught shoplifting and given the customary scare straight tactics that I encountered at another grocery store.

I paid for about ten dollars worth of groceries when I realized I forgot to purchase a can of soup. My pockets had lint, but no money. I walked back to the soup aisle, two shopping bags in tow, and dropped a can of soup into one of the bags. I then tried to leave the store without paying for the soup.

One of the store's clandestine shoplifting spies approached me and suggested the two of us take a walk upstairs to the office. A cop showed up about thirty minutes later to go through the scare and shame ritual. Eventually, law enforcement released me into society without any of the groceries that I purchased. I made it nearly thirty years abiding by the declaration that I would never be caught stealing again. The humiliating handcuff act probably scares most offenders into paying for all goods and services. My handcuff experience was only a reminder that I needed to be less impulsive.

Finally caught in the act was the payback for all of the times I have departed grocery stores with stolen goods. I used to take a bus to a grocery store just to steal bottles of Dewars. I walked into the store with an empty backpack and usually left with two bottles that sometimes made a slight clanging sound when I went through the check out lane to pay for a pack of gum. I must have purloined at least twenty bottles of liquor from the grocery store inside of the St. Louis city limits.

It is not just that I committed a morally bereft act. My attitude in general about stealing was morally reprehensible. I knew stealing was wrong, yet I got immense pleasure out of taking things that were not mine. When I watched or read a news story that depicted a flagrant act of theft, I was amused and sometimes laughed aloud.

After researching Disruptive Behavioral Disorders, my motive for stealing originated from an antipathy for authority and societal norms. Most of my larceny was directed at institutions or adults I did not like or respect. My predilection for stealing derived more from deep-rooted psychological motives than the need for economic gain.

My inclination to steal is the one impulse that I have consciously eradicated. Like an addict who has to guard against relapse, I am on constant alert to be cognizant of any situation that presents itself as an opportunity to steal.

Now I can play a game of Monopoly without stealing the bank money and property deeds.

"I went to a fight the other night, and a hockey game broke out."

-Rodney Dangerfield

KICK ME OUT OF THE BALLGAME

By the age of seven, I realized there was not one venue where I could maintain focus for any length of time. My wandering mind deflected instructions from teachers. Bible lessons were nothing more than hour-long sessions of futility; I thought about everything under the sun except for God and heaven. My attempt to follow conversation during Sunday family dinners was a vain exercise in concentration.

The daydreaming came to a sudden halt the first time I walked into the St. Louis Arena for a hockey game. My uncle took me to my first game at the old barn, a Stanley Cup finals game between the St. Louis Blues and the Boston Bruins. Bobby Orr skated around the Blues players as if they were statues and scored on the Blues goalie like he was shooting at a cardboard replica. Bobby Orr was truly great before the "Great One," but he is not the reason I fondly remember my first live hockey game.

The sights and sounds of the arena besieged me. The concourse was full of cavorting fans and colorful vendors. I turned my head at every sudden burst of laughter and towards every dangling hockey memento. The energy I felt stilled my racing mind. I was at peace with 20,000 lunatics.

My focus sharpened once the referee dropped the puck. I watched the entire game with a laser like level of concentration. Every time my uncle tried to explain something to me, I shook my head in affirmation without uttering a word. I did not need explanations. I was going to figure out the game of hockey on my own.

It was not just the old barn. I found my comfort zone in every sporting venue. My father and grandfather took me to St. Louis Cardinal Baseball games as a revered tradition passed to future generations of St. Louis fans. They both tried to explain the intricate rules of baseball, but I figured out most of them on my own because I was intent on watching the entire game with an incisive mind. The only time I left my seat was to relieve myself, and sometimes I did not do that.

I saved on my brain's hard drive a detailed set of sporting event files from all of the games that I have attended. I can download Bob Gibson's high leg kick before he releases the ball towards Roberto Clemente, which Clemente shoots back like a cannon discharge. The line drive shatters Gibson's ankle. I rewind my brain's version of a DVD and view Clemente running down a ball in the right field corner, turn 180 degrees, and in one motion fire the ball on a rope to third base that beats the runner by at least two seconds. I have saved in a brain video file the playoff game when Bobby Orr skated around the Blues players as if he was performing skating drills around a bunch of pylons.

I enjoyed baseball games so much that I connived ways to get out of school so I could catch weekday games at the old Busch Stadium. My first attempt using the truancy strategy was unsuccessful. I called the administration office from inside of Kirkwood High School. In a pathetic rendition of mom's voice, I told the secretary, "Don isn't feeling well and will not be coming back to school after lunch." I discerned skepticism in the secretary's voice, so I abruptly hung up the phone and ran down the hall as fast as I could.

There had to be a better way to skip school for baseball. I convinced a female classmate to write excuse notes for me, which I always delivered on the day that I planned to be truant. She only wanted me to complete one homework assignment for her. Mom was incredulous when she saw I had eight absence days during the final quarter of my senior year. I told her it must have been a typo.

Sporting events have always been a place for me to leave behind my distractions and enter the world of hyper-focused attention. Once I was able to attend games without the presence of adult supervision, a subtle, yet perceptible change came over me. I was still intent on catching every play of every game. Without adult supervision, however, the intensity of my hyper-focused attention spilled over into displays of bad behavior. My wound up disposition was unfurled, as hyperactivity and impulsiveness pushed aside penetrating focus to become the predominant trait at sporting events.

****

Amen- Verbally abusive to others (4)

The strongest defensive mechanism in my repertoire is the connection between my acerbic wit and flippant tongue. I rarely had to settle disagreements by displaying physical prowess. Most of my peers took a verbal tongue-lashing and walked away with their shoulders sunken. Authority figures tried in vain to reign in the harangues with a combination of punishments and inducements to be nice. I eventually learned to control my tongue in most social settings, but the urge to let loose with diatribes drove my already restless nature over the edge when I was inside a sports stadium or arena.

Larry Bird was the first athlete I tirelessly heckled for the course of an entire game. I made rude references to his trailer park upbringing, mostly screaming profane things about his family's internal bonding. He muttered something that was unintelligible. His rebuttals to my insults increased in clarity when I made statements about how Magic Johnson was a better player than he was. Bird set a Veteran's Memorial Auditorium record by dropping fifty points on the Drake Bulldogs. I still wonder if I should get at least some credit for the record.

I looked forward to the annual Drake Relays, a track and field extravaganza considered one of two amateur trials for the Olympics. I was not captivated by the level of competition. I certainly did not marvel at the display of athletic prowess. I liked the Drake Relays because it provided a stage to hone my heckling skills. I told pole-vaulters about a place where they could shove their poles. I did my best *Caddyshack* impression before an athlete took off for the long jump, usually screaming "scratch" right before the athlete hit the launch stripe. In a morbid display of behavior, I heckled the runners who lagged far behind during long distance races.

I turned my invectives towards other fans when I was too far from the field, rink, or court to disparage the athletes and coaches. It seemed the only reason I attended sporting events was to hurl insults at other people. There were instances when my runaway brain became so out of control that I emptied sections of seats after unleashing one of my verbal barrages. Even my companions sometimes left their seats because they were embarrassed.

I never got into any trouble heckling except one time during a doubleheader at the old Busch Stadium. Doubleheaders were a beer vendor's dream. I contributed to one vendor's dream during the doubleheader by consuming my fair share of

Budweiser. I abided by the adage to pace myself during the course of both games, which meant drinking one beer an inning.

During the second game, a beer cup came raining down on the bleacher fans. I looked up and saw some boisterous young adults saluting us with the middle finger. I yelled some obscenities before telling them I was going to kick their asses after the game.

I forgot about my unveiled threats by the end of the game, but the ruffians from the upper deck had not. One of the thugs cold cocked me across the bridge of my nose, releasing a torrent of blood onto the grimy pavement. I slammed my Yankees batting helmet to the ground and walked away with my companions to continue with our day of drinking beer and chasing mischief.

Heckling became such an obsession that I made two trips to heckle Albert Belle. Albert was the perfect candidate for carrying a sign that read "Heckle Me" on his back. My brother accompanied me on both trips to Tiger Stadium, where we sat within earshot of Albert and spent every inning of all six games heckling him. When we ran out of creative things to say to Belle, my brother and I turned our insulting comments towards other fans.

I realized after our Belle ringing trips that if I wanted more space at a sporting event, I could achieve the goal by sliding derisive comments off the conveyor belt that was stored inside of my runaway brain.

****

IRRITATION

Professional athletes deserved every acrid word that came out of my mouth. The problem was other fans disagreed. Fans have lectured me about my diatribes, with the most insolent coming from a woman who got in my face during a baseball game. I ridiculed a player who seemed to be loafing after a fly ball. She said one of the most asinine things I have ever heard.

"At least he's trying!"

Trying? Baseball players receive an exorbitant amount of money to do more than try. With the fly ball, the player was not even getting close to the trying phase of the competition. The naïve statement from the woman exemplifies the disgraceful adoration sports fans have for professional athletes.

Are professional athletes worth more than neurosurgeons? Which one can we do without as a society? Neurosurgeons are more vital to the progress of the human race than some insipid baseball player.

After our devastating freak summer storm in 2006, I volunteered to help distribute food packages to the people considered needy by the Salvation Army. The boxes of food were mostly off-brand canned vegetables and pasta boxes. About five miles down the road, a baseball game got underway where fans paid six dollars for lukewarm beer and five dollars for a hot dog that was rolled on the grill for two hours.

Here I was handing out boxes of food worth six dollars while people pissed away money for six-dollar beers. Should we be helping a fellow human being in need or contributing to an overpaid professional baseball player? I disagree with George Will. Baseball ***IS NOT*** that important. Our societal priorities disgust me.

****

Gary and I made quite a tandem when we attended a sporting event. The Albert Belle heckling caravan to Detroit was just one trip my brother and I took over the course of a ten-year period. We took some trips without a supporting cast of misanthropes. The more raucous trips involved other people who fueled our misconduct while we spewed venom throughout the sports arena or stadium. Most of our trips took us to Chicago, where we made our presence felt in such venues as Wrigley Field, Soldier's Field, Chicago Stadium, and Comiskey Park.

Dave Bergdorf was the perfect companion for our trips to Chicago. He not only had a great sense of humor, but he also kept us from crossing over the proverbial misconduct line. We made one trip that even Mr. "steady as they go" Bergdorf could not help but join the mischief.

The three of us went to Chicago over a Fourth of July holiday to catch the White Sox and Red Sox play a three game series. The Taste of Chicago was also going on during the holiday celebration. We spent some of our time in Grant Park gorging ourselves with some top-notch grub and ice-cold beer.

I knew we were in trouble the minute we stepped into our hotel room and opened the small refrigerator that sat by the television. Inside the fridge was an eclectic selection of airplane sized liquor bottles. I mentioned to the other two that it was nice of the hotel to supply us with *free* liquor before we stepped out into the Chicago night. We made drinks, did some shots, and headed for the elevated train that transported us to the game.

My brother was in rare form during the Friday game, displaying his classic alcohol-fueled cantankerous behavior for all to see. We were fortunate that security did not arrest us and the bleacher hooligans refrained from retaliation. My turn to spout off came on Saturday night, after we polished off the hotel liquor and stumbled into a cab for the second game.

Once we got to the game, I was on mission to create as much trouble as possible. I roamed the stadium, striking up conversations with complete strangers who gave me disgusted looks after I staggered away from them. I found a cute beer vendor to hassle for about thirty minutes, but she grew tired of my slurred speech. A rain delay, the worst nightmare for stadium employees, halted the game for about an hour. The game stopped, but the beer kept flowing like Niagara Falls.

I took my shirt off and danced around the outfield concourse. A bunch of little kids who found it amusing that an adult was having so much fun quickly joined me. The large Jumbotron screen directly above us in center field showed the dancing unbeknownst to us. I was having some harmless fun until the rain stopped, the game restarted, and one of the thousand ADHD light bulbs went off in my head. The light bulb reminded me why I actually came to the game. I was there because I hated the Red Sox and anything that had to do with the city of Boston, Paul Revere and Ted Kennedy included.

I ran down to the outfield bleachers and started hurling insults at the Red Sox outfielders. One of them turned around when I mentioned something about his mother and sister. Out of the corner of my eye, I spotted one of the Red Sox relievers warming up in the bullpen. I ran as fast as I could to the bullpen and immediately unleashed a profanity-laced tirade. He continued to focus on the catcher and that pissed me off. I proceeded to take my despicable behavior into the gutter.

I reached into my pocket and pulled out a handful of coins. As the reliever continued to throw, I took the coins and threw them as hard as I could at him. I quickly ducked below the railing, where I heard someone shriek so loud that it reminded me of how I sounded when struck with a foreign object. I scurried back up the bleacher stairs onto the outfield concourse, where I stood slouched among the fans waiting in concession lines. My brother later told me stadium security and uniformed cops spent the better part of an hour looking for me. I do not know why they could not find a 6' 3" drunk with his shirt off, but I am glad they did not.

****

My brother and I usually planned our sporting event extravaganzas. We bought our plane or train fares, hotel rooms, and event tickets months before leaving St. Louis for a three-day getaway.

In February 1992, we were watching television on a Saturday night and talking about how sick we were of the dreary weather. The length of the dank and gloomy weather spell started to wear on my agitated ADHD temperament.

"We need to get out of this shithole," I said.

My brother replied, "How about a hockey game? Better yet, how about a hockey game in Chicago?"

We looked in the sports page and saw the Blackhawks were at home the next night against the Pittsburgh Penguins. We looked forward to a road trip that included chiding the Blackhawks and rooting on the defending Stanley Cup champions.

The next morning, we got up early and high-tailed it out of St. Louis in my brother's truck. I concocted a wicked vodka punch that we started drinking before we hit Springfield. By the time we got to Chicago, we were both inebriated and in dire need of relieving ourselves. We pulled into Grant Park and took our respective leaks against a tree. We were out in plain view for the public or any police officer who happened to pass by. None did.

We had time to kill, so we killed it by going to a sports bar and guzzling pitchers of beer. We arrived at Chicago Stadium early so we could purchase our tickets before the game sold out. We had to relieve ourselves again. Since there were not any portable toilets, we decided to piss on the stadium entrance doors that were out in plain view for the public or any police officer that passed by. None did.

Once inside, our adrenaline took a bit of the alcohol edge off. We found our seats and immediately went in search of more beer. The first two periods were uneventful, both on the ice and in the archaic heights of Chicago Stadium. During the second intermission, we made one more beer run and then the whole day's worth of drinking caught up to us.

The third period started with a fight on the ice. The pugilism kicked my heckling engine into high gear. We were both vociferous with our acerbic outbursts, lambasting anyone who dared to pass us by and look us in the eye. Without a compelling reason, I reached into my pocket and grabbed all of the loose change. Some people in front of us turned around and asked us to "keep it down." I took the large handful of coins and threw them at the back of their heads.

I felt a firm grip on my shoulder and looked up to see stadium security hovering over the both of us. They forcefully escorted us out of Chicago Stadium on the side of the building that faced the housing projects. We staggered through the parking lot for twenty minutes while looking for my brother's truck. We eventually stumbled upon it.

I mentioned that we should get a hotel room and call in sick to work the next day. My brother insisted that we head back to St. Louis. He wanted me to drive. His insistence won me over and I took control of his truck. I rolled down the window, lit a cigarette, and proceeded to make the 300-mile trek back to St. Louis. My blood alcohol content level had to be at least twice the .10 limit. The five-hour drive put us at high risk for causing a calamity.

There are times when I look back in retrospect (for you, Yogi Berra) and wonder if a heavenly angel watches over me. I do not think I endangered us during our trip back home. Who knows? I was not the model of sobriety. The most amazing aspect of the poor decision to drive drunk was that we passed the Illinois Highway Patrol headquarters. The cops must have been at a donut convention. My angel got us both home safely.

I do not know if I had ADHD or Bad Decision Disorder (BDD).

****

FRUSTRATION

I do not absorb much when I am in a place of cultural or historical significance. Curators of cultural and historical sites lay them out in a progression that seems natural to most people. Well, they are not natural for me.

I bounce around the Art Museum, going from room to room in record time. I start in room one to view painting number one, then I hurry over to painting six before streaking out of the room into an adjacent area that displays pottery. I look at one piece of pottery and streak back into the first room to check out painting twelve. I then stroll back to painting one. Once in awhile, I stop at a piece that I am totally fascinated with and hyper-focus on it for an inordinate length of time. I become one of the museum's sculptures.

The animals at the St. Louis Zoo must think I am nuts. The bears greet us when we enter the zoo. I look at the first batch of bears, walk over to the mongoose display, check out the seals, and then race through the primate house before I go back and take in the second batch of bears.

Gettysburg is the most popular Civil War monument and rightfully so. The era actors are excellent and the story of Gettysburg is historically prominent. The only thing I recalled after visiting Gettysburg was, "Blah, blah, blah, blah, Pickett's charge, blah, blah, blah." And that many people died.

ADHD EPOCHS

"Every child is an artist. The problem is how to remain an artist once he grows up."

-Pablo Picasso

THE WONDER YEARS

Amen-History of ADHD symptoms in childhood, such as distractibility, short attention span, impulsiveness, or restlessness (4)

Jasper/Goldberg-Even when sitting quietly, I am usually moving my hands or feet (Very much)

There was not much evidence during my early childhood years that proves I had ADHD. My linguistic development was normal. I was not a bed wetter, though I did piss in my pants during a Little League baseball game. I started walking on my own at eleven months. I sucked my thumb about as often as Dick Cheney tells the truth.

My childhood medical record indicates that I had some substantial health issues. I had one bout with such a high fever that my parents submerged me in a bathtub full of water in an attempt to control the raging inferno. I had a hernia four months after I was born, caused by my reaction to being force-fed another spoonful of Gerber's vomit.

Overall, I believe my early childhood years were comparatively normal. Even so, ADHD does not lurk inside of a child and then suddenly launch its symptoms in early adulthood. All of the ADHD indicators were present during my childhood and adolescence. The signs and symptoms were perceptible enough to warrant adult scrutiny.

It is easy to refer to an event that happened last week, last month, or even last year. Retrieving ADHD examples from forty years ago requires a well-structured memory. I may forget to take my groceries from the self-service checkout line, but I remember the weather conditions on the day that I jabbed an umbrella into the girl's eye at Mt. Pleasant grade school. It was cold, windy, and overcast.

The girl from Mt. Pleasant was one of the first to find out about my overly sensitive disposition. Childhood was when I started to build a defensive wall and lash back at those who criticized or made fun of me. I never believed in the turn-the-other-cheek exhortations disseminated throughout the Bible. I believed in the axiom to slap the other cheek in a ruthlessly unforgettable manner. Most of my problems in childhood stemmed from an explosive temper and impulsive rage. I understood what it took to evade responsibility for my vindictiveness. I blamed others for my conduct and denied involvement in illicit activities.

The lunch box was an especially volatile topic. I was so embarrassed to carry a lunch box to school that I devised a plan to avoid humiliation. I took a brown bag from the pantry drawer in our kitchen and stuffed it inside my shirt or jacket. Once out of parental view, I grabbed all of the goodies out of my lunch box and put them in the bag. On the way to school, I hid the lunch box in a bush or trash container. If it was not there when I returned, I told mom that one of my peers stole it or smashed it with his feet.

There was not the contemporary understanding of ADHD when I was struggling with behavioral issues as a child and teenager. Most of the adult authority figures used the label "discipline problem" when they described my behavior. My parents say they never saw me that way. I am not sure if that is due to self-denial or lack of awareness.

I carried the anger, vindictiveness, and resentment from early childhood through my high school years and beyond. Overt aggression towards people, destruction of property, lying, stealing, and skipping school was omnipresent in my life. I was especially good at destroying property that was not mine, whether it was doing bicycle donuts on golf course greens, lighting fires on public property, or throwing chairs through hotel sliding doors. One of the more nefarious acts of destruction took place during the summer of 1975.

I lived near two sets of railroad tracks. One set of tracks transported new cars from a nearby assembly plant. The train came by with the glistening cars around seven in the evening. I stood back about twenty feet from the tracks upon an incline and fired huge rocks toward the train. I broke windshields, side windows, and put large dents into the new cars. I started out doing this with another kid, but I enjoyed the rush so much that I eventually did it on my own.

I now realize the vandalism was not committed simply because I was a bad kid, but because I demonstrated conduct disorder symptoms that were associated with ADHD. Kids today have professional support, medical resources, and medication to mitigate disruptive behavior. I was not as fortunate because nobody smelled a whiff of ADHD in my behavior.

I was fortunate that nobody witnessed my destructive behavior. The punishment would have been a stint in the juvenile detention system.

****

Second grade was a debacle. I rebelled at home. I rebelled at church. I really rebelled at school, where my daily disruption of Mrs. Gilkes' class led to a variety of lectures and punishments. By second grade, I developed an arsenal of profanity that I unleashed on classmates, teachers, and complete strangers. I single-handedly kept Johnson and Johnson in business with profane diatribes in Mrs. Gilkes' class. She continued mom's tradition of washing my mouth out with soap with such regularity that I answered to "Dial."

Once adults understood that washing my mouth out with soap triggered diarrhea, they started employing alternative forms of punishment. During another boring science lecture, I called the kid sitting next to me a motherfucker. Since she was out of soap, Mrs. Gilkes sent me down to see our principal. He was not intimidating by any stretch of the imagination, but he did like to use his three-foot ruler to mete out punishment.

I already felt the sting of the principal's lashings, so I knew what to expect when I went down to answer for the profanity. He decided to play a mind game with me, giving me two options to mull over as punishment. I could take ten licks with the ruler or sing the national anthem over the intercom for the entire student body.

He thought he was dealing with a cream puff, a weak little kid who would melt from the fear of his imposing ruler. He was wrong. I told him to give me the ten licks, which he gladly did with a little more exertion than his previous lashings. As I walked out of his office rubbing my ass, I smirked at the Secretary because I knew the pain would eventually subside. Singing the anthem over the intercom would have lingered throughout the rest of my school days.

I screwed with adults every chance that I got. The best venue to screw with them was Westborough Country Club, where eighteen adult quartets made their way around the golf course. I strategically placed M-80s that were set with delayed cigarette fuses along the tenth hole, including one at the bottom of the flagstick cup. I hid in the bushes and watched with glee when an M-80 exploded right before one of the members followed through with his putting motion. I am surprised one of the older members did not collapse from a heart attack.

The cigarette fuse also came in handy when I got revenge on the Glendale cops for wasting my time during the Hostess fruit pie incident. I walked into the station on a sweltering summer day and asked the cop behind the counter if I could use the bathroom. My ingenuous demeanor belied the ulterior motive.

I went into the bathroom, placed a lit, delayed fuse M-80 behind the toilet, and calmly walked out of the station. Before my departure, I turned to thank the officer for letting me use the bathroom. I quickly made it home and waited for the loud explosion. It came, as did the harried shouts of cops who were befuddled as to who did what inside of their police sanctuary. I snickered when my parents asked each other, "I wonder what that was?"

I was not through with the cops. Later that summer, I took the wire cutters from dad's workbench and headed towards the station. Just to the side of the station, and out of view from those inside, stood a pen where all of the stray dogs huddled to keep warm. I snuck up to the pen and started cutting the mesh that separated the dogs from freedom. A few dogs immediately jumped out of the cage and ran away. One dog stayed inside of the cage and yelped. I quickly finished cutting the mesh and then pulled the yelping dog out of the cage.

Two days later, the cops removed the dog holding pens.

****

FRUSTRATION/IRRITATION

People who fly through red lights piss me off. The self-absorption with their hectic schedules jeopardizes the physical well being of others. It is maddening when a traffic light turns green and I have to count to three before proceeding through an intersection. The protectors of our public safety need to make red light infractions priority number one.

PS-The camera strategy is not working. The scofflaws figured out how to beat the rap in court.

****

The loud noises that emanated from the fine arts building fascinated me. My peers made cacophonous sounds with a mélange of instruments, while a poised conductor named John Tolle blithely led the class through assorted compositions. Every kid loved band class.

I wanted in.

Once I was band eligible in fifth grade, I broached the idea of taking band class with my parents. I wanted to play the trombone, the instrument with three valves that emitted harmonious melodies. I did not tell my parents about the three valves, just that I wanted to play the trombone. Having no concept of money, I just shrugged when my parents asked me if I thought trombones grew on trees. I did not care if they grew in a field. My sole focus was to procure the instrument that my friends were playing.

Mom bought a trombone three days later. I opened the case and was stunned to see the instrument did not have three valves. The instrument had a peculiar shape that included an inordinately long slide for someone with my reach. The slide that moved up and down the instrument bewildered me. I was too embarrassed to tell my parents that I asked for the wrong instrument. I found out on the first day of band class that the instrument I wanted was a trumpet. There were just two of us in the back row playing a distortion of a musical instrument called a trombone.

I practiced enough to become an adept trombonist, though the sounds coming out from it drove my entire family bonkers. My usual practice area was upstairs in the bedroom. I played with the windows open and blasted sound after discordant sound for the enjoyment of the entire neighborhood.

I found band class to be a nice diversion from the tedious classroom lectures. By middle school, band class was just an excuse to screw with the other students. I enjoyed, with Dennis the Menace like glee, throwing coins into the wide, bell-shaped tuba and baritone apertures. My classmates reveled from hearing the loud clanging noises the coins made during one of Stanley Topfer's music cessation commands. I snuck into the storage area and hid other kid's instruments, stole their mouthpieces, and stuffed rags and towels into their baritones, trumpets, clarinets, saxophones, and trombones. I made sure to stuff my trombone with rags and towels so it looked like I was a victim and not the perpetrator.

Band was always my first class in high school, a smooth transition into the rest of the day. It was also an easy A and I needed every A I could get in order to inflate my grade point average. I actually learned something about music in high school because I sat with some accomplished players who were excellent teachers. Marching and jazz band provided an outlet to release my high-octane energy and untapped creativity. We played concerts, participated in band competitions, and welcomed Jimmy Carter during a presidential rally. My parents asked me if I wanted to continue playing the trombone in college, but I declined knowing that my skill level was not enough to match the talent at the next level.

The trombone also had little star power. Few musical numbers featured the instrument with the long slide. I regularly missed playing sections of a song because the trombone section had to wait long interludes until our services were required. The trombone exacerbated my penchant for daydreaming.

My parents were proud of me for finally starting something and sticking with it through my secondary school years. They did not understand that I stuck with band because I liked the down time to daydream. Above all, I enjoyed using my trombone as a weapon. I prodded classmates in the back of their heads with my trombone slide. The spit valve at the end of the slide was my favorite weapon. I blew huge amounts of trombone residue as far as the first row, where the dreaded flute section quietly sat through the entire class.

During one high school band practice, I spurted out a slimy liquid substance into Tom Thomas' hair. He spun around and started pummeling Greg Himebaugh. The brawl went on for minutes until a red-faced Dr. Kuzmich broke it up. Thomas never knew I was the one who used the sliding spit dispenser. Dr. Kuzmich handed out his punishment to Thomas and Himebaugh, and then tapped his baton on the podium to strike up the band.

****

The prospect of joining the Cub Scouts intrigued me. The uniforms that my friends wore to school on Wednesdays definitely captured my attention. The uniforms gave my friends panache. They looked so cool that I devised ways to break into their homes so I could steal their uniforms.

I joined the Cub Scouts when I was eligible and stayed in scouting until I earned enough merit badges for Eagle Scout recognition. I tell people that I am an Eagle Scout and their responses are incredulous. Achieving Eagle Scout took about fours years of dedication to complete the standard requirements. I was at a disadvantage because I did not have the patience to pursue a goal that took four years.

Twenty-one merit badges and an involved community service project formed the foundation for the Eagle Scout requirements. My community service project entailed placing identification tags on all of the valuable property at Glendale Presbyterian Church. I made sure we did not tag the furniture and kitchen accessories that I planned to steal.

I completed the Eagle Scout merit badge requirements even though I had to overcome my disdain for swimming. The Boy Scouts dropped the requisite lifesaver merit badge about the time I commenced with my badge accumulation. Lifesaver would have been nearly impossible because it required above average swimming skills and I could not even open my eyes under water. I had below average upper body strength at the time and an innate aversion to being under water. Some experts may decide upon further analysis that I had a fear of drowning.

Scouting was the one group activity that exploited my ADHD gifts. It harnessed my leadership skills, especially the ability to make quick decisions and formulate action plans. The unpredictable nature of scouting unleashed my creativity. My greatest creative achievement was leading a group of first time campers into a competitive spring camporee.

My brother was in the patrol with a group of his friends, so we coalesced and accomplished fourth place out of our troop's seven patrols. We had to cheat to get through the various competitions. The pioneering event was especially arduous since I did not know anything about knots except they pissed me off. I surmised that the only use for pioneering was to become a skilled mountain climber or a notorious serial killer. Neither job classification appealed to me.

I sat behind the pioneering judge during the question and answer portion of the competition. A couple of patrol members shielded me while I whispered answers to the kid who was on the quiz session clock. We ripped off completed pioneering projects from other troops and used them when it was our turn to fasten a bunch of wood together with some rope. We finished second in our troop during the pioneering phase of the competition despite not having anyone who knew anything about pioneering,

Scout leaders judged our patrol on every aspect of camping, including meal preparation and cleanup. Our patrol set a record time in preparing, cooking, and cleaning up after our last meal. I instructed our patrol to serve pancakes and sausage links straight from the frying pans into the hands of adults who had joined us for Sunday morning breakfast. I did not know at the time that I invented the McGriddle breakfast sandwich. The price of pancakes and sausage links for fifteen people: $5. The facial expressions of people served pancakes in their hands: priceless.

Boy Scouts extracted the creativity locked deep within my brain. I was creative in coming up with solutions to problems, so creative that I was referred to by adults as a maverick who used unconventional tactics. Some of my peers had the audacity to call me a cheater. I did whatever it took to win Boy Scout competitions, including devising strategies that violated the rules and pushed aside socially accepted behavior.

I was able to build a rapport with the members of my Junior Leadership Training Camp patrol by breaking the rules. One night, all of the patrols hiked into the wilderness to camp without tents. The scout leaders provided us with flint and steel to start a campfire. They expected us to cook a whole chicken over the fire for our meal. Most of the other patrols snuck matches and lighters into their personal gear in order to sidestep the flint and steel rule.

When our patrol got to the spot assigned for us to break camp for the night, the other members became agitated over the flint and steel rule. Some of the patrol members even tried to ignite kindling using the cave dweller's method for starting a fire. One kid broke out matches and lit the kindling. I walked over to the fire, took the chicken, and heaved it as far as I could into an adjacent pond. The patrol members were aghast, whining about what they were going to eat for dinner. I went to my backpack and pulled out eight sandwiches and eight bags of chips. I passed them out to the rest of the patrol. We sat around the campfire laughing about how I stole our dinner from the adult commissary.

During each meal of summer camp, one of the scoutmasters graded us on everything from meal timing to food quality. I organized a patrol raid to sabotage our closest competitor's cooking gear and fuel sources. We soaped their pots and doused their charcoal with water. After one soaping incident, the disciplinarian scoutmaster came down with a raging case of diarrhea and George Johnson's patrol came down with a dinner score of zero.

I stole a snake from the nature area and entered the slithery reptile in a camp-wide snake race. Our snake destroyed the competition. I ditched scoutmaster tents set up by other patrols. I rigged patrol camping areas with fishing wire. I will never forget the expression on one kid's face after he tripped over the fishing line while he carried a large stack of firewood.

Scouting was the best way to release my ADHD. The great outdoors provided the perfect setting for my impulsive, yet creative behavior. While the Boy Scouts had rigid rules and standards, I was able to break most of them down while accomplishing their greatest honor.

****

FRUSTRATION

I have always treated hiking as a race. I wanted to get to point B from point A as fast as possible. I rushed through an activity meant for a leisurely pace. I never took the time to take in the beautiful views that surrounded me at every vista. I have hiked some of the most scenic parts of America and missed most of the view. I am frustrated that I never took the time to slow down, put my head up, and look out into the horizon.

****

I have fond memories of childhood. The pain and confusion of undiagnosed ADHD did not have a significant impact until I left home for college. Still, I started feeling isolated from the world. Loneliness emerged when I was in junior high school. I found myself participating in activities without the camaraderie of friends.

Every Friday night after Nipher Junior High School's football game, one of my peers threw a party to celebrate a victory or lament a defeat. I always heard my peers talk up the party during school on Friday, but nobody ever looked me in the eye and asked if I wanted to come along.

One Friday night, Susie Straub hosted the weekly shindig at her house. She lived three blocks from our home. I did not get an invite or even an acknowledgement that I was the student who lived closest to her. That evening, I told my parents that I was going for a walk. Once I got close to Susie's house, I stood behind a tree and observed the good time had by all. I spent a lot of time on the outside looking in.

Adults gave me many labels in childhood. The first label attached to me was laziness. My third grade teacher gave me the moniker of lazy, which she later interpreted as a trait that prevented me from reaching my potential. For years, I misspelled my middle name Keith by putting *i* before *e*. I thought that was the rule: *i* before *e* except after *c*. My sixth grade teacher finally caught my mistake and referred to me as someone "who is too lazy to even take the time to spell his name right." I will never forget the mortification that I felt when she said that.

My answer to the incipient isolation and ridicule was to strike back with a vengeance towards other people. It did not matter if I knew the person or they were complete strangers. I devised elaborate schemes that bordered on criminal behavior. During a family vacation, I came up with a plan that should have put me behind bars.

During our first visit, I immediately became fixated on a small train that carried tourists for a quiet ride around the lake. There were many trees to hide behind and throw things. On a blistering hot day, I summoned my brothers and we headed down to the track.

I always liked to throw things. I threw snowballs at cars. I even waited at bus stops for the bus to pull up and open its doors so I could pelt the driver with compact ice. I threw eggs at houses. I threw mud balls at fellow classmates who played soccer. I really enjoyed throwing rocks through windows; the crashing sound was symphonic. When I told my brothers we were heading down to the railroad track, they should have understood there was going to be some throwing of something.

My brothers and I hid behind the trees and threw pebbles and sticks at the first train that passed by. The pelting of the train with small objects grew old after awhile, so I started putting soda cans and rocks on the track to see if the conductor would stop to remove the objects. He did and I became bored with that plan.

Finally, I hauled a huge boulder and placed it on a corner turn that prevented the conductor from stopping in time to remove it. I then put a public garbage bin over the boulder. We saw a train approach and decided to run back to our cabin. Before we got there, we heard a loud crash and started to run faster. My brothers ran out of fear; I ran with the pleasure of knowing we knocked the train off the track. Thankfully, nobody was hurt. The train remained turned over on the track for the remainder of the week.

Property destruction was a sign that I had some type of behavior disorder. I am not sure what acronym caused me to pull off pranks that humiliated other children. On another dull summer day, I ran out of things to do by ten in the morning and the H in ADHD was fervently boiling over. Wiffle ball was an activity that allowed me to release some of the hyperactivity. I asked my brother to bring his friend over for a game of wiffle ball. At least that is what I told my brother to tell his friend.

I told my brother to bring his friend under a tree that was in our backyard. He watched as I climbed the tree and sat on a thick branch. My brother left and came back with his friend about ten minutes later. I dropped my pants and squatted in between two tree limbs. They were conversing below when his friend felt something hit him on the top of his head. He ran his hand over his head, looked up, and saw me cackling like a hen. When he realized I defecated on him, he ran home in tears and told his parents. His parents hysterically informed my parents about the antisocial act. My parents responded by giving me the worst whooping of my childhood.

A few years later, as I stood in line waiting for my high school diploma, I was not reminiscing about all of the wonderful times I had at Kirkwood High School. I was not contemplating my muddled future. I did not even notice the principal butcher my name before graduate number 92 nudged me forward. The only thing I thought about as I left the stage smiling was the day that I crapped on the kid's head.

"Was it over when the Germans bombed Pearl Harbor?"

-John Belushi's character "Bluto" Blutarski, from *Animal House*

FOUR YEARS DOWN THE DRAIN

Amen-History of not living up to potential in school (4)

Amen- Chronic problems with self-esteem (4)

Amen-Test anxiety, or during tests your mind tends to go blank (4)

Jasper/Goldberg-At home, work or school, I find my mind wandering from tasks that are uninteresting or difficult (Quite a lot)

"Where do you want to go to college?"

My parents asked me the question during the summer of 1977, after I compiled a relatively successful academic record during my junior year at Kirkwood High School. Like most questions about my future, I did not have a clue about my college aspirations. I did not comprehend the college recruitment process and I was not cognizant of the financial burden placed on my parents. I thought college was a given, that everyone went to college after graduating from high school.

We were required to take two college entrance examinations. I loathed the ACT and SAT because the sterile testing environment made it more difficult to focus than when I was in a classroom. The only noise made during the four-hour tests came from the clock. I constantly glanced at it to find out how much time I had left in a section.

There were times when I lost my train of thought after glancing at the clock. I had to start a question over and that caused my frustration level to boil over into physical distress. I shook my legs, tapped my pencil on the desk, twisted about in the chair, and darted my eyes around for a panoramic view of the room. I was so anxious that my mind went blank. Somehow, as if a higher being engineered a genetic anomaly into my system for self-preservation, I always pulled out of the blank funk and continued with the test.

The sections I had the most trouble with were reading comprehension and critical analysis. Sage testing professionals placed the reading comprehension section of the test deep within the booklet. When it was finally time to start the section, my brain was low on fuel and the words were nothing but a series of vague impressions on paper. I quickly glanced at the multiple paragraph dissertations and immediately examined the questions, hoping I could skim back over the reading section to find clues for the answers. I implemented a strategy not recommended by the test preparation manual.

The analytical section had questions that made me want to ram my head into a wall until it became a bloody pulp. Johnny is taller than Abe. Abe is taller than Ken. Ken is shorter than Bill. Bill drives Karen to work. Karen is smarter than Beth. Beth is shorter than Ken. Ken freebases crack cocaine. How tall is Ron?

Who gives a rat's ass?

My test scores were strong enough to have reputable schools like Drake University accept my application for a four-year stint preparing for the real world. Other colleges sent literature and my parents and I visited some of them, such as Milliken University in Illinois and Grinnell College in Iowa.

After discussing the prospects with mom and dad, we eventually settled on Drake.

My parents definitely wanted me out of the house for that phase of my life, but within leash-reeling distance in case I irrefutably screwed up. Screwing up became my academic major. Drake University is the primary evidence exhibit for my ADHD case.

The one incident that should have alerted mom and dad that my brain needed a wiring adjustment was when we visited the Drake campus during the summer prior to my first year. We spent a steamy July weekend attending a freshman orientation session. My parents stayed in a motel and I spent the weekend getting to know my roommate as we shared our future dormitory room.

The orientation was an endless stream of seminars led by bland administration officials. The only words I remember mentioned were “truancy” and “party.” The nights, however, were raucous fun. The two nights I spent carousing were a precursor to how I was going to prioritize my college obligations. My dilemma was to figure out how I was going to integrate study time into my social calendar.

After one dull session about who-knows-what, we walked out of the auditorium in the student center and headed towards the recreation room. I was looking straight ahead when I heard video game chimes, pinball machine alarms, and pool table balls cracking against each other. I abruptly turned right as if my brain programmed a fun microchip. The fun microchip directed me towards the first video game that was open. I shoved a bunch of quarters into the machine.

Dad was visibly furious. He openly castigated me, using a tone that was both demeaning and inquisitive.

"What is wrong with you?” he demanded.

I felt smaller than Tattoo from Fantasy Island after dad excoriated me like a five year old. I was acting like one and deserved what I got. My parents should have realized that I was not a good financial risk and maybe the leash should have been shorter. They had to contemplate whether I was going to make the right decisions, like deciding between homework and pitcher night at the West End Lounge.

I did not make a sudden move into the recreation room because I had a premeditated desire to piss off my parents. The sudden turn was strictly impulsive, an instantaneous search for wanton gratification that plagued me throughout my four years at Drake. The story of Siren luring the sailors to their deaths is an appropriate metaphor for describing my reaction to the noises coming from the recreation room. During the summer orientation at Drake, the whistles and bells that lured me into the recreation room were the first of many distractions that negatively affected my academic pursuit.

****

I failed the first test before I even moved my possessions into the Goodwin-Kirk dormitory at Drake University.

The summer before my eagerly awaited Des Moines departure, my parents asked me if I wanted to join the family for a vacation to Wyoming, Montana, and southern Alberta, Canada. I was surprised by the question, "Do you want to join us?", because it was a given the entire family went on vacation. They asked the question because they knew I was working overtime at Six Flags, trying to save money for the first year of college. I thought about it for five seconds until I realized I would have the house to myself for two weeks. I told them that I needed to work as much as possible.

I got the standard ground rules and instructions for assuming the king of the castle throne. They did not warn me about throwing a party, just some instructions on how to take care of the house while they were gone. The minute my family pulled away from the driveway, I was on the phone excitedly calling friends and foes alike to let them know I was having a bash. I called over fifty people.

I do not know how many people showed up because by 8:00 on Saturday night, I passed out on my parent's bed after depositing six hours worth of drinking throughout their bathroom. Three of Glendale's finest startled me out of my stupor. They gave me a quick tour of the carnage left behind by the departed revelers. The house looked like a disaster scene from a movie, with broken windows and lamps in every room. The worst of the destruction was outside, where tire marks on my neighbor's lawn topped the vandalism list. I knew I was in deep shit. I was in shit so deep an emergency response recovery team needed to rescue me.

My parents hit the roof when they found out about the party. The cops never called as I expected them to, but half of the neighborhood did. To make matters worse, I did a poor job of covering up my big mistake by rushing through the cleaning process. I missed a lot of beer spots, broken glass, and items under the couches. Dad found a bag of marijuana under one of the couches as well as some bags outside in the bushes. I had ten days to cover my tracks and make the place sparkle; I could not even accomplish that. I was too busy partying after work, taking full advantage of a curfew free two weeks.

My parents must have wondered how I was going to handle being on my own after failing to exhibit any personal responsibility while they were on vacation. They had every right to question their decision, because the minute they pulled away from the curb outside of the Goodwin-Kirk dormitory, I began to unravel in an ineffable way. All of the regimens, words of encouragement, and parental mandated norms were gone. A swift torrent of anxiety supplanted structure.

****

My freshman academic schedule for the fall semester consisted of fifteen hours. The classes were introductory in nature. I did not make the same mistake I did my senior year of high school by impulsively selecting courses that were beyond my comprehension. I fell into a structured routine, especially after pledging a fraternity and participating in social events.

My fraternity class was a boisterous group of delinquents. We broke into a sorority house in the middle of the night and ransacked the girl's possessions. We pulled fire alarms together. We bonded! For the first time in my life, I felt part of a social network. Fraternity members elected me Vice President. My grades were meeting my parent's minimum expectations. I developed connections with prominent students and became involved in student activities. My first year was a successful start to my Drake career.

Still, my ADHD flourished in a college environment, especially the tendency to make impulsive decisions. I dropped one class on a whim in order to improve my grade point average and receive a higher activation number in the fraternity. I had to decide whether to go out and enjoy quarter draws, or stay home and study for a quiz. I would head towards a quiet study place, then abruptly turned around and race to the West End Lounge to be with my friends.

I became a complete mess two weeks into my sophomore year. I lived in a home with twenty other 19-year-old males and no adult supervision. That type of living environment was a recipe for disaster. My ADHD boiled over as I made bad decision after bad decision. My inattention in the classroom precluded me from achieving adequate grades. My hyperactivity entailed more than just letting off steam. My ferocious impulsive behavior started hindering my ability to establish social bonds.

Peers solely issued decrees about my behavior, instead of contributions from parents and other adults. In some ways, the peer judgments and reprimands were more painful to endure than an adult rebuke. One incident destroyed most of the relationships that I developed with my peer group. It also shattered my reputation on campus.

The fraternity held its annual fall theme party amidst hay bales and carved pumpkins. I did not have a date on the afternoon of the party and I was not seeking one. I was at the Drake football game when my pledge dad asked if I wanted a date for the party. Beer permeated my brain and I responded with a euphoric yes. My enthusiasm diminished about an hour later, after the alcohol haze subsided.

We met at the gala affair and made small talk. I was restless, as if she chained me to a pillar and I had to stay chained until the last of the drunken guests left the party. I suddenly excused myself and headed out the back door, taking my car as fast as I could down to the West End Lounge.

I sat at the bar for thirty minutes, downing draft beer and shots of whiskey. I staggered off the bar stool and went outside to take a leak. I stumbled by a mangy dog on my way back into the bar. I leaned over and muttered, "You look better than my date tonight. I'm taking you home." I drove back to the fraternity house and carried the dog inside. I brazenly went up to people and said, "Look at my new date!" The party photograph template prominently featured the dog and I.

My disreputable display of malice became an indelible memory for everyone to see. All I wanted to do was get in my car and drive as far away as I could to escape the degradation of being the biggest asshole alive. One of my fraternity brothers bought a copy of the photograph just so he could see my expression every time he showed it to me. A friend later told me that the girl broke down in tears and ran out of the party after witnessing my actions. It remains the most hurtful gesture that I have ever committed in my life. I will never forget how I treated her.

During my final semester at Drake, I got up the nerve to apologize for my despicable behavior. I ran across her at a bar and offered a sincere apology. She said she was over it and walked away to a large group of people who were laughing in the center of the room. I stood by the corner of the bar and watched a college basketball game for the rest of the night by myself.

****

FRUSTRATION

Knowing there is nothing I can do, no matter how hard I try, that will allow me to reestablish any type of relationship with the people I met in college

****

During the summer between my sophomore and junior years of college, I worked as an apprentice for an independent electrical contractor. Dad got me the job, with the declaration that "this job will improve your self-discipline." I spent three months learning absolutely nothing except that I hated installing CO2 systems in a sweltering manufacturing plant. Tedious jobs like wiring businesses for power and delicately laying cable for air conditioning systems were not commensurate with ADHD. My patience level for anything that took more than five minutes to complete was low. I hated the job and the people I worked with.

The crew realized my disdain for the work and they dropped me off at a plant where we had already finished a job. They would then come back at clock out time to pick me up. I finished the summer delivering telephone books and enjoyed the autonomy that came with setting my own schedule. It was the first time I realized that I preferred working by myself rather than collaborating in a team environment. The money was better too. I bought a couple ounces of marijuana with my telephone book delivery money before heading back to Des Moines to start my junior year.

I lived with three other fraternity members on Greek Street, a place passed down from year to year by other members of the fraternity. The house was called "The Alamo" and appropriately so, because it always seemed to be under some type of party siege. A few weeks into the semester, I met our newly hired twenty-five year old Greek Advisor. We instantly connected; she was attracted to my one-liners and smart-ass attitude. Like most of my ADHD impacted relationships, the relationship ended when she realized I was behind the maturity growth curve. Her affection bolstered my confidence.

As my confidence grew, I decided to become involved in more student and fraternity activities. I was part of the student fees allocation committee, the group responsible for deciding how to spend the money that enhanced student living. I always voted for expenditures that involved alcohol or adorning the student recreation center with more pool tables.

My work as chair of the student polling committee strengthened the pool table argument. I made up responses for the pool table issue, claiming that a vast majority of students wanted more pool tables in the recreation center. I took the results to a student fees allocation meeting and almost got the group to fork over the dough for the pool tables.

Campus involvement overwhelmed me. I barely kept my grades above 3.0, the self-imposed standard of excellence. My study habits were horrendous. Not one study environment defused my proclivity to be distracted or impulsively quit a study session. I tried studying in the student center, campus library, and in my apartment bedroom with the door closed. I did not have a study strategy that worked.

I eventually studied at a church on 34th street. The Pastor was kind enough to allow Drake students to study in the church classrooms. I did not like studying in God's house either. I spent most of my time slamming books on the floor outside of rooms where startled students sat with their notebooks wide open for mental absorption. I ended up shunning God's house for study time, after I stole some of the church's furniture for our apartment.

I was getting a reputation on Greek street as a volatile person. I was brewing a potent pot of animosity, fueled by creating a "me against the world" mentality. I sensed that even the fraternity brothers I hung out with were spending more time away from me.

I went home for Christmas break disheartened that once again I was failing to develop a consistent performance record. I was not finishing the innumerable projects I signed up for and was straining the friendships that I developed over the previous two years. I was entering the phase of college when students made career decisions, but the only decision I could make was closing the West End Lounge on fifty-cent pitcher night.

My course schedule was as incoherent as my thought process, with no discernible interest or area of expertise. When pushed to declare a major, I chose Public Administration over Political Science. I came back from winter break refreshed with at least an academic direction. I got back early and spent some quiet time in the apartment, mostly spending my Christmas money on booze and thinking about a woman I met during the fall semester.

I sat in the apartment one evening during Christmas break, drinking vodka and listening to the Beatles greatest hits. I knew Mary was back early from break as well. I polished off the vodka, smoked a couple of nerve calming bongs, and then called her. We chatted for a long time over the phone. I had a unique sensation after I hung up the phone. It took twenty years of separation to understand the validity of the sensation.

I became more at ease in social situations when I was with Mary. She brought structure to my academic pursuit. We spent countless hours studying together and I always seemed to absorb more of the material when I studied with her. People who were in constant contact with me noticed subtle changes in my behavior. I did as well.

The second semester of my junior year was the most consistent period of my life. Instead of wavering in social, academic, and personal environments, I was fast becoming a more stable human being. Mary's influence diminished all of the pronounced undiagnosed ADHD symptoms. I knew that our relationship was more than a fleeting romantic excursion during a segment of our respective college careers. Our relationship was more about our minds than our bodies. My mind prospered when I was around her.

During the winter break of my senior year, Mary went to England for a semester of studying abroad. I might as well have left with her. After we said our goodbyes, all of the negative ADHD characteristics immediately roared back and took firm control of my life. While stability was the common theme when I was around her, my unpredictable disposition vigorously retuned after she left for England.

My body was in Des Moines, but my spirit was in London.

****

The first time I experienced acute loneliness was during the second semester of my senior year. I was spiraling down with no interest in my academic endeavors and did not have a clue as to where I was heading in life. I was cycling through another group of friends, mostly my fraternity brothers who wanted nothing to do with me. I got so down on myself that I broke down at times and uncontrollably wept.

When I did snap out of my self-pitying mindset, I did so with powerful reprisals. I rebelled against academics by cheating on one of Dr. François Wilhoit's esteemed tests. He played the guilt card when he handed out the test, clearly stating that he was going to leave the room and anyone who cheated would have to "deal with their consciences." I did not have a conscience during my senior year, so I cheated. Not only did I cheat off other students, I was also a willing provider of information to students who wanted to cheat off me.

I rebelled against the fraternity system by burning down a float barely twelve hours before the Drake Relays parade in downtown Des Moines. A friend and I were staggering home from the bars when we crossed through a rival fraternity's property. I dropped my lighter while trying to light a one hitter. When I looked up and saw a wad of tissue hanging from a flatbed truck, I muttered, "Fuck them," and then lit the paper. My friend and I ran back to our apartment on 34th Street.

I even rebelled against my own fraternity by stealing the checkbook and writing bad checks before moving back to St Louis. I signed the checks with the first name of one fraternity brother and the last name of another. I was not content with just stealing the checks to buy steaks and beer. I had to mock the fraternity as well.

I came back to St Louis after graduation without a clue about what I was going to do for a living. I burned the bridge that led to the Public Administration department at Drake by not fulfilling my academic and internship obligations. I sent out resumes and made phone calls, but there was little interest in my background.

I knew my occupational future was unclear, but I did not realize how murky it was until I spent a day with dad at his place of employment. He wanted me to look up to him as a career role model, a person who diligently moved up the corporate ladder and provided for his family. We had lunch in the company cafeteria with some of his co-workers. They asked questions about my career aspirations. I made up answers as we went along.

I was twenty-two years old, confused about my future and confounded by the looming isolation of my social life. None of my high school friends wanted to spend time with me and I was not meeting anyone to establish another cycle of friendships. I sat in bars by myself and reflected on my troubled life. My mind raced so fast that I thought my head was going to either spin off my collarbone or explode from all of misfiring neurotransmitters.

I never seriously considered suicide until the night I stumbled from a bar at a Laclede's Landing watering hole. The booze, combined with a marijuana haze, provoked a depressing self-examination. I decided it was time to end the mass confusion that was my life.

I walked to an overpass that stretched over I-55/70 in downtown St. Louis. The wind began howling after I stepped over the guardrail to look down at the speeding vehicles on the highway. I spent at least ten minutes contemplating the final leap of my life. All I really wanted was someone to see the desperation in my eyes. The only person who could pull me out of my downward spiral was once again thousands of miles away on a Peace Corp mission.

I precariously stood on the ledge while making animated gestures to all of the cars and trucks that sped by underneath me. I cried out your name, Mary, with my arms outstretched in a defiant gesture towards a God that I believed gave me the short end of life's stick. A gust of wind suddenly pushed me into the guardrail, which I grabbed onto for dear life.

I then frantically pulled myself over the guardrail and away from the dark side.

"Great souls are grown through struggles and storms and seasons of suffering."

-Pastor Rick Warren

STRAIGHTJACKET

I came upon a fork in life's road when Mary and I worked on Gary Hart's presidential campaign. She suggested that I move with her to Colorado and pursue a graduate degree at the University of Denver. I made general inquiries into the school's energy management graduate program and she contemplated accepting the school's financial aid offer to continue her academic career. Tufts University was her first choice, but Mary was not confident the prestigious school would accept her application. She was also worried about the exorbitant tuition and cost of living on the east coast.

I was restless in Des Moines. The thought of enduring two more years of academe made me anxious. After a day of imbibing margaritas, I called my girlfriend to tell her I was moving to Chicago. Three weeks later, I was on the road to the Windy City. Shortly thereafter, Tufts accepted Mary's application. The school provided enough financial incentives for her to begin a new chapter in her life. I took the wrong fork in the road. The fork I should have taken was the one that led back to Des Moines.

In August of 1984, I moved to Chicago for what I defined at the time as love. I stayed for the cocaine. That summarizes the four most turbulent years of my life.

****

The relocation decision was an impulsive reaction. My girlfriend suggested that we take our relationship to another level. We were not going to reach another level living 300 miles apart. I blurted out an avowal over the phone and then arranged to move to Chicago in three weeks. I did not weigh the pros and cons of the move or considered the financial costs. The financial costs turned out to be significant.

I packed up a U-Haul and attached it to my Honda Civic for the 300-mile ride to my girlfriend's home. The Honda struggled to pull the U-Haul. The engine made strange noises on every uphill section of the interstate. The car's struggle to make it to Chicago was the perfect allegory for what was going through my mind. I pensively considered all of the possible outcomes, with the focus being on the relationship with my girlfriend. She was the only reason why I hastily left Des Moines.

My parents were less than thrilled with my move, which should have been a beaming light that illuminated common sense into my sclerotic brain. I never followed my parents' guidance when it came to life altering decisions. Dad was particularly concerned about my move to Chicago. He knew Chicago would bombard me with anxiety and inundate me with so many distractions that I would shut down after a short period.

He was right. The engine in my head struggled because of the relocation decision. I knew right away, during the first sleepless night at my girlfriend's home, that I missed Des Moines and made the biggest mistake of my life. I never expected my life to change so dramatically because of a simple 300-mile move.

I was fortunate to have a place to stay while I searched for a job and apartment. I did not possess the mental capacity to understand that I needed to find a job and an apartment before I made the move. I tried to find a real job that was commensurate with my academic background. My attempt was a futile exercise in career advancement. I was unable to follow a prioritized job search list in order to procure gainful employment.

I found a part-time bartending gig with the help of a fraternity brother. The drive from my girlfriend's home to the restaurant in Highwood took forty-five minutes. The long ride home from the part-time job gave me ample time to contemplate the move. I was not happy and became more anxious with every passing day.

I frequently went downtown and watched the frenetic tempo of the bustling business and shopping districts. The sounds I heard were omnipotent. My head moved towards each fleeting noise before another one blasted my senses. The pace of Chicago was overwhelming compared to Des Moines. I was full of disquiet on a daily basis, bombarded by sound and visual sensations that I never experienced before.

The bartending gig generated enough cash for me to rent an apartment with another fraternity brother. I finally took care of the two most important relocation elements. I found a job and a place to call home.

My world radically changed immediately after I settled into the Rogers Park neighborhood.

****

After about two months, I calmed down a bit and adapted to the upbeat tempo of the Chicago lifestyle.

The living arrangement with my fraternity brother worked well because our contrasting schedules kept us from spending much time together. I serendipitously found a better job at an upscale American bistro in Glenview. I responded to an advertisement and interviewed with the owner. I had no experience working in an upscale environment that had an extensive wine list. Nevertheless, Curtis Wierbicki hired me and immediately put me under his tutelage.

The learning curve was high, but I was exhilarated working in such a super-charged ambiance. Curt was instrumental is helping me thrive in an upscale restaurant. He mentored me professionally and took the time to refine my personal skill set. Curt is definitely on the short list of people who have accepted me for who I am, which in his case meant minimizing my ADHD weaknesses and exploiting my ADHD strengths.

After six months at The American Grill, a fellow employee asked me to help her open a fine-dining restaurant. Her husband and another couple were also part of the team that planned to launch the restaurant in a high-income Chicago neighborhood. I was flattered she considered me for such an establishment. Even though my income declined because of the employment move, the six months I spent at Les Plumes was like a paid apprenticeship.

Even with a tranquil living arrangement and provocative introduction to the restaurant industry, I felt a sense of isolation and loneliness. My girlfriend and I were drifting apart, and I compensated for our lack of intimacy by carousing long into the Chicago night. The fraternity brothers who lived in the Chicago area kept their distance from me. The only people I hung out with were fellow workers.

I longed for my friends in Des Moines.

I went back to Des Moines about six weeks after my move to Chicago in order to pick up the rest of my belongings. Before I relocated to Chicago, a fellow Gringo's bartender gave me a kitten. She kept the kitten for me while I settled in Chicago.

Cassidy was the anti-cat because she was affectionate and responsive to a few phrases like "Come here." She was the opposite of a stereotypical species renowned for its aloof nature and sneaky disposition. I left Des Moines with Cassidy and the rest of my furniture. When I returned for the Drake Relays six months later, my friends from Des Moines saw a vastly different human being.

Cassidy immediately became skittish in her new surroundings. She scratched the front door and left her scent throughout the apartment. She tried on numerous occasions to run out the front door, as if an invisible spirit haunted her. Finally, she was so agitated that she squeezed through a small gap in a window and jumped into a bush from a second story ledge.

I witnessed her plunge and went outside to look for her. I searched in the front and back of buildings connected by enclosed breezeways. I entered one breezeway and my face became ashen. Directly in front of me laid a woman on the cold concrete. Blood dripped from a gaping wound from her head into a mid-size cooking pot. The placement of the cooking pot underneath her head seemed peculiar.

I collected my racing thoughts, ran back to my apartment, and called the police. They asked me questions when they arrived on the scene, some of which intimated that I was a suspect in the woman's demise. It was obvious the woman did not slip, fall, and land on top of a pot that absorbed most of her spilt blood. Someone assaulted her and the cops knew it. My shock of finding a dead body subsided and grew into anger after the cops asked insulting questions that were thick with accusatory connotations. After two hours, the questioning ended and the cops left. They reminded me that they would stay in touch.

I heard from the police department two days after the homicide. They said the crime was unsolved but they believed the motive was robbery. My apartment buzzer went off while I was on the phone with the cops. I went downstairs to find Cassidy in the arms of my downstairs neighbor. Our reunion was short lived. Cassidy took another dive into the bushes later in the day. This time, I stayed inside and contemplated the horrific sight of an elderly woman's head bleeding into a cooking pot.

The welcome wagon used to leave amenities for anyone who moved into a neighborhood. My welcome wagon from the city of Chicago was a dead body. Within two months of moving to Chicago, I found a murdered woman and lost my cat. Okay, the lost cat was not a big deal, but the image of the murdered woman dominated my ADHD brain. My racing thoughts froze on her facial expression the moment I found her. I thought about her during every waking moment and in the middle of spectacular dreams.

I wondered if she was an omen.

****

My life has been full of wild vacillations. The vicissitudes have consisted of personal successes followed by downward spirals. I invariably fell into an abyss where I had to start over. The Chicago downward spiral became precariously close to ending my life and I have been trying to climb back up from the bottom of the abyss ever since. Two incidents clearly triggered the downward spiral while many other factors exacerbated my descent into personal hell.

My job and apartment situations were going well, but the relationship with my girlfriend took a turn for the worse. I felt there was not any passion in our relationship, at least not from her. I already experienced a number of dating relationships where the recognizable spark flickered on and off until it inevitably burned out. The sixth sense customarily kicked in, but I was never able to put my finger on the ultimate question of why.

My girlfriend put an end to the relationship rumination by dropping a bombshell on me: she was pregnant. My mind raced with thoughts about how we were going to take care of an infant. My girlfriend decided to go for a knockout blow. She followed the pregnancy declaration with a more devastating statement.

She wanted an abortion.

Abortion was a topic discussed during heated political debates in college. A couple of days passed before I registered the enormity of an abortion. I understood the moral consequences and was educated about the physical effects an abortion has on a woman. As I drifted in and out of an anxiety driven stupor, I finally deduced what an abortion meant for our relationship. My only reason for moving to Chicago was up in smoke. I faced a mordant reality.

We went to the clinic on a blustery Saturday in early January of 1985. I sat in the clinic by myself for six hours, with just my active mind to keep me company. It seemed odd that a magazine rack was in the waiting room.

"Okay, honey. You go with the doctor to snuff out a life while I skim through the collection of *Field and Stream* to occupy my time."

The worst six worst hours of my life moved in perpetual slow motion.

I had a furious internal debate during the six hours. Were we killing an innocent life? Should we put the infant up for adoption? How would my unpredictable lapses in concentration affect the child in the long-term? I did not even notice when my girlfriend finally came out from one of the rooms. I only focused on the vacuum like sucking sound that I intermittently heard during the previous six hours.

We pretended to be lovers during the following month. I knew something was amiss when she refused to make plans with me on Valentine's Day. Instead, she wanted to discuss something with me at a restaurant on the day before Valentine's Day. Not content with just springing the pregnancy and abortion issues on me, my girlfriend crushed me with one of the shortest, yet most defaming things I have ever heard.

"You're not any good in bed!"

She went on to say the fire was gone in our relationship and that it was best to be friends. I played the good stoic until she left and then the blood drained out of my body. I could not move for about fifteen minutes and barely acknowledged the server when she inquired about the check. That is right! I picked up the tab after my ex-girlfriend sullied me with the cruelest choice of words that I have ever heard.

Within five weeks, I acquiesced to my ex-girlfriend's abortion decision and absorbed the lowest form of verbal abuse. Everything I built to that point in Chicago, including saving money for a trip to Europe with guess-who, began to crumble as I wove a sinuous web around my tormented heart.

I drifted into a pattern of hard-core drug and alcohol abuse.

****

My self-destruction took root towards the end of 1985. The abortion experience rattled me. I wrestled with my moral principles about a decision I believe has more implications than those in our physical world. I have a strong moral compass that directs a pious conscience. Abortion is morally reprehensible. I have emotionally dealt with the abortion since my six hours in the clinic, listening to a sucking sound take the life out of my son or daughter.

The deleterious statement my girlfriend made about my lovemaking exacerbated the hand wringing over the abortion. Once she told me that I was not a good lover, my self-esteem obliterated like the countryside conifers in a nuclear explosion. My heart took the ultimate blow that pushed me over the edge.

I was convinced that life was not worth living. Procreation is the paramount reason why we exist. If I could not perform the intrinsic function, then what good was I to humanity? When my self-esteem walked away, it was easier to let it go than try to recapture it. It was easier to shy away from situations that may have caused more rejection. I stopped trying to forge intimate relationships with women.

After the rejection, I went on a sex binge that would make Wilt Chamberlain proud. I felt confident because I was sacking many attractive women. I had a false sense of bravado made worse by a weird looking bump on my penis, a reminder that unprotected sex with multiple partners can lead to bad things.

When I finished my sexual conquest phase, I felt empty and searched for ways to ease the pain of low self-worth. I always used alcohol as a crutch to keep me afloat during times of emotional chaos. As I was spinning into despair, I decided to turn to cocaine in order to ease the pain.

Cocaine became an impulse purchase when I was on a drinking binge. I liked the sharp mental edge cocaine gave me, a kind of focus that I could never establish sober. After the implosion of my self-worth, I used cocaine and alcohol in a blatant attempt to kill myself.

I spent the next three years snorting my way to oblivion.

****

My farewell bash in Des Moines turned into mayhem. Cocaine's vice-like grip caused me to lose control. We were having a pillow fight in a hotel room when somebody struck me in the face with a cheap shot. I picked up one of the heavy chairs that sat by the desk no one used and threw it through a sliding glass door. Talk about a buzz-kill. That was the first, and certainly not the last time, that the volatile mixture of cocaine and alcohol landed me in a heap of trouble.

I did not use cocaine much after that until I earned enough money in Chicago to afford its exorbitant price. Cocaine was an easy commodity to purchase in Chicago, so in another way dad was right about Chicago being a bad place for me to live. My running mate sold coke, mostly to people he knew and not on a scale that had a line leading out of his apartment.

My cocaine consumption increased once I started working at a new restaurant in the River North section of downtown Chicago. The restaurant was the trendy place that Chicago's movers and shakers frequently visited. A large contingent of New Orleans natives moved to Chicago to help open the Creole-Cajun themed restaurant. We made fistfuls of cash every night and looked for bars and nightclubs to burn through our newly found largesse. We formed a nightly party posse that ran its course into the wee hours of the morning.

At first, my coke usage was a recreational way to burn mental exuberance. I was happy with my job and the cash that I earned. After the one-two punch to the heart, I snorted so much cocaine that I became a zombie running on a continuous stream of white powder. Cocaine also snared the New Orleans boys. We used the American Express phone at the back of the restaurant to dial our dealer's pager. He always called back and we placed our order. All it took was for one of the New Orleans boys to look my way and yell, "Call him up!"

I usually called the dealer early in the shift. We knew we would make a significant amount of money during the ensuing six hours of business. The dealer brazenly walked into the restaurant at the height of our business volume. He strutted to the back of the restaurant, slapped a bag of coke into one of our hands, and took the cash we collected for the sack of white powder.

We called our dealer nightly and if we did not score from him, my running mate worked with us and he had coke to sell. We were living high on the hog, snorting coke and drinking our tips away like tomorrow was the end of the world. I even spent time with some cokehead traders at The Chicago Board of Trade. The stigma of the eighties was alive and well. I did not need a Personal Digital Assistant to remind me to buy cocaine. It was the first thing that came to my mind after I woke up from the previous day's white powder binge.

The cry to "call him up" became the first and only item on my daily task list.

****

I fear incarceration. I do not have the common fear that most people have about jail, the one where you become someone's personal sex toy. I could use my wit and cunning to get out of being someone's bitch. But ADHD would drive me insane locked in a small cell, with twenty-one hours out of each day spent pacing around and having my mind explode with rapid fire thoughts. The thought of imprisonment behind an iron gate like a dog at a kennel has tempered my ADHD and kept me out of jail for any lengthy period.

But I have seen the world from behind bars.

Just before the Christmas of 1986, one of my Cajun friends and I decided to leave our restaurant's Christmas party and wander Broadway Avenue to look for hookers. We passed a substantial amount of cocaine back and forth; the sack must have been at least an eight ball. What the hell, it was Christmas and we were going to spend our money and time pursuing iniquity on every street corner.

I propositioned a hooker who was across the street. Minutes later, a flurry of lights and sirens came rushing towards us. A bunch of people got out of the cars yelling, "Get down on the ground!" I did not see police markings on any of the cars, so I immediately thought they were going to rob us. One man flashed a badge and pushed me up against the wall, with a gun pointed at my head.

I did not whistle at a hooker, but at a decoy planted by Chicago's finest to catch solicitors like myself. A simple solicitation charge would have been easy to take. Pay the fine and scurry for the precinct exit. I, however, was the last one to have the sack of coke and the cop pulled it out of my pocket with the redoubtable question of, "What is this?"

Moments later, the cops hauled me away to the precinct station close to Midway Airport. They put me in a cell after confiscating anything that might cause me harm. I stewed in the cell for an hour before making the one call allowed and I made that to my ex-girlfriend. In turn, she called dad who immediately drove up from St. Louis to bail me out of jail.

I spent close to forty-eight in a holding cell, waiting for my turn in front of the judge. About halfway through my incarceration, two more men joined me in our now cramped quarters. One of my new cellmates snuck a joint into the cell by hiding it in his rather large Afro. I wanted no part of that and told him to take the steely bed I was sitting on. I stretched out on the cold floor and tried to catch some semblance of sleep. I never smelled the joint, so he probably forgot to stash matches in his Afro.

Early in the morning, an obviously agitated cop told me to follow the guards into a van. The van took me and the other miscreants to court. My volatile stomach finally gave in and I splattered a reeking load of diarrhea into my already soiled undergarment. I cleaned up in a court bathroom before a uniformed officer escorted me into the courtroom. Dad stood in the aisle and followed me up to the bench; he posted bail for me. I took my lecture from the judge and then dad and I left the courtroom.

We ate dinner at a seafood place by his hotel. I spent the night back at my apartment marveling at the even-tempered way dad talked to me. There were no scolding or abrasive words, just a polite suggestion that I should come back home and regroup. I thought about it and eventually decided to make a go of it in Chicago.

I reached another fork in life's road and once again, I went in the wrong direction. I cleaned up my act after the arrest because the time in confinement literally scared the shit out of me. Soon after the arrest, I was back to snorting it up and lashing out at the world.

****

Money was flowing from the restaurant at the rate of $1000 a week in take home cash. I was not taking home much cash, because between work and home were bars, nightclubs, and guys that sold cocaine. The Cajun boys were dropping like flies, becoming despondent at being away from New Orleans. Most of them moved back to the Crescent City.

I tended bar part-time at a small place on Rush Street for a man I met through restaurant connections. I frequented the bar to play pool, down a few drinks, and buy cocaine. I figured that I might as well make a little extra cash and snort cocaine on the clock.

My Cajun compatriot also filled in as a bartender. He was doing so much coke that his money ran out and, in what I referred to at the time as a suicidal thing to do, he ripped off our boss for over $500. That made our boss angry, so my Cajun friend hopped on a plane to Las Vegas. He left behind his fiancé to whimper in my arms. I never saw my Cajun friend again. He was the last friend I had except my running mate who kept me supplied with cocaine.

I wandered Broadway Avenue on my days off, hitting the bars and doing bumps of coke to the point that the booze was not having any effect on me. I was doing so much coke that I had constant nose bleeds and could move my nose back and forth, as if it was a screw loose on the side of a wall. An associate told me that unremitting cocaine abuse caused ligament damage to the nose. His warning did not scare me. I continued with my unremitting drug use.

I received a pleasant surprise one night while I was at work. My ex-girlfriend came in for dinner with her new boyfriend. She did not bother to call me in advance of her visit.

She asked me, "You are okay with this, aren't you"?

Sure I was! Men are always okay when women call them lousy lovers. On top of that, it was great she found true romance and decided to rub it in my face. I did even more coke and drank more booze to numb the pain of isolation and loneliness.

About four weeks later, I was hanging out at a bar that was one block from my apartment. A disturbance broke out in the adjoining liquor store as a man ran out and headed up Broadway. The clerk screamed and all of us, including the owner, ran outside after the perpetrator. That was a bad move because the robber had a silver plated pistol and sprayed some shots at us. Luckily, his aim was off and nobody got hurt. One of his shots zipped over my head. I heard a high pitch whistling noise, but the booze and drug combination prevented me from moving any part of my body. I did not even flinch.

I just stood there in a stupor and it was not until the following day that I reconciled the previous night's event. I wished his second shot had put me out of my misery. Things had finally reached the point when I realized it was time to leave Chicago and restart my life with a clean slate. I pissed away my savings and was binging daily, with no real purpose except to walk the streets with rage in my heart.

I made a veiled threat on President Reagan's life. The call came from my apartment, which led me to spend a day with the Secret Service in a subterranean building in downtown Chicago. I tried to play off the accusation by telling the agents I had friends over the night before.

"Maybe one of them did it," I told the agents.

They played the recording of the call; the voice was distinctly mine. The phone call instigated a series of psychotherapy sessions that I attended over the course of the next two years.

In early 1987, my last friend left in Chicago took me to a hospital for a psychiatric review after I made a series of late night phone calls. I know I made one to you, Mary, because I have my father's notes depicting the conversation.

"Don called and threatened to kill himself," you told my father. "He says he is getting screwed all the time."

My ex-girlfriend and her mother came over to my apartment on another night after I called and told them I slashed my wrists. I did try, albeit, not with the intent to sever a vein or artery. I only wanted to flee from the personal hell.

I saw a lot of therapists and psychologists, including a stint at a hard-core intervention facility. After all of the psychobabble, nothing changed because the cause of my malaise was undiagnosed ADHD. I was so frustrated with my life that I resorted to self-medication to get me through the day. I continued down the sordid path of self-destruction towards two events that individually should have altered my outlook on life, and collectively should have scared me into sobriety.

I was about to spend the worst Christmas of my life, high on cocaine and contemplating suicide. In addition, I was soon to become the victim of a violent assault that almost ended my life.

****

Over a span of twenty-seven years, I spent an occasional Thanksgiving holiday away from my family in St Louis. I did once in college and twice while I lived in Chicago, the second time being the Thanksgiving of 1987. My parents were not concerned in 1987. They reminded me to let them know when I was coming home for Christmas.

Their disposition dramatically changed two weeks before Christmas, when I called home and informed dad I was staying in Chicago over the holidays. I told him it was work related and I could tell he did not believe my explanation. He was skeptical, asking me if everything was all right. I assured him it was and that we expected a very busy Christmas week at the restaurant.

The problem with my statement was the restaurant permanently closed a month earlier. I was barely scrapping by at another restaurant that was located five blocks from my former employer. Barely scrapping by for me meant making enough money to buy booze and cocaine. I did not have enough money for a train ride to St. Louis or Christmas presents. I made it clear to dad I was spending Christmas with friends and that I would not be alone. On Christmas Eve, I sat in my spacious apartment looking out into the gloomy Chicago day.

I felt a gut wrenching, heart aching pain. I was isolated from the world, with no one to turn to for help. Alone on Christmas, with not even one invitation from anyone I knew in the Chicago area to share in the joy of the holiday season. I looked into the bathroom mirror and was disgusted with what I saw.

My roommate was at his girlfriend's home in one of the northern suburbs and I did not expect him back for a couple of days. He was also my running mate, the person who supplied me with cocaine when all of the other channels were dry. I wondered aloud if he left a little treat for me, so I searched his room for cocaine. I looked inside of his coat pockets, under his mattress, and behind his dresser. After a half-hour, I reached into his badminton case and felt a large object wrapped in a plastic bag. I pulled it out of the badminton case and was astonished to see a huge chunk of rock cocaine. I took a small sliver off and silently vowed to take nothing more from the rock. The rock was gone twenty-fours later.

I snorted a vast amount of cocaine on Christmas Eve night and Christmas day, 1987, and those twenty-four hours were full of immense self-doubt, anger, and thoughts of suicide. The more I became despondent, the more coke I did. I frantically wanted to talk with someone, anyone, who would let me bend his or her ear.

I picked up the phone numerous times to call home, but I always put it back on the receiver. I paced around the apartment, but I never left it the entire time I binged. I do not remember if I even ate during the twenty-four hour binge period. I do remember I racked up over one thousand dollars in

900 phone charges that I eventually passed off on my "son" in order to avoid paying the bill. My roommate came home and found his coke missing. He made me pay back a substantial sum of money.

Two weeks later, I finally made it home for a belated Christmas celebration with my family. My parents were visibly upset when they picked me up from the train station and saw my disheveled appearance and vacant expression. I put on twenty pounds since the last time they saw me.

They knew something was amiss and implored me to move back home. I did not even look them in the eye when I said I would think about it. After a couple of days, I decided to give Chicago one more try and vowed to make a concerted effort to clean up my act. I was stubborn and lived in denial, blaming others for my misfortunes and refusing to accept responsibility for my actions.

After nearly four years of misery, I still wanted to make it in Chicago. I was not going away until someone had to bury my corpse in a Chicago cemetery.

****

On the early morning of June 22, 1988, an intruder broke into my apartment and violently assaulted me while I slept. The implement used was a commemorative *St Louis Blues* Pepsi bottle that had a long neck and thick base.

My first glimpse of the assault occurred in a dream. When I finally came around, I noticed blood splattered on the walls by my bed and a pattern of shattered glass on the floor. There was a knife on the bed and a pair of handcuffs attached to the nightstand. I looked at the half-eaten pizza I ordered three hours earlier.

I stumbled out of bed and grabbed the first towel I saw to contain the blood, which was flowing out of a deep wound. My clothes were drenched with blood that dripped onto the hardwood floor. I staggered to the front door, frantically unlocked the dead bolt, and then fell to my knees by the neighbor's door. I pounded on their door for a few seconds with blood stained hands. They eventually opened the door and looked traumatized at what they saw. Shaken, my neighbors called 911. They helped me inside to wait for the ambulance.

The ambulance ride was interminable. I kept going back to the dream sequence to figure out who might have perpetrated the unspeakable violent assault. I was in shock by the time we got to the hospital because I lost a considerable amount of blood and the initial adrenaline had faded.

I waited in the emergency room for what seemed like hours. Nurses occasionally passed by with a fresh towel for me to apply on the gaping wound. I was agitated and not for the usual ADHD reasons. I was not waiting on a doctor to diagnosis a cold.

A large group of medical personnel finally wheeled me into surgery and put me under the knife. The surgery took four hours to close a wound that required over fifty stitches. The surgeon did a remarkable job. He not only sewed the wound shut, but he also cleaned out all of the glass particles from the inside of my cheek. When I came to, the attending physician claimed that I came within centimeters of losing my life. The person who assaulted me nearly sliced my jugular vein. I was lucky to be alive.

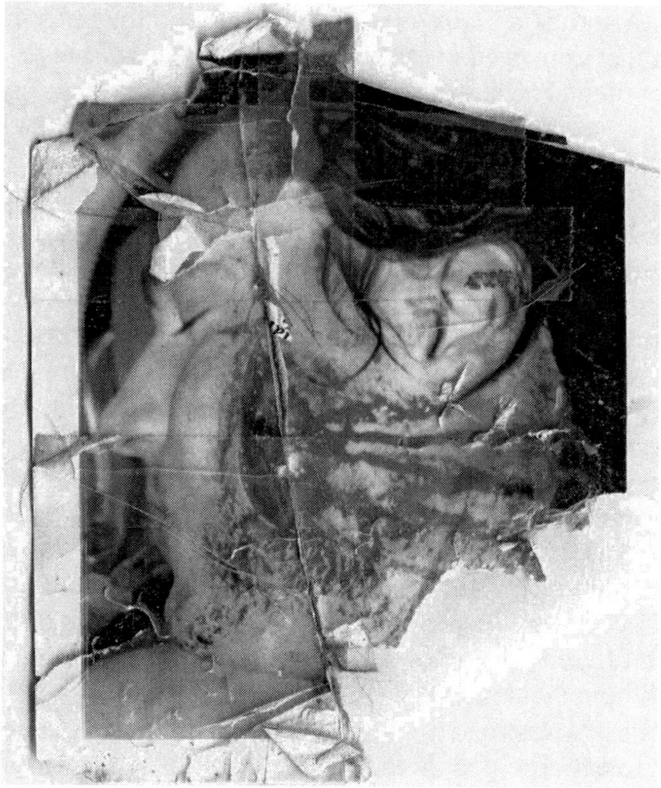

Assault Photo

Two friends picked me up at the hospital and took me to a coworker's apartment, where I mended my wounds by laying on a couch for eight days. I was in physical pain, but I soon realized that the emotional pain of being a violent crime victim was the lasting impact of the assault. I called my family and the few friends I had left in Chicago. Their lack of empathy amazed me. The consensus response I got was, "This isn't a surprise, Don. It was a matter of when, not if."

After the assault, I tried to turn around the behavioral pattern that consisted of daily cocaine and alcohol binges. My efforts failed. The self-pity and anger led to more drug and alcohol abuse. I constantly wondered when the next attack would occur during the middle of many restless nights.

I continued with the surreal act of living in Chicago for another four months. In early September, I showed up for work after a night of nonstop binging; I had not slept in over twenty-four hours. My bloodshot eyes gazed into my manager's inquisitive stare. He recognized my condition, but all he said was to be prepared for a shift that would last the next ten hours. I knew I would not last that long. When I stayed up all night using cocaine, I usually had enough to get me through the next work shift. My pockets were empty. After my manager walked away from the bar, I turned around and bolted out of a side door. It was finally time to bolt from Chicago.

I sat under a tree and reflected on the events that transpired during the previous four years. The events unfolded as an unfiltered collage of self-destruction. I waited until sunset to stroll home and plan my escape from Chicago. My last desperate act was to sell my trombone just so I had enough money to eat. The people that I asked for financial assistance turned their collective backs on me. I agreed to move back into my parent's home in St Louis.

I took the train home to start over with my life. All I had with me were two suitcases of clothes and many bad memories. I came home devoid of money, friends, and self-respect.

****

The transition to a more structured environment in St Louis saved my life. Even in a more stable environment, I could not shake the memories of the incredible things that happened to me. The more I thought about Chicago, the more my blood boiled until it percolated into a spiteful rage. I thought at the time my vindictiveness was due to some symptom of Post Traumatic Stress Disorder. What I did not understand was that I also had a raging case of ADHD. PTSD and undiagnosed ADHD combined to create a potent brew of mental instability.

I made phone calls to every person whom I felt let me slide down the slippery slope of a downward spiral. Sometimes the calls were short, profanity laced tirades, and other times they were lengthy, highly audible denunciations. Nobody escaped my wrath. I blamed everyone for everything that happened to me while I lived in Chicago. I was particularly hard on my ex-girlfriend and former boss at The Butcher Shop.

They treated me as if I was a child molester just paroled from prison. Nobody wanted anything to do with me. I went through another cycle of friends and the friendships did not just gradually fade away. My explosive temperament detonated the friendships. I spat on the people who tried to help turn my life around while I lived in Chicago.

I have been back to Chicago since my discomfiting departure in 1988. I never tried to reconnect with anyone until 1998, when I walked down Chicago Avenue to The Butcher Shop. The owner was my former manager, a man who did his best to help me when I was at the bottom of the barrel. I walked in from the gusty, cold night air and immediately saw him directing traffic out in the restaurant.

He looked at me without any hint of emotion and asked, “Are you still psycho?”

"Obstacles cannot crush me."

-Leonardo DaVinci

DÉJÀ VU ALL OVER AGAIN

Despite some minor setbacks, I made progress distancing myself from the horrific Chicago memories. I immediately connected with a tight-knit group of friends that included T.H. He was the first person I became friends with after I moved back from Chicago in 1988. We remained friends until the summer of 1996.

We were pleasure hopping on a stormy June evening when T.H. asked if I wanted to join his restaurant management team. The conversation quickly turned one-sided. T.H. said that before hiring me, he needed to be convinced that I had cast aside my personal demons and was ready to move into a leadership role.

"You need to control your temper and not get romantically involved with any of the girls," he said in a distinctly condescending voice.

T.H.'s statement floored me. Here was a reputed friend who struggled with money and job stability issues lecturing me about my personality defects. I simmered for a good two hours while we bar hopped around St Louis. ADHD and six scotches brought the simmering pot of discontent to a boil. I wanted to kick him out of the car as we sped down the freeway. Instead, I unleashed a tirade that exposed his many shortcomings.

After about a fifteen-minute verbal onslaught, I pulled the car into a parking spot and rested my head on the steering wheel. Tears began streaming down my face, but not because of T.H.'s stinging words. Emotion flowed from my tear ducts because the same words that I heard thousands of times were ringing inside of my head. A recurring sense of inadequacy brought the tears. Not knowing I had ADHD continued the ceaseless mental anguish.

T.H. tried to console me, offering to take me to a hospital for reasons I am befuddled about to this very day. I told him to get out of the car. T.H. told mutual friends I had a nervous breakdown, a blatant lie that bordered on slander. I was hurt and enraged when I heard about his unsubstantiated medical analysis.

I knew our relationship would never be the same. Another group of friends decided to ostracize me. The same pattern of behavior that plagued me in Chicago returned in full force. The behavior formed the perfect ADHD storm that led to another life-changing downward spiral. Two or more simultaneous demoralizing events usually punctuated my downward spirals. In Chicago, it was the one-two punch of the abortion and lousy lover declaration. In 1996, it was the stinging comment from T.H. and subsequent slanderous statements.

The central theme of my downward spirals has been failure. By 1996, I failed on a number of levels that were eerily reminiscent of other downward spirals. I failed at maintaining relationships with another group of friends. I failed to see a career-enhancing project to fruition. I failed at procuring my graduate degree, after patently telling people about my aspirations. I failed to keep a job for more than eighteen months, impulsively leaving one restaurant company for another without any pause for the ramifications. I was a failure in the eyes of my parents, peers, and even my brother, who usually provided ardent support despite my inscrutable behavior.

I was alone again, walking through the world without a confidant by my side. While I did not sink into the deep abyss as I did in Chicago, I was self-medicating at a good clip from late 1995 through early 1998. Once again, I did not give a shit about life or my place in it. I blew large sums of money, hopped from job to job in record fashion, crashed my car, and got a second DUI.

****

FRUSTRATION/IRRITATION

The American consumer is rapacious.

Unleashing a greedy horde of American consumers into a contemporary mall is akin to watching the old Pac Man game, where the game's central character gobbles up everything in sight. With such a gluttonous mindset, salespeople have developed a tactic called the up sell, or in restaurant lingo, the add-on.

Car sales representative used to be notorious for the up sell. They tried to push every accessory available in their inventory on a consumer, from plush seats to state-of-the-art audio systems. When Saturn emerged on the scene in the early nineties, their sales team employed the novel soft sell strategy. Saturn's motto was no haggling, no pressure to buy. The established players in the car industry followed Saturn's lead and slowly adopted a more restrained sales pitch.

Corporate restaurants used to train their service personnel to up sell, until they also realized that a pressured consumer does not return for another visit. I worked with servers who insisted that their up selling skills were the reason they made more money than their serving brethren. I have always maintained that someone who is dissatisfied with a purchase, mostly due to buying pressure, will not return and become a repeat customer. Repeat business is the easiest way to grow sales. Selling people things they do not want alienates them and they end up buying similar products elsewhere. The up sell is still a popular tactic in many industries including, much to my chagrin, the restaurant industry.

Some corporate restaurant chains still have not trained their employees to soft sell. I stopped going to one family-dining restaurant because they would not stop trying to sell me pies. My last visit there occurred on an early morning when I picked up breakfast on the way to work. A pie pusher already spoke to me over the phone when I arrived to pick up an omelet. When I got to the counter, the woman handling my order asked me if I wanted a blueberry pie to take with me. I just wanted some greasy food and enough coffee to make me tremble for the ensuing eight hours. I looked her straight in the eye and said, "Why the fuck would I want a pie at eight in the morning?"

Banks and insurance companies are a pain in the ass. Calling for a simple balance validation results in a flurry of questions to either upgrade an account or buy other services the company has to offer. If the companies are large, they route calls overseas and I just hang up the phone. I do not understand what the Pakistani, who calls himself John, is saying on the other end of the line.

Dentists are one of the original up sellers. My parents were somehow convinced to slap braces on my teeth for two years and then a retainer for another two years for my perceived overbite. Four years of metal on my teeth caused a slight under bite. Dentists take advantage of the public's ignorance of dental concepts and they parlay the ignorance into scare tactics that lines their pockets. "Your face will fall off if you don't have those two glistening white teeth yanked" is something a dentist might say to exploit a lack of dental knowledge.

Jiffy Lube employs another pushy sales force. They try to sell me services I do not need and act like if I do not buy their pitch, my car will catch fire on a bridge and tumble down the banks into a raging river. I have to plan my Jiffy Lube visit. I drive up slow, turn the engine off, and coast to an open bay. I see the salesperson (not mechanic) and immediately jump out of my car. In one deft motion, I throw him the keys and sprint away while shouting, "Just an oil change!" When I return, he still tries to sell me shit that I do not need.

The most pathetic up seller is the Veterinarian. Vets manipulate pet owners because of the sentimental attachment we have for our animals. That pisses me off. If a vet ever springs the two thousand dollar surgery routine on me, I will ask him where Jasper can find the nearest gas chamber.

Two years ago, the Vet tried to instill fear by saying Jasper needed a tooth yanked. Last year, Jasper supposedly needed an intensive teeth cleaning procedure. I didn't bite on either sales pitch and my file must have read," Need a new strategy to get this asshole to buy something he doesn't need." This year, the Vet tried the weight loss tactic. He claimed Jasper gained one pound over the past year. His solution was for me to invest in an expensive weight loss regimen.

One fucking pound? That's one pound in seven dog years. Humans cannot even keep off one pound for seven minutes. I just shook my head and walked out. I am sure they are devising a new way to get me to buy an add-on next year. The Vet's next pitch will be to up sell a simple annual examination by suggesting that I buy a fifth leg for Jasper, claiming the extra leg will improve the dog's self-esteem.

****

My grandparents were parsimonious. They did not use credit cards for purchases, making sure that their hard-earned cash paid for whatever they bought. They never brandished their nest egg in the form of extravagant gifts or high-ticket items for themselves. Grandma was the first person to exhort me with the adage, "Save it for a rainy day!" I wish I assimilated at least some of her venerated advice when Thanksgiving 1996 rolled around.

We finished devouring the Turkey and dressing, and were either slumped in our chairs or farting our way to the moon. Grandma got up and helped, as she always did, with clearing the licked-clean plates. She came back into the dining room holding an assortment of envelopes and began handing them out to each of her seven grandchildren. I was ready to explode out of my chair in anticipation of what was in the envelopes.

As I opened mine, grandma said the money was a one-time gift. I tore into the envelope the millisecond after she uttered the word money. Staring at me was a check for five thousand dollars. She admonished us to take good care of the financial windfall. I did not hear her sage words because all I could think about was how and where I was going to spend the money.

Grandma did not explain why we got the money or where it came from. I eventually surmised, after researching financial topics online, that it was a tax-free gift from her estate. Grandpa died in 1993, so the mutual trust in their names became exclusively hers. In order to avoid estate taxes, the tax code allowed her to give a certain amount tax-free and the recipients did not have to claim the gift as income.

I had absolutely no thought of saving at least a small portion of it. Not even a slight reflection about donating a percentage of my windfall to charity. The check was like the photo Michael J Fox held of his siblings in *Back to the Future*. The check melted before I deposited it in the bank.

The next day, my brother and I booked a flight to Oakland for a football trip to see the Raiders. Why invest in an IRA when I could invest in FUN. In honor of the new job I was to begin in January, I went out virtually every night between Thanksgiving and New Years Day. The five thousand dollars shrank faster than a dot com stock price. It did not take long for the entire sum to disappear.

I dozed off and ran into a large, sturdy mailbox stand that was located at the entrance of the condominium complex where I lived with my brother. I glanced off the mailbox and hit a garage, waking the neighbors with a thunderous noise. My first reaction after I snapped out of my trance was to high tail it out of trouble. The condominium I shared with my brother was only a quarter of a mile away. The car's damage prevented me from making a getaway.

By sunset the following day, I impulsively bought a used car that committed me to another loan agreement. That made two outstanding car loans, one car, and about four hundred dollars left of grandma's money. Within six weeks, the money was gone and I had nothing to show for it except more debt. The car I impetuously bought was in fair condition and was worth much less than the car I wrecked.

The irony of running out of Grandma's money was I had to ask her for more money during the summer of 1997. It was acutely embarrassing to ask for a loan and then lie about how I burned through her check. Surprisingly, we all got another check at Christmas. Mine was smaller than what the other grandchildren received because I did not pay back the money I borrowed in the summer. I used the second check to live on until I found a job. Subsequent holidays came and more checks followed. I spent them all without saving a dime.

The cavalier manner in which I handled grandma's gift was one of the many examples of how undiagnosed ADHD ravaged my lifestyle. My grandparents lived in a modest home when they could have afforded a more lavish residence. They rarely splurged on anything, except on vacations after grandpa's retirement. They exemplified the virtues of thrift. I did them both a disservice by recklessly spending their hard-earned nest egg.

****

I was stuck in an ADHD funk during 1997.

I was not showing up for work, setting a record for the number of different restaurant training programs completed in one calendar year. I finished one training program and immediately quit to start a training program with another company. I drove by or walked past my places of employment on scheduled days, only to abruptly turn around and head back home.

The horrible experience I had as a manager in training for Boston Market exacerbated my itinerant employment record during1997. Once again, I had trouble maintaining focus in a structured environment. My ADHD blew up during a corporate training session in Overland Park, Kansas. I could not sit still during the classroom sessions and I incessantly blurted out smart-ass remarks while the other trainees were trying exchange ideas. The training team openly ridiculed my behavior and the ridicule had a profound effect on my confidence.

I cut off all ties to the people I was close to, including my brother who was mired in a mini downward spiral of his own. He hated his job and, among other personal issues, embarked on occasional drinking binges that unpredictably erupted during any night of the week. He directed a lot of his wrath towards me, which is why I stopped coming in the door when I heard loud music. I returned to my car and drove straight to the nearest hotel.

My money situation was on shaky ground. Without a steady stream of income, I maxed out multiple credit cards in a spending binge reminiscent of my days in Chicago. Texaco was kind enough to give me a card that I maxed out in three days. I did not max the card out with gas purchases. I pushed the plastic limit by buying beer and cigarettes. I singed another revolving credit card by making a string of superfluous purchases. The purchases occurred during a job interview trip that I took to Dallas.

One morning, I woke up on a mission to get a fresh start in life and move to another city. One month prior to my morning revelation, I contacted a restaurant company in Dallas with a resume submission and they responded with an open interview invitation. I called the restaurant company on the morning of my fresh start revelation and arranged an interview. I left for Dallas two days later.

My thought were scattered like leaves on a blustery day. I did not prepare for a move nor was I ready for a management interview. I drove to Dallas in the older model car I impulsively bought after my condominium crash. When I arrived at the motel outside of Dallas, I immediately thought to myself, "What the hell am I doing here?"

I ate dinner at one of the chain's restaurants in a half-hearted attempt to prepare myself for the interview. After a steady stream of margaritas, I bought a twelve pack of beer and polished it off in the motel room. I overslept the next day, waking with barely enough time to shower and make it to the company headquarters in time for my 1:00 interview.

My drive to the company headquarters was a sequence of events straight out of a Charlie Chaplin film. I missed the headquarters exit and spent the next thirty minutes recklessly driving around trying to find a way back to the interstate. When I finally located the headquarters, I jumped out of the car and uttered some audible obscenities. I was in such a frazzled state that people in the parking lot gave me strange glances.

I entered the building. The receptionist looked at me with jaw-dropping amusement. My clothes were soaked with sweat and my hair looked like I had just spent a day in an airport wind tunnel. I rushed through a personality profile form and waited impatiently for the corporate recruiter to summon me for the interview.

The interview barely lasted fifteen minutes. I knew I poorly presented myself in front of the corporate recruiter. I drove directly from the company headquarters back to St Louis, forgetting some personal possessions at the motel.

I did not want to live in Dallas. I wanted out of St. Louis to move as far away from my problems as I could. The ADHD carnival ride was plunging into rapid descent. I decided to crash into the abyss with a reintroduction to cocaine.

****

There has always been a strong correlation between the rough patches in my adult life and the availability of cocaine. Cocaine was only a few steps away during my Chicago downward spiral. By 1997, I was in another position where cocaine came knocking at my self-pitying doorstep. The impromptu decision to walk out on a bartending job in the middle of a busy Friday night shift was bad enough. The decision to work behind a competing bar that attracted drug dealers sealed my fate.

I did not learn my Chicago lesson: do not work behind a bar that has late hours and provides opportunities to abuse drugs and alcohol. I closed the bar at 1:30 five nights a week, which meant I spent five nights a week carousing until the wee hours of the morning. There were other similarities between 1997 and Chicago. In both instances, I developed a petulant me versus the world mentality, embittered at the cards handed to me by our impregnable God. I blamed others for my predicament, never assuming even a slight measure of responsibility for my actions. I felt very alone in a very distant world.

There were acute differences, however, between 1997 and Chicago. I was close in proximity to my family in 1997; living with my brother prevented me from tail spinning into a free fall. The toll that cocaine took on two people I knew scared me into white powder abstinence. I was still doing stupid things, but not in a life threatening manner.

My second DUI in eight years highlighted 1997. I slept off the night in a Des Peres police station cell. The next morning, I felt as drained as I have felt in my entire life. There I was, thirty-seven years old, staring out from behind a Mayberry type jail cell and thinking to myself that I may never turn my life around. I could not fathom reaching for the stars when a personal chasm sucked in my arm. I could not take another beat down. Maybe the time had come to make good on my previous attempt to jump off an elevated platform into the arms of God.

The Jefferson Barracks Bridge frequently appeared on my mental conveyer belt.

I do not know why I thought jumping to my death was the way to go. Maybe it had to do with the vivid dream sequences, the ones where I euphorically soared towards my final destination. If I jumped off a bridge, I could fly away and my problems would disappear. What actually disappeared was the urge to jump. Before my twisted soul reached the point of Chicago or the night when I looked down on Interstate 70, it made an amazing transformation. I got angry, but for a good reason. I was going to come back strong from the 1997 version of a downward spiral. I was going to be resilient in the face of despair.

****

By the end of 1997, I was back to taking the bus as my primary mode of transportation. People who know me evaluate where I am in life by how I get around. If they see me waiting at a bus stop, they surmise that I am going through a difficult phase. It would not be a stretch for them to think that legal issues precipitated the difficult phase. If I am driving a car, then people conclude that I am making a comeback from my financial woes. The combination of poor money management and a DUI forced me to once again stand along the busy roads of St. Louis and wait for the bus.

I did not mind taking the bus. I enjoyed the stress free ride, unless there was someone sitting next to me incoherently mumbling or emitting a malodorous stench that made my eyes water. Taking the bus did negate the capacity to manage time. Just an extra five minutes on the toilet made me forty minutes late for work. When I was behind the time curve, I often jumped the fences that surrounded Interstates 55 and 270 and dashed across the highway as if I was playing the human version of *Frogger*.

I often rushed to get ready for work because I was so worried about missing the bus. One day, I left the faucet on in haste and my brother came home a few hours later to find water all over the bathroom floor. Some of the water made its way to the condominium below. My brother was not a happy camper. I intuitively knew he was tired of sharing the condominium with me. Leaving the faucet on was the last straw for him.

He knew I was strapped for cash, had no car, and walked long distances to catch a bus or run errands. I never asked him for rides, nor did he offer them. I stuffed my backpack full of dirty clothes and walked a mile to the nearest Laundromat because the washing machine in the condominium was broken. I never complained about the washing machine or my situation in general.

I drained the last of Grandma's second check late in the winter of 1997-98. The DUI cost me more than I expected. I could not find a job close enough where I could walk to work without any time management hassles. My bed was in such poor condition that the coils sprung out from the mattress. The money issue became so desperate for me that I took the last of my stash and tried to derive a little income from gambling at the downtown casino. In my most financially perilous moments, I have always seemed to pull away from the brink of destitution. I made enough money to stay afloat until February of 1998.

In early February, I responded to a job fair advertisement. The local paper promoted the job fair for Busch Stadium. A manager hired me as a bartender and assigned me to work in a busy sports bar. I raked in the cheese while Mark McGwire and Sammy Sosa ingested performance-enhancing drugs. I made enough money to make a comeback for hopefully the final time of my life.

****

IRRITATION

Have you ever wondered what weather forecasters do outside of the five minutes allotted to them on the nightly newscast? My theory is they check the price of grocery chain stocks after predicting another eight-inch snowstorm that never happens. On the other hand, they may be brushing up on their weather lingo.

Weathermen and Weatherwomen (no gender bias here) are notorious for using catchy phrases like "a surge of Gulf moisture," "a pesky cut-off low pressure system," and "into the northerly flow we go" as standards for their weather segments. I cannot figure out why they are the only ones in a newscast predicting what is going to happen to us while everyone else is telling us what has already gone down.

I have nothing personal against television weather forecasters. They are fine additions to the human race. They speak to scouting groups, pitch in to help at civic events, and volunteer their time for the next good cause that comes down the pike. My problem is television weather forecasters have celebrity status. How in the name of Katrina did we place weather forecasters at the top of our celebrity list? How in the name of Rita did we create icons that constantly screw up on the job? How in the name of Ike did Al Roker become famous?

Besides baseball players, television weather forecasters are the biggest frauds going. They make a good salary plus cash for any public appearances on the side. The biggest claim they can make on their predictive resumes is that maybe, just maybe, they are correct fifty percent of the time. Television weather forecasters go on nightly with devilishly fake shiny teeth smiles and tell us tall tales.

Most people do not think it is a big deal when weather forecasters screw up. Here is a short list of professions that depend on weather forecasts: restaurant managers, EMS personnel, construction workers, couriers, truckers, pilots, farmers, cops, golfers, and lawn care specialists (grass cutters).

When I was in sixth grade, our science teacher taught us how to forecast the weather by using five simple instruments: thermometer, barometer, wind vane, humidity gauge, and a cloud chart. I can use those five tools today and out duel any weather prognosticator who has his or her head glued to the local Doppler radar. Modern technology has not advanced weather forecasting. It has just given it more sex appeal.

Hurricane Charlie was the last straw. The National Hurricane Center correctly forecasted the hurricane's landfall. However, they advised people in Tampa Bay to evacuate to Orlando. Lo and behold, the storm veered straight into the city of Orlando. Nice job, National Hurricane Center!

We may laugh at weather forecasters, but God does not. When he sees a weather forecaster at the pearly gates, he pushes St. Peter aside and says, "I got this one."

"Okay Mr. Weatherman, you have broken three of my commandments. You act like me because you think you can determine what only I know will happen with the weather (false icon). You lie nightly to others (bearing false witness) and you take money for your services without providing any service (stealing). So, I've come up with a forecast for you in eternity."

"HOT!"

"The great and invigorating influences in American life have been the unorthodox; the people who challenge an existing institution or way of life, or say or do things that make people think."

-William O. Douglas

FIRST IMPRESSIONS, SECOND THOUGHTS

I awoke on September 11, 2001 to the beeping sound of my answering machine. The only message was from my friend who screamed, "Those bastards have done it again!"

I clicked on the remote and immediately became transfixed by what materialized in front of my eyes. Both Manhattan towers were infernos and Steve McQueen was not rushing in to save the desperate souls trapped by the carnage. Every television station, including *The Weather Channel*, showed footage of the planes that slammed into the twin towers.

The horrific images and nonstop bombardment of tragic news took its toll on me. PTSD kicked into high gear and so did a sick, empty feeling in my stomach. The images repulsed me to the point that I felt nauseous. All I could think about was how the passengers on the flights must have felt the moment before their demise. Compassion for the victims and their families was my first impression.

My mind was on switchboard overload as the hyperactive component of ADHD took control of my disposition. I was cognizant of the fact that watching wall-to-wall coverage of the historic event would be emotionally draining. I turned off the television, left my apartment, and took a long drive in my car.

I drove to a restaurant company that was recruiting for a new store. They requested to review my credentials four days before 9-11. I promised the manager I would stop by on Tuesday, September 11 to deliver the resume. It never occurred to me that the terrorist attack would shut down an entire nation. I contemplated if it was in good taste to conduct business on such a tragic day. Nonetheless, I left my resume in a folder by the restaurant's locked front door.

When I returned home, my mental state shifted from sadness and empathy for the victims to utter rage against the perpetrators. Six hours after the first plane struck the twin towers, Bush administration officials began dropping not so subtle hints that Islamic extremists based in Afghanistan were responsible for the terrorist attacks. The Islamic attribution became the impetus for the subsequent march towards war. On September 11, 2001, I could barely contain my deep hatred for the Islamic faith.

Drinking fueled my rage. I do not remember if I ate anything after I got back from dropping off the resume, but I know I drank the rest of the day away. There was no need to go to work or perform any other task for the remainder of September 11, or for the following five days. My only job was to sit in front of the television and pour shots of whiskey and beer into my system to agitate an already hyper-focused wrath.

My thoughts were excessively dark on the days after 9/11. I repetitively visualized the gruesome videos of the mayhem. The movie screening room in my mind played graphic dream sequences of heart wrenching horror. I felt an aura of vulnerability like I did immediately after my Chicago assault. I did not realize the deep impact that 9/11 had on my life until I demonstrated some disturbing ADHD behavior.

****

Amen-Sense of impending doom (3)

Amen-Frequent feeling of demoralization or that things won't work out for me (4)

Jasper/Goldberg-I make quick decisions without thinking enough about their possible bad results (Very much)

T.H. and I rekindled our professional relationship in 2001. He approached me about becoming the General Manager for a Louisiana themed restaurant. His offer was flattering. We spent a few days in New Orleans with the Executive Chef researching ideas for the food and drink menus.

The offer from T.H. to assume the General Manager's position demonstrated that I was slowly gaining re-acceptance into his group of close friends. I put a lot of effort into coming up with a recruitment strategy and pre-opening employee training program. T.H. and I seemed to restore our personal and professional camaraderie.

It was business as usual for T.H. He and Barney Chiselhead did not communicate with me. About four weeks after I accepted the offer, T.H. told me that my responsibilities would differ from what we had previously discussed. What he failed to tell me, and what I had to find out through other sources, was the restaurant lacked the necessary funding to open a full-service restaurant. His reticence about the lack of financial support was the final straw.

I began preparing for a graceful exit after hearing the news from T.H. My plan for a graceful exit quickly turned into an unprofessional departure. Two days before 9-11, I left my resignation letter for T.H. at the company office. It was certainly a cowardly way to quit, but I did not feel T.H. deserved a one-on-one discussion.

I felt lousy about leaving the note, another hit and run departure that was my professional legacy. The lousy feeling I had dissipated two days later after the terrorist attacks. I did not think about T.H. or the restaurant again. All I could think about were the events that unfolded on the fateful September morning. Because of my preoccupation with 9-11, I made some bad decisions that drained my bank account.

I purchased two cars within four weeks that were lemons. I used a rental by the week plan that was expensive. With a credit rating that was pathetic, I had no choice but to succumb and rent a car so I could make it to work and back. I chose to work in St. Charles, a forty-five minute drive from my apartment in south St. Louis. There were plenty of restaurants between my apartment and St. Charles, but I elected to make an hour and a half round trip drive for a restaurant chain that I abhorred.

9-11 scattered my brain way beyond any previous ADHD pattern. I was making such poor decisions that I was not entertaining alternative options. I struggled to get out of bed, lethargic from my 9/11 preoccupation. I fell into a depressed state, constantly thinking about how the victims felt before the explosive end to their lives.

9/11 was the day many Americans vowed they would never forget. It was also a day many people claimed would change them as they tried to pick up the pieces and move forward. I made the same claim that I was going to change. I understood that life is short and not guaranteed. I would be a better person. I made a vow to stop drinking but the vow only lasted for two weeks. Like most Americans, I reverted to the gluttonous, self-serving lifestyle that preceded 9/11.

****

IRRITATION

I am glad I dumped my cable service. Now I am stuck with our local affiliates, which means I watch the local morning news first thing out of the sack. I notice each affiliate tries to mimic their parent company's morning programming format.

First, everyone on the set seems too damn chipper for seven in the morning. Second, each network affiliate rolls out a clown (cannot call him a reporter) who is strung out on caffeine, or something more potent, while reporting on the most frivolous story of the day. Most of us prefer to be eased into our day by gradually sliding sugar laced cereal and high-octane coffee into our systems. We do not need some overly active loudmouth trying to get our attention. We certainly can do without news anchors hem hawing their way through a story.

The local Fox affiliate has taken the absurd to a new low. They run at least one story a day about *American Idol*. I know it is a shameless ploy for ratings, but it says very little about the intellect of their viewers. I guess morning viewers do not want to learn about Wall Street's meltdown, immigration reform, Iraq, energy prices, outsourcing, the sub-prime mortgage fiasco, political corruption, global warming, education, and the superfluity of local news stories that have an impact on our lives. Viewers who care about important issues must be in the shower when the Brittany Spears soap opera makes its daily appearance on the telecasts.

The leaders of our country pray for this type of ignorance. The more tuned in we are to programs like *American Idol*, the more tuned out we are to their malfeasance and incompetence. 97.5 million Americans either dialed in or clicked online for their

American Idol, or about ninety percent of those who voted in the 2004 presidential election. More adults know who the *American Idol* finalists are than the names of their state representative.

I do not see how we can lament the state of our education system. We have become poor role models for teaching our children what should matter most in our lives. *American Idol* should be nothing more than a last call topic, not a lead story on a local news program-ratings gimmick or not.

The success of *American Idol* does not surprise me. A majority of Americans are infatuated with the lives of those who live in the spotlight of fame. Nevertheless, there are hundreds of issues more worthy of our energy and attention. I may have ADHD, but I am glad I do not have the malady that poisons society: Priority Deficit Disorder (PDD).

****

Dr. Edward M Hallowell contributed the book *Driven to Distraction* in 1995, a virtual ADHD bible co-authored with Dr. John J Ratey. Nearly ten years after releasing their first book, the tandem followed up with *Delivered from Distraction*, a book that stresses the many positive attributes of ADHD. Hallowell and Ratey both provide erudite insight into the evolving science and psychology of ADHD.

Hallowell consistently highlights the positive characteristics of ADHD. Some of the more noteworthy traits are original thinking, keen intuition, and an attitude that challenges the status quo. ADHDers have many creative talents, says Hallowell, which are usually underdeveloped until an

ADHD diagnosis. ADHDers are mavericks who walk to the beat of a different drummer.

I have always been a maverick. I take the opposite side of an argument, regardless of whether I am for or against its central premise. I am always determined to find a better way of doing things and my tendency to question the status quo has given me the reputation of not being a team player. I would rather think for myself than follow lemmings that fall into an ocean of conformity.

My first taste of challenging the status quo came at an early age. I was fascinated by the Kennedy assassination and the hypothesis that one person murdered him as depicted in the Warren Commission Report. I bought books on the subject and tried to engage adults who remembered the events of November 22, 1963 in discussions about the merits of the lone gunman theory. I never believed the assertion that a single bullet wounded both Kennedy and John Connelly. I am even more skeptical that a shot fired from the Book Depository forced Kennedy's head back instead of forward. Newton's Law of Gravity defies the Warren Commission's explanation of Kennedy's fatal head wound.

I certainly do not accept conventional wisdom. Some of the topics taught in history class turned out to be spurious; look at the myth of Christopher Columbus. History is surely someone's version passed down through multiple generations, which leads to the embellishment of events. I have always lived by the creed that unless I directly experience a historical event, or until I meet someone who recounts a historical event, I cannot make an accurate assessment in a historical context. If that makes me a maverick, a trait according Hallowell that is common in ADHDers, then I must confidently project my maverick persona in a world dominated by lemmings.

I do not cross the line into the realm of conspiracy theory. I focus on the most suspect statement of fact proposed as the status quo. In the JFK assassination, the statement of fact comes from the Warren Commission's ludicrous explanation that one gunman killed Kennedy. Challenge that, and only that, and the status quo considerably weakens.

I have examined the government's explanation of 9-11 and the 9-11 Commission's official report on the terrorist attacks. What really happened to the smaller building that reportedly collapsed after the twin towers crumbled to the ground? Did it collapse or was it demolished by detonation? Closely examine the reaction of President Bush the moment his aide informed him of the terrorist attack. His facial expressions signaled more of an affirmation than one of indignant surprise.

We were spoon fed a load of crap when it came to disparaging the Islamic faith. I regret that I blindly accepted that load of crap as the status quo.

It is not normal to accept the status quo.

"The real dignity in life is not winning the battle; it's being in the fight."

-Cory Booker

FRESH START

Undiagnosed ADHD is like riding a roller coaster. The highs are exhilarating, followed by demoralizing freefalls into desolation. I have been riding the ADHD roller coaster for the past three years. The freefall has not been as abrupt or pronounced.

A relatively stable lifestyle slowly unraveled after I decided to resign from my management position after the 2005 baseball season. The uncertainty surrounding my future led me to ponder an occupational fork in the road. My decision set the stage for the past three years.

I received a nice offer from Jack in the Box to enter their fast track management program. At the same time, a friend presented an intriguing partnership proposal. The proposal was to purchase and take over operation of a venerable St. Louis restaurant and bar. I contemplated the fork in the road for a good month before deciding on which career path to take. After mulling over my friend's business proposal, I bid adieu to Jack in the Box and took the entrepreneurial fork in the road. I felt the restaurant was a once in a lifetime opportunity.

My partner and I spent the better part of three months writing the business plan, meeting with the owner, and coming up with a financial package to buy him out. The process was educational, but in the end, it seemed like a waste of my time. The restaurant owner tried to conceal financial improprieties.

We had to pry information out of him, like digging for how much he took out of the business to pay alimony. I had a premonition that we would never assume ownership, but I wanted to see the process to fruition. I believed my consistent behavior during the entire process would embolden others to look at my ownership potential.

My friend called one evening to inform me the owner decided to take in a partner. The owner's new partner planned to invest a substantial amount of money in the restaurant. Both roads that led from the fork had irrevocably closed. Once again, a wrong decision manipulated my confidence.

I really wanted a crack at owning a restaurant. I toiled for years learning the restaurant business, mostly from the mistakes of proprietors and general managers. I was disappointed that the deal fell through, but I refused to let the outcome taint my optimism. I enthusiastically went through the interview process and received two job offers that would have put me on the fast track to assuming a general manager's position.

Then out of nowhere, T.H. came back into my life for the third time.

A friend invited me to a Super Bowl party at one of the restaurants T.H. co-owned with Barney Chislehead and a third partner. Everyone had a good time. None of the past interfered with my favorite sports event of the year. About a week after the Super Bowl, I stopped by to check out the construction work on the partner's new restaurant. The impromptu visit turned into an opportunity.

I helped T.H., Barney Chiselhead, and the other owner prepare for and operate the cash cow that is Mardi Gras. It was their first Mardi Gras as owners and they wanted to make sure the day went as smooth as it could under trying circumstances. I left after the sixteen-hour day with a little green in my pocket and a fatigued driven beer buzz.

I heard back from T.H. a week later. He invited me to interview for a management position with his restaurant brand. For the first time, I informed a prospective employer during an interview that I had ADHD. The owners agreed my revelation was not a problem. They offered me the general manager position at the new restaurant.

I resigned after six weeks, disgusted with the owner's continued lack of business ethics and personal compassion. They humiliated me during a meeting, questioning the restaurant acumen of someone who worked twenty years in the industry. Barney Chiselhead, whose expertise is construction and not restaurant operations, questioned an employee schedule I prepared for the meeting. I stormed into the restaurant the next morning, threw my keys on the bar, and took my paycheck without saying a word to anyone.

Former friends made disparaging comments about my relationship with T.H. I heard derisive comments about my character, particularly my mental capacity and inability to work under pressure. I am sure T.H. had a gut-ripping time belittling me. I drifted apart not only from his social group, but also from the world in general.

Self-doubt was back in full force.

****

FRUSTRATION

I reach the pinnacle of my frustration when my shoelaces tie into an inextricable knot or the phone cord tangles into a plastic ball. All a doctor needs for a clinical analysis of my ADHD is to video tape a session where I try to unravel Jasper's walking leash. I know Jasper is perplexed when I stammer and curse my way through such an ordinary task.

****

I have experienced self-doubt for most of my life. The self-doubt has snowballed from a steady stream of negative events that I trace back to childhood. The lingering thought of not reaching my potential and disappointing others erodes my confidence. The more I reflect on my performance record, the more likely I will take fewer chances. The fear of failure is a difficult thing to deal with and a seemingly impossible hurdle to overcome.

Past failed attempts to make changes in my life provided the self-doubt foundation for the recent events that did not go my way. I constantly beat myself up over a number of issues. The predominant issue is why someone with such a high intelligence level consistently sinks into quagmires. I know what I need to do to in order to move forward, but getting it done is an enduring struggle. Self-doubt leaves me frozen in a time warp. I do not know where to start and, when I think of a game plan, I often decide to watch television or play video games.

Immense self-doubt presages low self-esteem, which in my case is lower than most people realize. Self-esteem is how I view myself, the analysis of my contribution to humanity. It should measure values such as compassion and honesty. Our avaricious society measures self-esteem by academic achievement, career success, physical appearance, and material possessions

My material possessions pale in comparison to what my peers own. I never moved into a subdivision with a SUV and HDTV. I do not wear the latest trendy fashions, nor do I wear earrings or have any tattoos that adorn my body. I do not own a car. The perception of others always comes back to one central theme: I am an underachiever. They perceive a forty-eight year old single male as a human aberration. That perception hurts.

The years of listening to comments on my miserable failures has taken its toll. After every imploded relationship, I pull back and build a protective wall around my tormented soul. I would rather stay home and play a computer game than risk another installment of public humiliation. I have made it a point not to enter into relationships. I prefer isolation to camaraderie.

After the latest debacle with T.H., his tight-knit group of friends permanently ostracized me from their exclusive circle. A few people from the group joked about my experiences with T.H. They treated the situation as a comic routine that I performed for their amusement. It was not close to being funny.

The rejection caused a familiar round of job-hopping. I quit four jobs in a six-week period during the summer of 2006. I was at a point in my life where my confidence was at its nadir. I could not shake off my ignoble experiences with T.H. and questioned some of the career decisions I made earlier in the year. A pending sense of doom enveloped my mind.

I felt sorry for myself. My shoulders drooped when I walked and my eyes were not looking much above the ground I covered. The empty feeling of loneliness I was accustomed to during my life once again reared its ugly head. Any of the spiritual advances I made over the previous year were obliterated by the blame everyone else but me routine. I was angry with God for dealing me the crappy hand that he gave me in this life.

I received two startling wake up calls that happened within a month of each other during the summer of 2006. The first was a freak violent storm that hit St. Louis on July 19. The second was a car accident on August 15 that demolished my car.

****

The July 19, 2006 storm began when a squall line moved across eastern Iowa along a stationary cool front. Part of the line dropped south into northern Illinois, eventually skirting across Springfield as it headed for central Indiana. At least that is what the weather gurus thought. During the 5:00 news, the television meteorologists downplayed the storm. By 6:00, the tone in their voices told a different story.

The radar was ablaze in red as the storm dropped straight for the city of St Louis. I thought it was a good idea to get Jasper out for a walk before the storm. An unusually strong gust front preceded the storm and hit the neighborhood while I walked Jasper. The wind blew trees over and busted limbs off huge Sycamores, hurling them like missiles into the ground. Jasper and I ran home and beat the resultant onslaught by minutes.

I have been through my share of violent weather. The July 19, 2006 storm was the most violent I have ever encountered. The wind was relentless, breaking off branches and downing huge trees. I heard a couple of loud crashes. I looked out of my window and saw my neighbor's car crushed by a towering Sycamore. A strange sound emanated from the eerily green sky. It was a sound similar to the one discussed on *The Weather Channel*. The sound was a fifteen to twenty second mid-level roar, like a small train engine starting up at the depot. Debris swirled and the rain moved horizontally.

The storm lasted thirty minutes but the devastation it left lasted for weeks. My power flickered on and off until finally it went off for good. I wondered if the power went off because I muttered, "make up your goddamn mind." I went outside and was stunned to see the widespread destruction.

I knew the power was going to be off for days. The searing heat forecasted to engulf St. Louis would aggravate the hardship of an electricity outage. I called my parents to explain the situation. There was some hesitancy on the other end of the line when I told them I was driving out to drop off Jasper.

I drove through the worst of the storm destruction, veering off streets in order to avoid debris that blocked my way. I thought I was in good shape to reach the interstate until I came across a huge tree that fell in the middle of Holly Hills Boulevard. I detoured through Carondolet Park, hoping to find an open road that would take me to the interstate. The only way out of the park was to drive across a softball field and onto another road. I went the wrong way on the one-way stretch of road until I came to the interstate, where I immediately floored the gas all the way to my parent's home.

I was breathless when I reached their humble abode. My thoughts were running on full steam as I pulled into the driveway. I anxiously pondered where I was going to spend the night and possibly the following nights. Mom greeted me at the garage door. Dad strolled up the stairs with the two dogs. He initially thought I exaggerated about the storm's intensity. He did not believe the storm was as bad as I made it out to be until he turned on the news and saw the property damage.

My racing mind came to an immediate halt. My own father thought I exaggerated about a serious situation. His statement challenging my veracity felt like a forceful punch to the nuts. I quickly left the house and drove back home to retrieve some personal items for an indefinite hotel stay.

My brain misfired neurons at a furious pace as I dwelled on the same odious thought. Would someone come to my aid if I choked on something or would he or she assume my antics were an exaggeration? It is sad when people doubt my authenticity. Now I understand why nobody believed me when I described all of the chicanery that went on at the old Busch Stadium. They would listen to my account of events, nod in affirmation, and then walk away.

People do not take me seriously. ADHD plays a big part because the impulsive and hyperactivity components beget animated behavior that borders on histrionics. Everyone who knows me well has seen my agitated side at least once. Unfulfilled commitments have given me the label of being unreliable. My warped sense of humor gives people the impression that I am not serious about anything. It is difficult to garner respect when people do not know when I am joking or when I am serious. Not even a humble entreaty can change that.

I understand that people do not respect me. I certainly deserve the brush off after years of demonstrating hyperactive responses to tense situations. It still hurts when my father thinks I am making up a story about a wicked storm. It hurts when I tell family and friends I am writing a book and they shrug it off like dandruff flakes brushed from their shoulders. It hurts when people ostracize me as if I have some type of incurable disease.

I can take it when people keep me at a distance because of ADHD related behavior. I cannot fathom why they treat me as if I just escaped from a Leper colony.

****

FRUSTRATION

People call me derogatory names. They apply a mixture of reproachful labels. Some of the insulting remarks and labels are true depictions of my character. Laziness is not one of them.

Just hearing someone call me lazy provokes rage, when my mind goes blank and my face turns red.

I have fought long and hard to overcome ADHD, a condition that I unknowingly lived with for 44 years.

I humbly suggest that certain people reacquaint themselves with the definition of lazy.

****

I was as lonely as I have ever been on August 3, 2006. It might have been a dream that ignited the mental spigot, but August 3rd was the day I took an introspective journey through my life.

I did not like what I saw.

I tried calling you, Mary, on the cell phone number you gave me when we met in 2005. I got a disconnected message and furiously tried to find some way to reach you. I called your alma mater and left a message on their website. I could not find a way to reach out to the one person who has fervently stood by my side.

I knew drinking my thoughts away would not change things. But I tried anyway. I wanted to forget the past forty-six years by wiping the slate clean with an alcohol lobotomy. I got home from a bar and sat on the edge of my bed. The complicated organ that is my brain did an incredible thing and unleashed a flood of images.

I thought about fatherhood, how I will never be able to share in the joy of raising a family. I thought about the rebukes of "Don't do it that way," "Your way is wrong," "Wait your turn," and "You're just lazy." I thought about the emotional baggage I carried around for forty-six years.

I surveyed my relationships landscape and detailed every negative comment made to me from virtually every person I have known. I realized that I was not anyone's best friend. I reflected on the "friends and family" restaurant training events that I have worked, when I could not come up with one lousy person to invite and share in some of the free grub. I thought about Jasper being the only living creature that trusted me.

August 3, 2006 was a time for reflection. I wondered if my life would have turned out different if the medical establishment had diagnosed my ADHD in childhood. I reflected on how an active intervention program could have helped me cope with the ADHD symptoms. I have made many erroneous conclusions about my chronic under achievement, lack of discipline, and numerous failures. After absorbing criticism throughout my life, I built a wall around my feelings and developed a distorted self-image. Finding out about ADHD was not the panacea for grappling with the adult symptoms.

Adults who find out about ADHD late in life have to deal with the "what if" question. The "what if" question visits infrequently, but when it does, it drowns my proud, self-reliant nature the way a tsunami wipes out a tropical island. The "what if" is not about money management, professional status, or education achievement. It is about relationships, or in my case lack of relationships. When "what if" surfaces in my brain, the storage disk unleashes a torrent of painful memories of flawed interactions with a lifetime's worth of people.

It is the perceptions of me that hurt the most. I can only take so much belittling. August 3rd was a day to let all of those verbal jabs and demeaning impressions come to the forefront. When I have one of those days and realize I have nobody to share my feelings with, the situation becomes hopeless, and I slide into a depressed state. I do not think about suicide anymore; that is a chicken shit way out. August 3rd, however, was the rare day that bailing out on life once again made an appearance in the back of my mind.

The pain on a day like August 3rd really hits hard, making it tough to breath at times. I self-medicated myself with booze but I could not get one morbid thought out of mind. What would happen if I suddenly I died? How many people would pay their respects? Not many would show, if any at all. My body may rot in the apartment for days until Jasper desperately crashes through a window to freedom. Nobody checks on me, so who knows.

What if I never had ADHD and was able to cultivate and maintain relationships with a diverse set of people? I would not be sitting alone on my bed in a drunken stupor and wallowing in self-pity. Finding out about ADHD as an adult helped me work out some complicated issues.

That does not mean living with undiagnosed ADHD was easy.

****

I burst out of my funk on August 15, 2006, when I was involved in a car accident on the section of Interstate 270 that approaches the I-55 southbound exit. I was in a three-car link that was part of a twenty-plus car pile up during rush hour.

Traffic moved at a slow pace until it came to a grinding halt. The pace picked up again to around forty miles an hour. I dropped my cell phone on the floorboard and reached down to retrieve it. I looked up and saw that the car in front of me had come to a complete stop. I applied the brakes with as much force as I could, but it was too late. I skidded into the car in front of me at thirty miles per hour. My head hit the steering wheel and my elbow rammed into the dashboard.

We gave our statements to a county police officer. The accident obviously overwhelmed him and his partners. He told me it was okay to drive off in my severely damaged car as long as I went slow and immediately took the car to a repair shop. I drove off at a speed of no more than twenty miles per hour. After a half-mile, the hood flew up into the windshield. The shattered glass particles exploded into the car. The force of the impact caused my head to slam into the steering wheel.

I woke up the next morning with a lemon size lump on my elbow. I was concerned, but over time the lump subsided and there was not much pain. While I was preoccupied with my elbow, I started getting headaches at odd times of the day and felt lethargic the minute I got out of bed. I did some research and discovered that I sustained at least a mild concussion. The last thing I needed was another blow to an already amorphous brain.

I assumed total responsibility for the accident. The distraction of the fallen cell phone prohibited me from averting the tangled cars. For one of the few times during my life, I actually accepted responsibility for something I did! Accepting responsibility for the accident gave me the elusive fresh start that I have always wanted.

Like many individuals with undiagnosed ADHD, I have gone through periods of my life when I thought things would never work out. I hit the downward spiral and locked into a tenacious holding pattern, using all of my intellect, ingenuity, and resiliency to keep my head above water. There were times when I felt like a boxer on the ropes, pummeled by fists of fury. I have always bounced back because the real dignity in life is brushing myself off and remaining in the fight. A fresh start is impossible to achieve unless someone has the will to keep fighting.

Before the car accident, I had a relapse of self-pity that is a typical sequence of the downward spiral. I quickly got a hold of myself and moved on. Encapsulating the life of an ADHDer is simple: it is about dusting ourselves off and moving on. If we piss everything away, from relationships with loved ones to overdrawn bank accounts, we need to maintain our resolve to fight back and use our ADHD skills to climb out of the rock bottom hole that we have created. Starting over to me denotes a repetitive phase in an ADHDers life. A fresh start means never looking back.

We have to accept who we are and move on to the next phase of our lives. We must eagerly anticipate the events that unfold on a new day. If we do not, we will become engaged in the mundane process of starting over when we should be rewarding ourselves with a fresh start.

****

IRRITATION

I used to rail at people who drove and talked on their cell phones. The St. Louis Post-Dispatch noticed my criticism in a commentary piece that I submitted for publication. Since I was guilty of the same thing, I will avoid the haughty hypocrisy of "Do as I say, not as I do." Instead, I have some simple requests for those who use cell phones.

Do not talk on a cell phone when you are ringing up my groceries. Do not answer your cell phone when we are engaged in conversation. Do not check your cell phone messages when you are taking my dinner order.

****

Adults with ADHD typically have visionary imaginations. When our imaginations fail to advance past the visionary stage, we tend to become overwhelmed in a sea of self-pity, much like the state I was in on August 3, 2006. When we see dream after dream collapse, we become limp and lose all hope. Nevertheless, we are considerably resilient. We rely on ingenuity to help us adapt to situations that are not conducive for someone with ADHD.

Resiliency does not manifest unless someone is fully accountable for his or her actions. For forty-six years, I was not accountable for my behavior. That has changed over the past two years. We already have a deficit of stand up people in this country. We certainly do not need more.

Instead of making excuses by deploying the acronym ADHD every time something goes wrong, I am more cognizant of the wonderful gifts derived from the condition. Instead of playing the cynical and narcissistic game of "what if," I reflect on some of the more poignant lessons I have learned from my mistakes. ADHD may be a neurobiological condition that requires a tremendous number of intervention strategies. Maturity is a condition of the heart.

My ADHD has changed in more ways than by my acceptance of personal responsibility. In some ways, it has dramatically changed. In other ways, the changes have been more subtle. I have stopped watching television ever since I got rid of the madness called cable. I tossed my video game console and games into the alley dumpster. The hyperactivity and impulsive components have weakened significantly over the past ten years. I am less inclined to drop whatever I am doing on a whim and start something completely unrelated to what I am trying to achieve. The first day is not the social hurdle it once was. The biggest stride I have made is developing relationships.

I ran into Tiffany during the fall of 2006. We worked together for a short time in 1996. She and her husband lived a couple blocks away, but we rarely saw each other unless it was a quick greeting while we drove by in a hurry to nowhere. I was walking Jasper in the park when I noticed her with her two small children and German Shepard. My instinct was to do nothing more than give a hand waving hello, not to shun her, but to evade a situation where I had to listen to a drawn out conversation.

Her dog came towards us to play, so we met about halfway and started some small talk. Her husband told her about my writing project and she asked how it was going. I was a little hesitant to discuss the book with anyone because the people I already told reacted with a shrug or replied with a snide remark. We engaged in about a thirty-minute discourse on ADHD, a world record for me talking about a subject for that length of time.

We mostly talked about her daughter, who was being home schooled because of ADHD. The little girl had a hard time paying attention, but she was an intelligent and creative person. She understood linguistics, but could not comprehend the value of money. She loved to draw pictures and was good at it, but could not remember the previous day's math lesson. Many of the young girl's traits resembled the same traits that I struggled with in childhood. Tiffany and I further discussed my diagnosis experience, her daughter's ADHD evaluations, and the impact ADHD drugs have on children.

We leisurely strolled through the park when I realized I missed the salient part of life by not being able to focus and pay attention to others. Now that I am better at focused conversation, I do not have to be evasive when I talk with someone. I do not have to give a halfhearted hello and keep going on my way. People have unique perspectives to offer and my impromptu discussion with Tiffany was a prime example. I learned a lot by listening to her.

A day before I ran across Tiffany in the park, I was delivering telephone books to a Catholic church/school when a woman approached and inquired about taking one of the books home with her. My initial reaction was typical. I curtly said the company allocated a certain amount of books per route. I started walking away when I turned around and said, "This is church property so maybe I should be in the giving spirit." That brought a smile to her face, which immeasurably brightened my day.

I have experienced a number of similar situations lately. An elderly woman needed to use my cell phone to find a residence. A complete stranger came up to me in a grocery store parking lot and asked me to jump-start her car. Unexpected encounters have always made me anxious, an invasion into my own little ADHD world where my timeline is of paramount importance. That was I how I initially reacted in the park with Tiffany. I just wanted to move on after the salutations from afar. I am thankful I did not.

I learned from Tiffany some more about ADHD and its impact on children. I also learned about interaction, about how much I missed it by building a wall around my unique disposition. My aversion to social situations because of ADHD limitations has caused me to miss an important life lesson, which is nurturing the growth of human bonding. I lived in a shell so I did not have to reveal my darting eyes, impetuous interruptions, and demeaning condescension.

What I have missed is only part of the undiagnosed ADHD tragedy. I have failed to share all of the wonderful elements that make up my personality. I was a shining star that faded in the presence of other people. I cannot take control of my future without making strides in social settings.

I need to start now with every chance that I get.

WHAT ALL OF THIS MEANS

"Nothing is particularly hard if you divide it into small jobs."

-Henry Ford

EUREKA!

I envisioned writing about my anomalous experiences during the summer break between my junior and senior years of college. I kept a lengthy journal with the intention to develop it into a manuscript. I never progressed past plotting the basic outline. Other book projects did not even get to the outline stage. It was not until I left your house three years ago, Mary, that I had enough clarity to start the most involved project of my life.

My initial goal was to collaborate on a book with a psychologist. The combination of an ADHD medical professional and a forty-four year old undiagnosed adult might have made a compelling read. After the Dr. Kia fiasco, I was hesitant to contact anyone affiliated with ADHD.

I did contact two local ADHD specialists over the phone and a few more via the Internet. I received the brush off. My conclusion, especially after meeting Dr. Kia, is the ADHD medical establishment would rather make money off ADHD than help us reach our full potential. I moved forward with the book project on my own.

I purchased a tape recorder. The analog relic recorded my thoughts whenever I felt the urge to let it all out. I started talking into the tape recorder the day after I last saw you, Mary, and did not stop until September 2006. The recordings were seventeen months of incisive commentary, muddled ramblings, and painful recollections. I brought the tape recorder with me everywhere I went.

When I came up with an idea while I drove to work or when I ran errands, the idea became a flickering thought before I got home and pulled out the keyboard to begin a writing session. The tape recorder allowed me to play and replay hours of personal anecdotes, opinions, and research. It allowed me to capture my spontaneous wit and rapidly moving thought process.

The tape recorder gave me an outlet to vent without offending anyone during my homilies. Psychologists claim the primary way they help clients is to listen and let them work things out for themselves. Instead of paying someone to listen, I took the inexpensive route and worked out my personal demons by listening to the vitriolic monologues. The tape recorder was my psychologist.

I began audio tape one with some short stories and my take on contemporary topics. As the tapes moved forward, I described how ADHD affected me in an emotionally devoid manner. There was no energy in my voice. I was not peeling away the layers of my psyche by probing the emotional scars. My demeanor changed when I spun into a freefall during 2006. I confronted the demons head on with penetrating descriptions of my experiences.

After writing the rough draft, I decided to listen to all twenty-two and a half hours of audio one more time before I initiated the editing process. It was painfully obvious that I missed some important material. Even with the headphones blaring audio directly into my ear lobes, my wandering mind did not assimilate all of the content.

The twenty-two and a half hours of recorded audio tapes were not enough to get me moving on a book. I concluded that I needed to limber up my fingers and post daily blogs on a free

Web site. The blogs were mostly about ADHD. I did not edit any of the blogs. They expressed the lava flow of thoughts that poured out of my brain. The blogs prepared me for the prodigious task of completing the one and only long-term project of my life.

****

I told some people about my plan to write a book. Sometimes, I mentioned the topic of ADHD and sometimes I did not. Most of the people I told did not even ask about the topic. They just paused and said something like, "That's great, Don!", and we moved on to discuss something else. I could tell by non-verbal cues that people were skeptical of my planned endeavor.

Gary was the most supportive. His response when I told him about the book was, “That’s great! Good luck! You’re good at that.” When I told mom, there was silence on the other end of the phone line. I am sure she was thinking to herself, “Oh great. He will start another project that he will not finish. He will get bored and start something else like he has been doing the past forty-six years.” Other people offered little in the way of encouragement or discouragement.

I was not angry because of the skepticism. After all, I have spent my entire life informing people about my unfinished business. My success rate for completing a task that required a long-term commitment was appalling. The irony of writing the book was I surmounted the symptoms of ADHD that have diminished my past productivity. Writing a book of this magnitude required traits that people with ADHD lack and in my case were indisputably absent.

Procrastination foiled my previous attempts to complete lengthy projects. I started many projects with vigor, only to see my enthusiasm wane. I finished projects with a poor effort or I did not finish them at all. I needed to write every day in order to see this writing project through, even if I was uninspired before transmuting my thoughts into words.

Most writers and writing instructors talk about writer's block. I sat before the computer with trepidation, wondering if the feared writer's block would pervade my thought process. It was tough enough to finish a lengthy writing project and have to deal with the ADHD components of distraction, impulsiveness, and hyperactivity. It would have been impossible to complete the project if the sign in my brain read "vacancy." Fortunately, my mental spigot gushed on most days.

I was more concerned about quitting the project on a whim when another brilliant idea emanated from my pulsating mind. Another issue was if my hyperactivity, even in its diminished form, would make it impossible for me to sit and hammer away on the keyboard. Moreover, there was the chronic sense of underachievement that persisted every time I recalled an aborted project or unfulfilled obligation.

The key to ADHD is learning how to manage our lives by eradicating the inevitable lapses in discipline. I took what I learned about ADHD and came up with a game plan for writing the book. The original game plan fell apart three days after I conceived it.

****

FRUSTRATION

Martha Stewart is the anti-Christ.

She takes tongue depressors and spends thirty minutes on her show making a Christmas display. She spends an entire show showing us how to cut ribbons for ornamentation on some other project she has created in her warped mind. If the icing is not perfectly frosting a cake, she takes forever smoothing over the rough edges while using a satanic voice that describes whatever the fuck she is doing.

I sit throughout her entire show, unable to move from my seat or flick my fingers onto the remote control. She casts a hypnotic spell over someone with ADHD.

****

My first objective was to find a job that gave me the time and energy to write the book. I knew a management gig would not cut it, because babysitting a bunch of overweening brats would have diverted my attention from a lifelong dream. I tried finding a restaurant service job where I could make money and get out in time to add a few lines into one of the book's chapters. I bounced around from job to job, frustrated I could not find a job that gave me an uncluttered perspective.

Compounding the perfect job search was my restlessness. I started looking for places to live that were conducive to writing a book. I must have driven my landlord and family crazy with all of the proclamations I made about relocating to another part of the area. I almost moved to Washington, Missouri. I almost moved to St. Charles, Missouri. I almost moved to Pacific, not the ocean. I think the manager at U Haul thought I was running from the law when I called him for the third time to make a rental truck reservation.

In between moving decrees, I rearranged the furniture around my apartment in order to create the perfect book-writing ambience. My initial strategy was to move the desk and computer into a room that had a window air conditioner. The stifling St Louis heat would have made it impossible to write in a room that did not have a window unit. Once out of the unbearably hot office room, I was going to write day and night until the book was finished. I only wrote a few blogs during the summer of 2006.

I found the consummate revenue-generating job in October of 2006. I was not keen on waiting tables, but I had to swallow my pride and look at the bigger picture of completing the book project. There was not any responsibility attached to the job except to show up and give a decent effort. I liked working at night since most of my creative juices flowed the minute I got up in the morning, probably due to my subconscious writing the book for me while I slept. I also decided to stay in the apartment that I rented the previous seven years.

The morning after I decided to stay, I sat down at my computer and typed the first few lines of the book. I worked with an outline that I constantly revamped and continued to do so until the book was finished. The tapes were an invaluable asset, although it was hard to understand what I was saying on the first few because I spoke too fast into the recorder. I found a slower rhythm as the tapes progressed.

My original intention was to provide information about ADHD. I read everything I could get my hands on about the condition. I wanted to convey every perspective, from the drug treatment debate to the ambiguous causes. I noticed a change in my monologues starting with the fifth tape. I described my personal experiences living with undiagnosed ADHD.

I also noticed my thoughts about ADHD changed over time, mostly due to all of the personal artifacts that my parents gave me during 2006. Besides my memory, the artifacts were the only link to my past and they provoked some deep underlying emotions when I started laying them out on the bedroom floor. They were the pieces of evidence I needed in order to prove I had a stronger version of ADHD. I wonder about the circumstantial timing of the artifacts. They appeared when I was having trouble developing a coherent outline.

The great flood of 1993 swept away a trunk full of my high school and college artifacts. I did not cry the sentimental cry after finding out my cherished possessions floated down the Des Moines River. I had many chances to retrieve the trunk full of memories before the flood. Every time I made it back to Des Moines, I either forgot about the trunk or was too occupied partying with old friends to retrieve it from the dusty storage area at Gringo's restaurant. After examining the personal artifacts that my parents gave me, the trunk would have offered more evidence to strengthen my ADHD case.

People with ADHD have an erratic short-term memory, but our long-term memory is a vault brimming inside of our brains. The personal artifacts my parents gave me unlocked the vault. The words that came from my fingers felt like lightning bolts.

I was on my way to completing my first long-term project.

****

I have always been passionate about writing. My first published piece of work was a letter I wrote to the high school newspaper. The letter contested my suspension for allegedly throwing a snowball at one of the vice principals.

First Published Writing

Snow throwing

Dear Editor,

I was recently sent home from school for throwing a snowball at a fellow student. This is the first time I have been suspended from any kind of function. I believe firmly that suspending me was too harsh a punishment.

Other crimes at our school are committed daily without the apprehension of the guilty party. Furthermore, in my three years on the Kirkwood campus I have seen more people evade punishment for crimes of a more serious nature, than the one I committed.

I have walked past the smoking area and witnessed snowballs being thrown by other students.

A person who skips a class is not sent home from school, but is required to pick up trays in the cafeteria. I threw the snowball without thinking of the consequences. It was a mistake on my part, but I believe a warning in this instance would have been sufficient enough to prohibit me from doing it again.

Students who destroy property or skip a class are slapped with a punishment as severe or less severe than mine. The administration probably will say injury can be the outcome of snowball throwing. This is true, but students driving to school or playing Hoc-Soc in gym usually run the same risk of injury.

I feel humiliated about the incident and I realize my teachers are going to have a lower opinion of me because of my suspension. I wish to tell the readers of the **Call** to tie a string around their finger to remind them that throwing snow is wrong.

Respectfully yours,
Don Potochny

Without any formal training as a journalist, I submitted articles and commentary to the editor of Drake's school newspaper. Meeting a deadline meant handing my submission to my roommate, who was also the school's newspaper editor. I was at peace when I wrote for The Times Delphic. I did misquote a few people because I did not pay attention to their responses. I did better at pure commentary because I got a rush putting my opinions into written form for the world to see.

Once I moved back from Chicago, I submitted letters to both St. Louis daily newspapers. I looked at writing as a hobby, a pursuit I would follow in my spare time while I tried to make it in the restaurant industry. I took a writing class at a local community college and garnered high praise from the instructor, Carol Niederlander. I eventually submitted commentaries to The St. Louis Post-Dispatch and Nation's Restaurant News. The periodicals published most of my submissions. I still have a copy of the first check that I received for a published commentary.

As I headed towards the finish line with the manuscript, I surreptitiously found an online writing community that enhanced my writing style and created a succinct voice. Helium is wonderful enterprise comprised of over 100,000 writers. After I started posting articles on Helium, I incorporated writer feedback into sections of the manuscript. I particularly paid attention to punctuation and structure issues. I highly recommend Helium for any writer who wants to join an authentically supportive writing community.

I find writing to be the ultimate release, a way for me to pass on the convoluted thoughts that backfire in my brain. While I lose many verbal debates, people look at me in a different light when I put my side of an issue into words. Instead of a rambling rant that borders on arrogant piousness, I type 750 word commentaries that neatly convey my ideas, moral convictions, and point of view.

My love for writing was the main reason I was able to push aside self-doubt. I was finally doing something that implemented my natural ability and unconcealed passion. I wrote when I was sick. I wrote when I was full of energy. I wrote when I was hung over. I wrote with a stiff alcohol buzz (not recommended). I wrote at all hours of the day and awoke during some nights with the inexplicable exigency to write. For all of the positives that gave me momentum to write the book, I still had to deal with the multifarious symptoms of ADHD.

And deal with them I did.

****

Carol Niederlander was my lone writing supporter. She stood alone against the vast majority of people who doubted my writing ability.

One of the most disappointing elements of graduate school was the critique I got on one of my writing assignments for a Business Communications class. The professor wrote on one of my papers that my work was "disjointed" and had "a lack of organization." I did not even know what disjointed meant until I looked it up in the writing bible, the mighty Thesaurus. I though the word meant a joint that was cut into pieces. I vehemently disagreed with her assessment and she went on to call me "disputatious."

I am grateful she uttered her critique. She was right, though I would not admit it at the time. My thoughts disconnect, which is why I make little sense when I verbalize them. They just bounce around inside of my head without rational order. Her comments have been an inspiration while I have traveled through the book-writing journey.

Putting my thoughts into coherent order was a challenge, but a challenge I had to meet if I was going to produce a capacious work for print. I worked meticulously to make sure my writing was cohesive and connected. I used the Cut and Paste command from Microsoft Word, sometimes cutting an entire section of one chapter and pasting it into another. An ADHDer must have created Cut and Paste.

I did not set a deadline for the book's completion, which meant I did not have to storm through the project and produce an inferior product. Nonetheless, the urge to rush through the book was present and it took self-control to negate the impulse to wrap up the project. I tried not to look at the finish line, but I sure daydreamed about it every day.

My mind constantly flashed self-doubt images. My inability to complete graduate school ten years ago was the one endeavor that shackled my enthusiasm for making any book assertions. I told everyone about graduate school and most people said, "Looks like Don has finally turned the corner." I did turn a corner right into an oncoming truck.

Some parts of the book were extremely difficult to write. I literally slumped in my chair when I finished Straightjacket. There was just so much going on in my head when I described the most painful period of my life. I also had moments of intense internal struggles, when I wondered if the material I was putting in was relevant to the principal theme of the book. My biggest concern was whether writing the book was going to heal or rip open old wounds, not just for me, but for anyone else familiar with my story.

I want to thank one person for helping me overcome the ADHD hurdles. Thank you, Oprah! When the going got tough and I refused to get going, I daydreamed of appearing on your show to talk about my revolutionary ADHD perspective. I daydreamed that you asked me question after question about the book as I beamed in front of your adoring fans.

My answer to one of your questions bothered you.

"So, what is your favorite book, Don?"

"Oprah, I don't have the patience to read a book."

****

IRRITATION

This is an idea for Congress to chew on. Make the first Monday in February President's Day. That Monday would be the day after the Super Bowl, a day in which nobody gets anything accomplished. We already lump all of the Presidents on a day when people spend more time shopping than reflecting on our country's history. It is not hard Congress. All you have to do is expunge "third" from the statute and insert "first."

Some windbag will probably get up in a vacant House chamber and give a monotonous two-hour speech in front of C-Span. He or she will express outrage that the day after the Super Bowl cheapens President's Day. Here is some input: you and your cronies in Congress have already cheapened the holiday! Now do us a favor and give us the day off after the Super Bowl to recover from our hangovers and empty wallets.

"Let me tell you the secret that has led me to my goal. My strength lies solely in my tenacity"

-Louis Pasteur

DISAPPOINTED

What was the seminal event during my life that clearly demonstrated that I needed active intervention and remedial treatment? Was it my time in Chicago, when the incessant cries for help were disregarded as undisciplined outbursts by a chronic underachiever? Alternatively, did the seminal event occur when I spewed profanity at the woman on Ruckert Street?

There was not a lot of publicity about ADHD when I was a child. The ADHD phenomenon gained momentum in the nineties, long after I distanced myself from the four miserable years of Chicago. There was enough information about ADHD to make a conclusion about my behavior and performance. None of the therapists or psychologists that I saw mentioned ADHD. The best they could do was flippantly voice hackneyed Freudian interpretations.

The sex therapist did not understand why my mind moved at such a rapid pace during sex. When I made the rounds among Chicago psychologists, the focus was always on my drug and alcohol abuse. There was never any exploration into the deep-rooted cause of my drug addiction. It turns out it was my way of coping with a strong version of ADHD.

Ninety-nine percent of the book-writing journey was a glorious ride that allowed me to discover the gifts of ADHD. I prepare for the future armed with the knowledge I have gained from the many mistakes that I made. I look to the future by accentuating the positives of ADHD and controlling the negative symptoms that previously tarnished my life.

There certainly were moments of weakness, when the "what if" question seeped into my consciousness. I will not enumerate the variations of "what if." There were so many that all the time I endured asking "what if" turned out to be an exercise in mind-numbing futility. I got angry. I became melancholy. I headed down the same dead end path by blaming others for my past behavior.

Asking "what if" is a self-destructive mindset. I have to remain positive and move forward where the future does not depend on retrospect.

That does not mean I am not disappointed.

****

In December of 2007, I moved out of an apartment that I rented for eight years. Staying in one place for eight years is directly against my nomadic temperament. I had six different addresses during my five years in Des Moines, three apartments in Chicago, and another five places I called home within four years of moving back to St. Louis. My favorite make believe game as a child was to pack up the toy wagon and pretend that I was moving to Texas, California, or anywhere but where I was at the time.

I was ready to move a year earlier and not because I was restless from trying to write the book. The second urge to move was because of the car accident and subsequent medical issues. Another round of impulsive job-hopping strained my finances to the breaking point. The new job was not paying the bills and I fell behind with car payments. I investigated some type of financial protection through the legal system.

I bought the car one week after I received a settlement check from the insurance company. I am not sure if the concussion and/or ADHD had anything to do with the careless way I shopped for the car. I had a budget limit, but that went down the toilet minutes after I laid my eyes on a 2002 Honda Accord. I completed the entire car purchase process in a little more than two hours. Dad is shaking his head while he reads this.

A looming car repossession forced me to alter my living arrangement. I had to find a place to live within walking distance of our light rail system. After searching for three months, I found an apartment close to a public transportation hub. I met with property owner and decided the apartment he had for rent met all of my needs. I gave him a deposit check for $550 and planned to meet with him within a week to sign the lease.

I informed my landlord about the move and he immediately offered me a two-month rental grace period. His offer came three days before I was to sign the new lease. I called the property owner and informed him of my decision to stay put. He made some unsettling noises, mostly sighs, and proceeded to lecture me about how he had "jumped through hoops" to get me to sign the lease.

“You didn’t have to jump through hoops when you took my $550 check,” I said over the phone.

That ticked him off a little, but he got downright angry when I asked him about his Jesus vanity license plate.

“Jesus would give me back my deposit and let bygones be bygones.”

His parting shot was the familiar refrain I have heard from many people throughout my life. He said he was "disappointed in me.”

I cannot calculate the number of times I have heard people say were disappointed in me or disappointed with me. I have heard people say they were disappointed in me as far back as early childhood, when I got the disappointed lecture from an adult after committing some type of punishable offense.

I disappointed Mr. Matheny after he caught me cheating on a math block quiz in the sixth grade. I disappointed Mr. Wolters for letting Rocky Emins cheat off of me during a ninth grade citizenship test. I disappointed Mr. Welch for handing in a calculus test that had nothing more than a "please fail me" on the piece of paper; he gave me a D minus. I disappointed Dr. Walter Roettger after I failed to complete an internship project during my final year at Drake University.

I disappointed my parents, mostly by failing to reach my potential. Dad expressed his disapproval without even knowing about ADHD. He did not utter the word disappointed, but his classic look of disappointment made words unnecessary. I disappointed my brother for over staying my welcome at his condominium. I disappointed my grandmother when I went to her for money just five months after she cut me a trust fund check. The look of disappointment on her face still breaks my heart.

I disappointed all of my coaches for failing to follow the rules. I disappointed my scouting peers during a two-week wilderness excursion. I disappointed friends because of my loutish behavior, college peers because of my insolence, and teachers because of my academic inconsistency. I disappointed girlfriends and their respective families. I disappointed employers when I fell short of their expectations.

Just hearing the word disappointed made me cringe and pull back from social interaction. When I disappointed someone, I ran like the wind to get as far out of audio range as possible. I spend so much time alone because I am weary of hearing "I'm disappointed in you." People have set expectations for me without realizing the obstacles I have overcome to moderate my ADHD symptoms.

People should ask themselves how I felt going through life hearing time and again that I disappointed them. Have they thought about how their words made me feel? I spent over half of my life living with a condition I did not know about. I worked hard to come up with creative ways for adapting to environments where my peculiar personality and maverick perspective did not fit in. Tenacity is my greatest attribute. Without it, I would have faded into oblivion long ago.

Now it is time to turn the tables. I ask the people who articulated the condescending disappointment lectures just one question: Do you know what disappointed me?

I am disappointed in an education system's failure to recognize that hyperactivity and inattention precluded me from thriving in a classroom environment. The educational hierarchy should have promoted an individualistic methodology for my schooling. That approach worked for Mrs. Ogles and it worked wonders for mom.

I am disappointed in a sausage grinder system that administered standardized tests for the discernment of my mental acuity. Standardized tests do not measure innovation, creativity, and tenacity.

I am disappointed that I do not know my true Intelligence Quotient. I will never know, because I become distracted and restless about two-thirds of the way through an IQ test and make imprudent mistakes on the remainder of the questions.

I am disappointed in the people responsible for my academic and professional education. They never understood that I learned more in an interactive or computer environment.

I am disappointed that home schooling was never offered as an option for my education.

I am disappointed in the coaches who manipulated my weaknesses. Your job was to make me better, not to give up on me.

I am disappointed in employers who made me sit through the same laborious training sessions as everyone else, even when they knew I could not sit still for more than thirty minutes at a time.

I am disappointed in restaurant managers and owners who failed to harness all of the wonderful gifts I bring to the restaurant industry: energy, enthusiasm, teamwork, and knowledge. All of the managers or owners I have ever worked for needed a healthy dose of foresight and compassion. That is, except for Curtis Wierbicki, Paul Hamilton, Alvin Watkins, and Cynthia Early.

I am disappointed in the people of faith who do not honor the teachings of Jesus. The Bible instructs you to forgive others for their transgressions.

I am disappointed in family, friends, peers, teachers, and employers who preferred to lecture me about my failure to live up to their expectations rather than congratulate me for implementing creative ways to cope with ADHD. Oh, I forgot. You did not realize I have ADHD. I am disappointed in that as well.

I am disappointed in all of the people who thought I was joking about writing a book. Is it a joke now?

I am disappointed in T.H.

I am disappointed in the people who think normal behavior is paying six dollars for a tepid beer to support over paid baseball players, while some people cannot afford their electric bills in the midst of a one-hundred plus degree heat wave.

I am disappointed in the people who gladly fork over six dollars for a tepid beer to support overpaid baseball players, yet bitch about paying four dollars for a gallon of gasoline.

I am disappointed in the people who believe I am full of hyperbole. Look again at the photograph of my face split open. Does it look like I exaggerated about what happened to me in Chicago?

I am disappointed in the people who shrug their collective shoulders when asked about the rampant use of performance enhancing drugs in baseball. They believe steroid ingestion by baseball players is normal behavior, yet they chide me for my ADHD idiosyncrasies.

I am disappointed in the people who perceive me as a failure, when Ivy League "experts" who cannot come up with viable solutions for societal problems miserably fail at their jobs.

I am disappointed in the people who perceive me as a failure, yet give a pass to the greedy suits and Wall Street con artists who directly caused the near collapse of our nation's financial system. All of those scumbags should spend time behind bars. I thought my stealing was detestable.

I am disappointed in the people who perceive me as a failure, but remark, "these things happen" when offering their respective kernels of wisdom on the Minneapolis bridge collapse.

I am disappointed in the Ivy League establishment for shoving diversity down our throats. Diversity is not about skin color, gender, or religious difference. Diversity is accepting people of any race, gender, or religion who present contrapuntal viewpoints to the status quo.

I am disappointed in the people who complain about airport security measures when millions of children throughout the world have daily sustenance that consists of a fucking bowl of rice.

I am disappointed in the people who feel they have to kiss ass in order to climb up social, professional, and economic ladders. I am more disappointed in the people who drop their pants.

I am disappointed that my name appears in jury duty databases.

I am disappointed in the psychologists and therapists who wasted my time. Their respective evaluations of me were no more intuitive than if I gleaned insight from Dick Cheney.

I am disappointed in Dr. Kia, who used the hour prearranged for me to rant about his personal demons. I am also disappointed in him for not asking me what I wanted out of the diagnostic process. It certainly was not a Ritalin prescription.

I am disappointed in the people who do not recognize the wonderful gifts of ADHD. They would rather ridicule someone for being outside of "normal" behavior parameters than take the time and energy to comprehend the gifts of ADHD. I call that being lazy.

I am disappointed in the people who throughout my life exhorted me with phrases like "It's all in your head" or "Be mentally tough." Educate yourselves before giving me your insulting opinions about what goes on inside someone's head.

I am disappointed in television sports anchors that use the words integrity and St. Louis Cardinals in the same sentence.

I am disappointed in the people of Kirkwood, Missouri for selling their soul to the devil.

I am disappointed in a psychotherapy culture that promotes prescription drugs as the panacea for refining the rough edges of ADHD.

I am disappointed in the people who drive to Earth Day.

I am disappointed in the people who would rather spend time watching *American Idol* than give their time and money to help our returning war veterans. They need our help.

I am disappointed in the people who decry global warming, yet drive their children from one activity to the next in a gas-guzzling automobile.

I am disappointed in a lobby that feels a background check to ascertain mental fitness is considered gun control.

I am disappointed in Mothers Against Drunk Driving for not holding anyone accountable for the uncontrolled inebriation that occurs at sporting events.

I am disappointed in Montel Williams for deriding the ADHD condition as fraudulent.

I am disappointed in the ADHD medical establishment for not making it clear to people like Montel that ADHD is a real condition.

I am disappointed that an ADHD diagnosis is a guessing game.

I have kept my head above water by cutting corners and punching through societal norms in order to compensate for my lack of ADHD awareness. I tried to meet or exceed the expectations of others so I did not disappoint them.

What are my expectations? More important, what are God's expectations of me? All that really matters is that I lead a purpose driven life and not waste my energy trying to placate artificially set expectations. A few people have accepted my unique personality. Mary Packard tops the short list.

I do not care if I meet your expectations. Let me wrestle with my conscience when I fail to meet my own expectations. After all, it has been your unsolicited expectations that have left me the most disappointed.

"If we think we have the answers, we are not open to a deeper understanding or exploring other ways of seeing the world."

-Dr. Laura Honos-Webb

THE GUESSING GAME

In 2003, Montel Williams devoted an entire show that attempted to controvert the legitimacy of ADHD. His guest list was replete with people who questioned all facets of ADHD, including actress Juliette Lewis, who said she believed ADHD was a fabricated disorder. There was only one doctor on the panel, Dr. Mary Ann Block, and she refuted the notion that ADHD was a discernible condition. There was not one person on the show who disagreed with Montel's central theme that ADHD was a myth.

I read articles from ADHD related web sites that blasted Montel for inaccuracies and an imbalanced point of view. Montel pissed me off because I thought he directly offended anyone who experienced ADHD symptoms. Who was Montel, I thought in disgust, to question the existence of ADHD?

Montel is not alone. Polling data suggests that a majority of Americans are skeptical ADHD is a genuine medical condition that affects seven to ten percent of children and four percent of adults in the United State. They believe ADHD is either made-up by the medical community or an excuse people use to cover for their personal problems.

There are many reasons why people doubt the validity of ADHD. First, in our stressed out day-to-day- lives, many people exhibit the hyperactive component of ADHD by frantically trying to complete all of their scheduled daily activities. They rush from place to place, sometimes forgetting to pick up dinner or neglecting to stop at a red light. Parents who escort their children to multiple events within an eight-hour period exhibit the manic signs of ADHD.

Second, there has never been a cogent explanation for the root causes of ADHD. I recently reviewed an article that stated heredity was the most likely cause of ADHD. The article went on to mention other possible causes: difficulties during pregnancy, prenatal exposure to alcohol and tobacco, premature delivery, significantly low birth weight, excessively high body lead levels, and postnatal head injuries.

There is not anything close to unanimity among the experts. The possible causes promulgated by the experts are as numerous as the number of ADHD symptoms. Most scientists believe the ADHD brain lacks neurotransmitter activity. They cannot agree on why the chemical composition is different. The conclusion of a recent brain-imaging article was succinct: "The evidence suggested here is simply an introduction. Unfortunately, there is a lot of variance in ADHD data and it is difficult to know what to believe."

Finally, a heated ADHD medication debate dominates the mainstream media and Internet discussion boards. The drug industry has followed in the contemptible steps of Big Tobacco by the way they have gained influence on the medical profession and Federal Drug Administration (FDA) approval process. People are concerned about the widespread prescription of controlled substances like Ritalin.

There are so many unanswered questions. Does the genetic puzzle impede the brain's chemical composition? What are the reasons for the differing types of ADHD? How does a concussion affect ADHD? What are the various strengths of ADHD? Is there an ADHD genetic link to the early onset of

Alzheimer's disease? Does ADHD generate bi-polar and depression disorders?

There are so many unproven aspects of ADHD that even I have become skeptical about certain facets of the condition. I do not blame all of the doubters that dismiss ADHD as some fad or over-hyped phenomenon. They want hard evidence, and that is hard to find in the current ADHD diagnostic world where everything is one big guessing game.

****

Concussions and ADHD share similar diagnostic procedures. For a concussion diagnosis, doctors ask patients how they feel and then give a nebulous assessment of the condition. "You might feel better in a week or two, or you might not," were the comforting words of wisdom I received at the conclusion of my concussion analysis.

An ADHD diagnosis is similarly vague. I was given personality profile tests, followed by an interview with Dr. Kia before I was guaranteed that I had ADHD. I still had to come back for a second session with a significant other even though Dr. Kia was eighty percent sure that I required a Ritalin prescription..

There must be a standard, physically perceptible test to diagnose concussions and ADHD. Why are we guessing about the most vital organ in our body? Why do we receive physical evidence of our heart ailments and metastasized stages of cancer, but do not receive an unadulterated view of brain injuries or malformations?

The brain is an organ, just like the liver, heart, kidneys, and lungs. If there is something awry with the liver, heart, kidneys, or lungs, there are physiological based tests that provide a diagnosis. When it comes to the brain, too much of the analysis derives from conjecture and indistinct tests. The brain is the vital link to cell formation and organ performance. The brain is the CPU that operates the body. Why does the medical profession insist on relegating the brain to second tier status when it comes to a diagnosis?

Asking for superficial evidence in the form of report cards and testimony from significant others is insulting to someone who spent their entire life compensating for ADHD. I am dismayed when a psychologist claims there is an eighty percent chance I have ADHD. Start making brain scans affordable and an insured process. Stop making a brain diagnosis part of a medical dart game.

The enigmatic brain is not just about ADHD and concussions. My cousin received a brain tumor diagnosis in 2005. One night while in bed, he inexplicably had a violent seizure that his wife fortunately detected. He received a diagnosis that used physical instruments, a tangible piece of evidence that proved he needed medical intervention in order to stop any further life threatening events. He still does not know why he had a brain tumor. There is not a brain tumor connection on either side of his family. Even though my cousin received an unequivocal diagnosis, his case further demonstrates that our inscrutable brain is an organ that demands intensive study.

****

While I despised Dr. Kia and his tactics, I liked his description of the *normals*. He was correct in his assertion that they are cynical ADHD exists as a physiological condition. Nevertheless, Dr. Kia did not mention the most salient reason why the *normals* are cynical.

The *normals* argue that ADHD is a made-up disorder because the preponderance of intervention strategies encourages the use of stimulants for easing or eliminating ADHD symptoms. Critics contend that a drug prescription for ADHD is the newest strategy for pharmaceuticals to expand their market by transforming normal variants of behavior into a mental disorder. They feel ADHD is an overly prescribed condition that lines the pockets of the drug lobby. The *normals* pervasive skepticism about ADHD is why the condition requires two separate debates.

First, ascertain whether someone has ADHD by implementing exacting measuring standards and guidelines. Physiological tests that clearly show chemical markers in the brain, like PET and SPECT scans, will dispel the myth that ADHD is an over-hyped malady. The tests must show hard evidence of what causes distraction, impulsiveness, and hyperactivity.

Contemporary research implements brain-imaging technology. Some results show a direct link between an underdeveloped frontal cortex and people who demonstrate ADHD symptoms. The frontal cortex coordinates executive functions like problem solving, planning, reasoning, and attention. The research data supports close similarities in the symptoms between ADHDers and people who suffer frontal lobe damage due to illness or accident. Some evidence suggests the right frontal lobe is smaller in an ADHD child than it is for a child who does not have the condition. Neurotransmitters also play a role, as low levels of Norepinephrine make it difficult to focus and pay attention. Low levels of Dopamine increase the level of impulsiveness and hyperactivity.

ADHD medications increase the amount of Dopamine and Norepinephrine. How do ADHD clinicians know if there is a depleted supply of either neurotransmitter by simply asking a patient questions and looking at report cards? They do not, which is why the *normals* question the validity of an ADHD diagnosis and subsequent treatment regimens. ADHDers ingest prescribed medications without an incontrovertible, physiological examination. The current ADHD diagnostic process is flawed.

The second debate is about treating ADHD. Prescription drug treatments are not the only remedy for alleviating ADHD symptoms. The role pharmaceuticals play in the rise of stimulant prescriptions needs more medical and journalistic scrutiny. As far as I could tell, Dr. Kia was nothing more than a street hood trying to push a narcotic stimulant on me.

ADHD research needs to focus on the chemical dynamics of our brains. We are getting close, but scientists need to conduct more brain imaging research and perform fewer studies like the ones that link smoking to ADHD. Stop squandering promising breakthroughs in physiological research. Once the diagnostic process becomes more certain like it is for heart disease and cancer, we then can move onto the next great debate as to what intervention, or what combination of interventions, will help someone with ADHD modify the more egregious aspects of their behavior. The time for smoking studies is later. The time to get serious about ADHD is now.

Undiagnosed ADHD is a complex condition with a seemingly infinite number of bad consequences. The ridicule, rejection, and general lack of respect leave mental scars that an MRI cannot detect. We owe it to those living in the quagmire of undiagnosed ADHD to come up with physical evidence that decreases ambiguous psychological testing. We then move on to how to treat ADHD. Treatment can include medication, a combination of interventions, or subtle personal management. The premise of any ADHD treatment program should be that one size does not fit all. It should depend on the strength of the ADHD ***AND*** the wishes of the patient.

Under the current ADHD diagnostic guidelines, I blow every symptom survey and checklist out of the water. I want more. I have looked into some research studies online, particularly those conducted by the National Institute of Health (NIH). I would like to participate in at least one study to help the ADHD community reach a consensus about the condition's causes.

I do not care if your diagnosis happened when you were five years of age or fifty-five. One of the ADHD gifts is a razor sharp intelligence that challenges the status quo. Do not accept the current diagnostic criteria. Thoroughly research the topic from every conceivable angle before formulating a game plan to confront ADHD symptoms. Take online surveys and complete the checklists as honestly as you can in order to measure the strength your of distraction, impulsiveness, and hyperactivity. The online checklists and surveys are similar to the ones you will complete at a psychotherapist's rate of $330 per hour. Seek second, third, and fourth opinions from specialists who may give you other perspectives.

And if you walk into a psychotherapist's office and are immediately inundated with a Ritalin sales pitch, turn around and run away as fast as you can from the pill pusher who is only out for himself and not the improvement of your ADHD symptoms.

****

FRUSTRATION/IRRITATION

ADHD is a conundrum.

Despite the efforts of scientists, we are nowhere close to defining the causes of ADHD. That leaves the door wide open for speculation and ambiguity. The door is also wide open for the pharmaceutical industry to gain a toehold on another condition that affects a segment of our society.

CHADD is the preeminent advocate for people with ADHD and they extol the virtue of a prescription drug remedy. Why is that? With so many alternative points of view about the interventions for ADHD, why does CHADD continue to advocate drugs as the primary mode of treatment? What about the scores of other treatments and interventions that help people who have ADHD? How much influence does Big Pharma have on organizations like CHADD? Some evidence suggests there is considerable financial influence.

We should not prescribe anything without knowing the physiological reasons behind the affliction, disorder, or condition. With ADHD, we know very little at this point. We also know very little about the short-term side effects and long-term implications of prescribed stimulant use. Why do ADHD experts predominantly inundate us with prescription drugs as ***the*** remedy to ease ADHD symptoms? Who gains financially from the over prescription of Ritalin? Are pharmaceutical companies manipulating people who have ADHD? Are ADHD drugs only about expanding market share?

I am surprised my ADHD diagnosis did not occur when I was twenty-four years old. Imagine all of the money the pill pushers would have made off me.

"Only those who dare to fail greatly can ever achieve greatly."

-John F. Kennedy

THANK YOU

I am grateful for the people who helped me navigate the choppy waters of ADHD. None of the people who were supportive of me knew about my ADHD. They just accepted me, for the most part, for who I am. Some left me to my own devices. Some encouraged me when times were tough. Some were mentors, taking the initiative to assist in my personal and professional growth. Some helped me understand the meaning of true friendship, love, and compassion. Some were running partners, providing me with an outlet to unleash my ADHD gifts upon the world.

One person was all of the above.

My Parents-I am the luckiest person on the face of this earth to have such supportive and loving parents. I never understood, until recently, the level of patience they needed to have in order to keep me on the straight and narrow. They provided the strong hand when I needed discipline. They gave me the opportunity to find answers to my complicated life. They provided the instruction, guidance, and stability that I needed during times of desperation. They were my moral compass during the formative years. They taught me the difference between right and wrong.

Gary-You did not care about my idiosyncrasies. You were always respectful of your older brother, despite all of my appalling predicaments. You helped me out when I needed a place to stay and showed uncanny patience before giving me marching orders. We have a lot in common, but not as much as we thought. That is what makes our relationship work at this point.

My Grandparents-I never heard anything the least bit disparaging come out of their mouths. I think my grandfather had some idea I was different by the way he showered me with attention, even after the other grandchildren were born. When I was down with few close friends, I could always count on my grandparents to provide love and care. I miss them both.

Mrs. Ogles-The only teacher I ever had, at any level of education, who had the remarkable patience to tutor me. She encouraged me to demonstrate my intellectual gifts and refused to exploit my personality weaknesses. There were times when other kids started to pick on me and she intervened on my behalf. My finest report card at any level came while I was in the fifth grade. That is not coincidental.

Denver Miller-The only organized sports coach who saw the shining light of my personality. He had a good time riding me on the basketball floor, but he taught me more about the game of life than any other adult did during my adolescence. There was more to Denver Miller than being a renowned high school basketball coach.

Curtis Wierbicki-Curt is the role model for aspiring restaurant managers. He saw something in me that few other people did. He brought out my energy, enthusiasm, and passion for the restaurant industry by displaying the same energy, enthusiasm and passion himself. He taught me about the technical aspects of service and the way to work a dining room on a busy

Saturday night. He never chided me for my impish behavior. He encouraged it.

Bill Entrikin-Men have a difficult time opening up to each other. Bill and I do not. We are able to discuss personal issues, like being the victims of a violent crime. The best therapy for someone whose brain explodes is a healthy does of humor. Laughter has always been my best friend. Bill is the engine of the laugh machine.

Carol Niederlander- Carol was the only writing instructor I had who encouraged me to write. Somehow, her criticisms of my style or content were delicate enough for me to accept. There were times when I was writing this book that I pulled out a creative writing piece from her class. The assignment was to use all five senses to describe a place that meant something to me. She praised the piece I wrote about Wrigley Field. Her written encouragement motivated me to keep on keeping on.

Eric Halluska-Where have you gone my friend? There must be something similar in our personalities if we stayed friends via the telephone for all of these years. We connected the first time we met, by virtually disagreeing on every topic we discussed. You were the first person I ever met who did not piss me off by differing with my pompous declarations.

Tony and Kristi Reyes-You will never fully realize the impact both of you had on me. Besides introducing me to my ADHD double, you unknowingly provided a social support system during my time of need. You always got me involved with group activities, like bowling and staggering around Herman. I never grasped your significance in my life until I wrote the chapter on relationships, particularly the sub-chapter that described social skill deficiencies. When I was around the two of you, I lost all of my social inhibitions and gained invaluable interactive skills.

Mike Donatt-I really believe the reason I finally sat down and started pounding out sentences for this book was your kindness. Like some other phases in my life, 2006 was a year when I was spinning my wheels in a hole of nothing. I tried hard to settle down and start this book. You greased the process with your humanity. You are one of the few stand-up people I have met in this life.

****

Dr. Mary Packard-Winkler did as much as humanly possible to keep in touch with me during the past twenty years. She sent me holiday greetings on a regular basis. She apprised me of her whirlwind life and described her close-knit family.

We set up a get together in Springfield, Illinois in the mid-nineties. Mary and her family were on their way to Sioux City and she suggested that I meet them for a few hours in Springfield. I told her it was a great idea. Like most of the great ideas in my life, I did not follow through with my plans to meet her.

I stiffed the person who has shown more assiduous attention to my personal affairs than anyone I have ever met. I stiffed the person who pulled me out of a self-induced gutter while I lived in Chicago. I stiffed the person who meant the most to me, the person who I have loved more than anyone else.

I bought *Who's Next* on a whim about six months before I made plans to visit Mary in 2005. I immediately put the CD in my car stereo and skipped around until I found "Getting in Tune." I had not heard the song for years and was perplexed as to why I wanted to hear it at that particular moment. I knew why after I heard the opening piano chords. The wistful chords evoked the vivid memories I shared with Mary. It was the song I heard when I nervously approached her front door.

Mary answered the door with the same reassuring smile I have seen thousands of times. It was the same smile that exuded equanimity and comfort when we attended Drake University, and later when we worked on the Gary Hart campaign. The same reassuring smile greeted me after I made a trip from Chicago at the beginning of my downward spiral. We embraced and I walked inside for the most important five hours of my life.

I will never forget that day. I was determined to pay Mary back for all of the blood, sweat, and tears she put into our relationship.

I read *The Purpose Driven Life* in 2005 after watching the account of Ashley Smith's encounter with her crazed, but soon to be saved abductor. The book is thick with religious references and at first that bothered me. The more I read the book and supplementary biblical passages, the more I understood what my purpose is in this life. Pastor Warren writes about burying fear by putting our faith in God. He writes that we all have a unique SHAPE for fulfilling our purpose in this world. I wanted to use my SHAPE to thank Mary by writing a book.

I still needed a sign that I was doing the good work intended for me. One night while sitting at the end of my bed, I prayed the most heartfelt prayer of my life. I prayed so hard that God got a headache. I asked God for a sign, any sign, which demonstrated to me that writing a book about undiagnosed ADHD was the right thing to do.

The next morning I logged on to my email account and was astounded to see a message from Mary. Eighteen months had passed since we spoke, wrote to, or saw each other, and there sitting in my inbox was a message from my long lost friend. I do not remember the content of the message. It was the sign that I asked for.

Thank you, Mary, for accepting me for who I am. Thank you for being the best friend that I have ever had. Thank you for being the inspiration for this book.

ADHD RESOURCES

www.ADHD-Information-Exchange.com

www.addisagift.com

http://adderworld.ning.com

www.amenclinics.com/ac/tests/add_test1.php

www.psychcentral.com

www.oneaddplace.com

www.add.org

www.addwarehouse.com

www.livingwithadd.com

www.ADDitudemag.com

www.visionarysoul.com

www.addresources.org

www.chadd.org

www.thomhartmann.com

www.add.about.com

www.adultadd.com

Driven to Distraction-Dr. Edward Hallowell and Dr. John Ratey

Delivered from Distraction- Dr. Edward Hallowell and Dr. John Ratey

Journeys through Adulthood: Discover a New Sense of Identity and Meaning While Living with Attention Deficit Disorder-Sari Solden

The Gift of Adult ADHD-Dr. Lara Honos-Webb

BIBLIOGRAPHY

Bailey, Eileen, "ADHD and Sleep Disorders," http://add.about.com/od/adultadd/a/sleepdisorders.htm

Carver, Joseph M. Ph.D., "Attention Deficit Hyperactivity Disorder (ADHD)," http://www.enotalone.com/article/4121.html

Fellman, Wilma LPC, "Career Challenges and ADD: We Have a Choice," http://www.add.org/content/work/wilma1.htm

Hallowell, Edward M. and John J. Ratey. *Delivered from Distraction: Getting the Most out of Life with Attention Deficit Disorder.* New York: Ballantine Books, 2004.

Hallowell, Edward M. M.D. and John J. Ratey M.D., "Adult ADHD: 50 Tips on Management," http://www.addresources.org/article_50_tips_adult_hallowell_ratey.php

Richardson, Wendy M.A. LMFCC., "The Link Between ADD & Addiction: Getting the Help You Deserve," http://www.add.org/images2/addiction.htm

Szegedy-Maszak, Marianne, "Driven to distraction," *U.S. News and World Report.* 26 April 2004, 53-62.

Watkins, Carol E. M.D., "AD/HD Co-Morbidity: What's under the tip of the Iceberg?" http://www.ncpamd.com/ADDComorbidity.htm

American Psychiatric Association (2001). *Diagnostic and Statistical Manual of Mental Disorders, Fourth Edition, Text Revision.* Washinton, D.C. American Psychiatric Press.

"AD/HD in Adults-Fact Sheet #7," http://www.chadd.org/fs/fs7.htm

"AD/HD and Coexisting Conditions: Disruptive Behavior Disorders (WWK 5B)," http://www.help4adhd.org.en.treatment/coexisitng/WWK5B

"Attention Deficit Linked to Smoker's Self-Medication Needs," http://www.cfah.org/hbns/newsrelease/attention11-19-01.cfm

"Behavior Disorders that often co-occur with ADHD," http://www.helpforadd.com/oddcd.htm

"Ritalin & Cocaine: The Connection and the Controversy," http://learn.genetics.utah.edu/units/addiction/issues/ritalin.cfm

"Self Doubt-The self fulfilling prophecy," http://www.addcorridorcoaching.com/aug05.asp.

"Social skills in Adults with AD/HD (WWK 15)," http://www.help4adhd.org/en/living/relandsoc/WWK15

"The Neurobiology of ADHD," http://www.adhd.org.nz/neuro1.htm

"We have learned so much…," http://add.about.com/cs/addthebasics/a/montelwilliams.html

"What causes ADD?"
http://www.add.org/content/research/causes.htm

PERMISSIONS

"Adult Self-Report Scale (ASRS) Screener," copyright c 2003 by the World Health Organization (WHO).
Reprinted with permission of WHO.
The WHO does not endorse any specific company or products

"Jasper/Goldberg Adult ADD Screening," copyright c 1992 by John M. Grohol, PsyD.
Reprinted with permission of John M. Grohol
Source: www.PsychCentral.com

"General Adult ADD Symptom Checklist," copyright c 1995 by Daniel G. Amen, M. D.
Reprinted with permission of www.addresources.org
"This educational material is made available, courtesy of Dr. Amen and Attention Deficit Disorder Resources. We are a non-profit organization, based in Tacoma, whose purpose is to help adults with ADHD achieve their full potential. We have numerous materials as well as a quarterly newsletter for sale. Our address is ATTENTION DEFICIT DISORDER RESOURCES, 223 Tacoma Av S, Tacoma, WA. 98402 Tel 253-759-5085, contact form and web site: *http://www.addresources.org/.*"

Lightning Source UK Ltd.
Milton Keynes UK
03 February 2010

149502UK00001B/91/P

9 781601 456229